Becoming a Lion

Becoming a Lion

JOHNNY SEXTON

PENGUIN BOOKS

PENGUIN BOOKS

Published by the Penguin Group
Penguin Books Ltd, 80 Strand, London WC2R ORL, England
Penguin Group (USA) Inc., 375 Hudson Street, New York, New York 10014, USA
Penguin Group (Canada), 90 Eglinton Avenue East, Suite 700, Toronto, Ontario, Canada M4P 2Y3
(a division of Pearson Penguin Canada Inc.)
Penguin Ireland, 25 St Stephen's Green, Dublin 2, Ireland (a division of Penguin Books Ltd)
Penguin Group (Australia), 707 Collins Street, Melbourne, Victoria 3008, Australia
(a division of Pearson Australia Group Pty Ltd)
Penguin Books India Pvt Ltd, 11 Community Centre, Panchsheel Park, New Delhi – 110 017, India
Penguin Group (NZ), 67 Apollo Drive, Rosedale, Auckland 0632, New Zealand
(a division of Pearson New Zealand Ltd)
Penguin Books (South Africa) (Pty) Ltd, Block D, Rosebank Office Park,
181 Jan Smuts Avenue, Parktown North, Gauteng 2193, South Africa

Penguin Books Ltd, Registered Offices: 80 Strand, London WC2R ORL, England

www.penguin.com

First published by Penguin Ireland 2013
Published in Penguin Books 2014
001

Typeset by Jouve (UK), Milton Keynes
Printed in Great Britain by Clays Ltd, St Ives plc

ISBN: 978-0-241-96635-8

www.greenpenguin.co.uk

Contents

Prologue

Two hours before kick-off and we are gathering for the coach's final address. It's a standard hotel conference room, carpeted, with rows of chairs, flip-chart and projector screen. But given the enormity of what lies ahead, and the tension in the air, it feels more like we've been summoned to the headmaster's office. Our coaches – Gats, Andy, Rob, Wig and Jenks – are sitting to the side of the room as we arrive in dribs and drabs and take our seats. There is no chat, just the odd whisper as the seconds pass until the appointed time. The only noise is from the Lions supporters outside. This hotel is barely a hundred metres from ANZ Stadium, so there are thousands of them gathered outside and they are already in raucous form. There are narrow gaps between the large panes of glass which form the outer wall of this room, so that while they can't see us, we can certainly hear them. I'm trying to hear what it is that they're chanting. Something about the queen. They're taunting the Australian fans, to the tune of the Beatles' 'Yellow Submarine'. Eventually, I figure it out.

> Your next queen is Camilla Parker-Bowles!
> Camilla Parker-Bowles,
> Camilla Parker-Bowles.
>
> Your next queen is Camilla Parker-Bowles!
> Camilla Parker-Bowles,
> Camilla Parker-Bowles.

Over and over. As I twig, I realize that pennies are dropping, or have already dropped, all over the room. Like the boy in the headmaster's office, I am ready to explode with laughter but also determined that

I won't be the first to do it. I exchange glances with both Andy and Rob and realize that they're the same, struggling to suppress giggles. I study Gats, too. In a way, he's under more pressure than any of us. It's the deciding game in the Test series. The whole concept of the Lions is on the line. His own reputation is on the line, you could argue, given the controversial nature of his selection. So there's a lot on his shoulders. But unless I'm mistaken, those shoulders are quietly shaking with laughter.

You've got to love the Lions supporters, but for most of this afternoon I've been cursing them. It seemed a clever idea by the management to check us into the Novotel around lunchtime, in order to avoid getting stuck in a traffic jam this afternoon – Homebush, where ANZ Stadium is located, is the guts of an hour from the centre of Sydney even outside rush-hour. Once we'd checked in and had some lunch, myself and Seanie O'Brien grabbed a room, and after watching TV for a while we decided to get some kip. But how can you sleep to a constant soundtrack of 'Delilah', 'Ireland's Call', 'O Flower of Scotland' and 'Swing Low, Sweet Chariot'? For the love of Jesus, would you put a sock in it? Please?

I went down and bought some earplugs from the little shop at reception, then back up to the room where Seanie was snoozing happily. But the earplugs brought no relief, only discomfort. I took a pillow and went down to the team room, which was in a slightly quieter part of the hotel, found a corner and lay down on the carpet. I think I got a few minutes' shut-eye. But to be reduced to this, a few hours before the biggest game in my career, is not ideal.

To be honest, very little about this week could be described as ideal. I've been bunged up with a chest infection and on medication, hacking up gunk all week. It probably didn't help that the weather in Noosa was pretty grim. You head up to the Sunshine Coast for a couple of days' R&R, having been assured that the weather will be perfect for the beach – temperatures in the low twenties and constant sunshine – then you get there and it's piddling down.

A good few Lions let off steam when we got to Noosa last Sunday evening – some who knew their tour was already over, some who knew they'd be involved today but just felt like having a few beers to unwind. I remember wondering what it would have been like up there if we'd been 2–0 up in the series! But we weren't 2–0 up. It was 1–1 and Australia had momentum after winning in Melbourne. We needed something different. And that was when Gats dropped his bombshell.

I didn't see it coming. I knew that with Jamie Roberts coming in at 12, there was a decision to be made at 13. With Sam Warburton injured, Brian looked the obvious choice to take over the captaincy. When I saw him doing media on Monday, I made the same assumption as everyone else. But Gats dropped him. He was such a focal point last week and suddenly he's not even in the twenty-three. He has handled himself with great dignity, even though all of Ireland seems to be outraged on his behalf.

After I sympathized with him, I had to put the whole selection issue to one side. It's not easy, because Brian's a friend of mine, but there are times in professional sport when you have to be selfish. This is a Test week, and it's one with its own particular difficulties. It was hard to shake the end-of-term feeling from our training session in Noosa on Wednesday. We were sloppy, lacking in precision, and it pissed me off no end. Andy Farrell tried to reassure me afterwards, saying that it was always going to be a difficult session after we'd had a couple of days off. But it was just as bad on Thursday and I let rip at the forwards. I don't think it went down very well.

But maybe we needed a bit of narkiness to give us an edge. Back in Sydney yesterday, everything seemed to fall into place in the captain's run. We did some contact just to liven things up and it went well. When we ran as a team, we were crisp, accurate. Alun-Wyn Jones, our skipper in Sam's absence, spoke well afterwards. Back at the hotel, Andy spoke really well about the need to find a new level of intensity, an intensity that would set us apart from the Wallabies. Last night I was feeling a lot better about things. Sometimes you can train crap for most of the week but then produce a performance when it matters.

So I'm feeling positive following Gats's final address, positive as I stand on halfway thirty seconds before kick-off, when the referee, Romain Poite, gives me a quick wink. It's incredibly noisy in here.

This stadium was home to the 2000 Olympics, so I was expecting it to be one of those soulless arenas where the players are separated from spectators by a running track. But the track has been covered over with extra rows of seats, so the crowd is right on top of us. There's a strange intimacy for a stadium with nearly 84,000 people in it.

I survey my options for the kick-off. The Wallabies have two-man pods – catcher and lifter – scattered evenly around their half of the pitch: Ben Mowen and George Smith to the right just short of the ten-metre line, James Horwill and Ben Alexander to the left of the posts on the twenty-two, Kane Douglas and Benn Robinson level with them but hugging the right touchline. They are also offering me Israel Folau, all on his own on the ten-metre line to my left.

Folau has been one of Australia's players of the series, but their key man is undoubtedly Will Genia. He is their director of operations, their pace-setter, the one who can deliver in the tightest of corners. I see him lurking behind the Douglas–Robinson pod. Maybe if I can kick high and long beyond them, our chasers can catch Genia, man and ball, and take him out of his director's role for the opening couple of phases of the game. Maybe we can unsettle the Wallabies.

Sure enough, as the ball drops from a noisy sky into their twenty-two, Douglas loses his bearings and decides to leave it for Genia, who is taken by surprise and makes probably his first mistake of the series . . .

ONE

New Season, Old Nightmares

Aviva Stadium

Dan Carter is at the end of the room, frozen on an eight-foot screen. It looks like he's about to launch one of those inch-perfect restarts in Auckland, or maybe Christchurch. I don't really care where he is, to be honest. Ireland's tour to New Zealand was over two months ago. I've seen enough of Dan.

When the summons arrived last week from Mick Kearney, the team manager, I assumed this get-together would be designed to look forward to the new season. We're already five weeks into pre-season training – can we not park New Zealand? But deep down, I knew I was kidding myself. Sometimes you can get away without reviewing the final Test of a summer tour, and just run off to the sun. But when you've been thumped 60–0? You have to be accountable for a scoreline like that. You have to trawl through the wreckage for clues. You have to experience the pain and humiliation again. So the blinds are drawn in the Havelock Suite, blocking out the summer sunshine, and there's Dan, up on the screen, on pause. We know what's coming next.

It's a kick in the balls, to be honest, sitting there in the semi-darkness, reliving it, complete with the soundtrack of the Kiwi commentators. We watch some clips from our heartbreaking near miss in Christchurch but mostly it's the Hamilton horror-show – Aaron Cruden and Sonny Bill Williams carving us up, Hosea Gear biffing tacklers aside, Israel Dagg cruising over the try-line. It's as if we're being told, 'This is not acceptable for a team that considers itself contenders.' No shit, Sherlock.

I've thought plenty about the tour so I know what *I* need to do to move on. I had four weeks' holidays to get it out of my system – though not with any real success. I arrived back in Dublin the Monday morning after Hamilton, and by that afternoon I was on a flight to Portugal, where Laura was waiting for me. Girvan Dempsey has an apartment in Luz, which he kindly lets us use from time to time. Lovely spot. The only problem is that most of the apartment owners in that particular complex seem to be Irish and they'd probably seen our embarrassment a few days previously. I'm sure I was recognized by people at the pool, but they seemed to know I needed space. My general expression probably made it obvious.

Defeat hurts some people more than others. I suppose it depends how much you put into it. I know some lads can go away on holidays and set it to one side. Compartmentalize. I can't do that. Maybe it's a good thing, seeing as I'm the playmaker, the man making most of the decisions. Sometimes I wonder, though. I agonize over games, especially if we lose. Lying in the darkness hours later, I'll replay large chunks of the action in my head, wince at a poor option taken, then imagine the play as it should have developed. If we lose the last game of the season, I have to live with that through the summer break.

Laura knows me pretty well at this stage – you'd hope so, seeing as we've been together since we were both fifteen – and she pretty much left me to myself for long stretches of that week in Portugal. I'm a bit of a cliché, staring at the same page of a thriller for hours, barely taking in the details of some gruesome act of violence because what I'm really thinking about is another gruesome act of violence, on a rugby pitch somewhere in New Zealand. I wish there was a switch I could flick, but there isn't.

After Portugal, we popped home briefly for Gordon D'Arcy's wedding before heading off to Mexico for a fortnight in Cancún, where there were plenty of welcome distractions. Without them, I find my mind drifts back to the stadium. This isn't to wallow in self-pity, more to try to come up with a solution. Setbacks like the one we suffered in New Zealand can make you hungry, which is good. I've trained myself to take positives out of every situation. But having all that stuff bouncing around in your head doesn't make for the most restful of holidays.

The final weeks of last season were a ridiculous jumble of emotions. With Leinster, I'd won another Heineken Cup medal, my third in four seasons. The final against Ulster at Twickenham hadn't been as dramatic as beating Northampton in Cardiff the previous year, but that didn't make the experience any less wonderful. Eight days later, however, we lost the Pro12 final, our third straight league final defeat, and our second to Ospreys at the RDS. To see them jumping up and down on the podium again, on our patch, was head-wrecking.

With Ireland also, I'd been through emotional extremes. Having lost the first Test in Auckland heavily, there was a dramatic shift in Christchurch the following week. No one gave us a prayer but we probably played well enough to beat the All Blacks, and definitely well enough to get a draw. It was amazing to see how human they could look when they were put under pressure: McCaw spilling the ball; Carter looking flustered as, for once, he wasn't being given an armchair ride; Dagg needlessly getting sin-binned.

But should I have tried that long-range penalty when they were down a man, or put it into the corner? What was Nigel Owens up to, suddenly penalizing our scrum when it had been on top all night? Finally, how come Carter's dodgy first drop-goal attempt flicked off Sean O'Brien's fingertips on its way wide, giving the Kiwis an attacking scrum that they didn't deserve? That was their escape hatch.

Mostly, though, I was haunted by Hamilton. If you look at it rationally, the result shouldn't have been too much of a surprise. We were running on empty at the end of a season that had begun fifty-three weeks previously because of the World Cup. We were without senior figures like Paul O'Connell, Stephen Ferris, Luke Fitzgerald and Tommy Bowe. Add in the fact that we were emotionally drained a week after coming so close to a historic result. But when you're in the middle of it, you don't allow yourself to see things that way. We reckoned Hamilton was another opportunity to make history and beat New Zealand. That's how I was thinking, at any rate.

I've never received a tonking like it. Not at school, not in club rugby, not with Leinster. Down 26–0 with half-time approaching, you're standing there as they're lining up a kick at goal and you're thinking, *When does this nightmare end?* The All Blacks were relentless. We'd seen the previous week that if you can build a lead against them, they can be rattled. But give them a lead and then take risks to haul it back, and they pounce ruthlessly on every mistake. The scoreboard can click along at shocking speed.

I was pretty upset afterwards. I was thinking, *Is my international career always going to be like this? It just seems to be plain sailing with Leinster. I turn up, concentrate on my own job and everything seems to fall into place. How come it can't work like that with Ireland?*

No one really said anything in the dressing room in Hamilton. We all went out and had a few beers and tried to have a laugh about the hiding we'd just taken. We are Irish, so that is what we do. We take the piss out of a bad situation. We make jokes at funerals. If there's a national scandal or a natural disaster, it will be just a matter of hours before the sick jokes start circulating. Sometimes when this happens, you can see the look of disbelief on the faces of foreign players in the Leinster squad. How can you joke about something as tragic as that? Because we're Irish. It's the same with being beaten 60–0. Laughing eases the pain. For an hour or two, anyway.

It's now eight weeks later and we have to take a more sober look at things. Honesty sessions, truth sessions, call them what you will. Ireland don't do them enough. At Leinster, we'll have one at least once a season. The senior players will sense when it's time for a pow-wow, and what needs to be said. Because we're with each other most weeks of the season and know each other well, some of the chat can be pretty blunt – 'What the hell were you doing X for, when we'd agreed Y?' And so on.

With Ireland, it's more difficult. You wouldn't be questioning a guy from another province so readily. You're treading on eggshells some of the time. When you're speaking, half of you is wondering, *What are the lads from the other provinces thinking about this?* or *What do they say about me when they're behind closed doors in Munster, or Ulster?* If there's that uncertainty, they can become half-truth sessions.

Not today. We were broken up into four groups according to our Test experience, with a view to finding ways of improving performance and then sharing them with the larger group. I was in a group with Keith Earls, Jamie Heaslip, Donnacha Ryan, Stevie Ferris and Cian Healy. Earlsy surprised everyone with his outspokenness – when someone who doesn't say very much suddenly speaks powerfully, people definitely take more notice. He said he had the impression that the provinces were more important to players than the national team, and he thought that was totally wrong. Ireland should be everyone's number-one team but, as he saw it, this wasn't the case.

He wasn't pointing the finger at any province in particular. He just thought we should all be less selfish with our information. For example, he let us know that he likes to get his hands on the ball early in a game and take on an opponent. It gets him into the game. He reckoned he should be able to tell Leinster players this, and not have to worry about us knowing this in the lead-up to a Leinster v. Munster game. We should be better at sharing plays that we find work for our provinces. We have to put our country first.

My main contribution was about getting more value out of national training camps, especially as the time we have together is so limited. If we have a two-week lead-in to a Test match, we need to get more out of the first week, in particular. Often, a player will come in from a big Heineken Cup game carrying a niggle or two and will treat the first week almost like a week off. You would have guys resting up, slacking off training. It's almost like wasting a week.

Over the past couple of years, pretty much ever since I'd been involved, we have come in and gone through a lot of the moves in the first week of a camp, but come the following Monday we would have to go through them again because guys weren't fully clued in. So we set some standards for ourselves, especially for the first week of camp before the autumn internationals. By the end of that week, we must be mentally ready to take on the Springboks.

I found myself contributing more as the afternoon wore on. Basically, I feel we've been underachieving, given the quality we have, so I said as much. Yes, we have a few key players out of the mix – Paulie, Stevie, Drico and now Rory Best and Sean O'Brien are injured – but we have a new generation of leaders coming through. I reckon we still have enough ability. We've done it at provincial level, now it's time to do something with Ireland.

The best thing about today is that the next time we come together, towards the end of next month, people will know what's expected of them. That's why it's so important to talk. I said as much to Declan

Kidney today. The last time we'd had a truth session like this was in Enfield four years ago and Ireland had won the Slam the following spring. Coincidence? I don't think so. Today went well. Watching the clips from Hamilton was no fun, but in some ways it was the best thing we could have done. That result has been following us around all summer, like a bad smell. Today we cleared the air.

Thursday 30 August

Newstead Building, University College Dublin

After New Zealand, the Ulster and Munster lads were half-anxious, half-excited about meeting new bosses: Mark Anscombe has joined Ulster and Munster have Rob Penney. With Leinster, the novelty factor was going to work in a training facility that's as good as anything in professional rugby.

There's no other way to describe our new set-up in UCD, a brand-new complex that houses the entire Leinster operation – administration, marketing, medical, media, academy, video analysis and, of course, rugby. It's amazing. Apparently when Toulouse heard about our €2.5 million development, they released a statement saying they had spent a million more on their new stadium, which supposedly has hyperbaric oxygen chambers to aid recovery from injury. It was as if they couldn't be seen to fall behind. All I know is that I've been training in UCD for nearly six weeks now and arriving here every morning is like a shot in the arm.

The main training space has a state-of-the-art gym and a running track, with a recovery area right beside it – hot and cold hydrotherapy units, including a giant jacuzzi with treadmills inside it, so you can use water resistance when rehabbing from certain injuries. Everything is in immediate reach but at the same time there's a great sense of space and of independence. Previously, we were based at the David Lloyd Fitness Centre down the road in Riverview, which was grand, but we felt like tolerated guests. This new facility feels like it's ours.

Last year we were training on bumpy old pitches on the other side of the university. The kickers had to pop down to Donnybrook in our cars to have a practice session. Now we train on pristine surfaces, either grass or 3G all-weather. We recover in an Olympic-size swimming pool. We do our video analysis on the mezzanine level, where there's an array of glistening Apple Macs. Our team meetings take place in rooms designed specifically for that purpose, with massive flat screens built into the wall. Everything still smells so new! And the dressing rooms? Joy. It's like what you get at the Aviva – your own spot, with drawers and loads of space. Your locker is outside in the corridor, which is right beside the cafeteria, which is right beside the gym.

In Riverview, our changing room was basically a converted office which had belonged to Michael Cheika, Leinster's coach when I first came into the side. There'd be thirty-five of us crammed in there, benches and bags everywhere. This was actually a massive improvement on the previous situation, when we didn't even have a dressing room. Back then, people turned up already in their training gear, and showered when they got home, or else they were changing alongside members of the fitness club. Crazy, when you think of it.

Moving into Cheika's office meant there could be no cliques. We bonded as a group. Eoin O'Malley might have changed beside Brian O'Driscoll, Sean O'Brien beside Felipe Contepomi. There was more banter, more togetherness. Leo Cullen and Shane Jennings had been the ones who insisted that we should be all together because they'd seen the benefits of a dressing-room culture in Leicester, where they'd spent a couple of seasons. I don't think it's any coincidence that the year we all squeezed into that room was the year we won our first Heineken Cup.

Still, that set-up wasn't good enough for European champions and in fairness to Leo and Jenno – and Cheika – they kept pushing for training facilities that would put us on a par with the most successful English and French clubs. We were incredibly fortunate to have a benefactor in David Shubotham, who's a friend of our chief executive, Mick Dawson, and who put up most of the money for the project. We're also lucky that UCD were so keen to be involved.

So I've been mustard-keen this pre-season. The strength and conditioning (S&C) lads are calling me Ben, after Ben Johnson, the disgraced Canadian sprinter. They reckon I must be on the juice, because I'm recording all sorts of personal bests in our spanking new gym. The main thing I learned from the New Zealand tour is that the Kiwis are fitter, faster and stronger than us. It helped them that they were in the middle of their season, whereas we were at the end of ours – when you're carrying niggles, sometimes it's impossible to do weights.

Someone like Sonny Bill Williams was born with physical advantages over the likes of me – the lads call me coat-hanger, because I've a slim frame and no shoulders to speak of. So I have to work hard to make any gains at all, because that's my body type and because I was late starting in the gym, nineteen or twenty, whereas some of the younger pros have been weight-training properly since sixteen. But I've put a special emphasis on my own S&C since coming back and it's beginning to pay off.

The one test that's killing me is my drop-jump. It's this exercise when you jump off a box onto a special mat and then spring over a hurdle. A device in the mat measures how much more powerful you have become from all those squats in the gym. I can't get the technique right. Maybe it's because of an accident last season when I flipped and landed back-first on top of the hurdle, which was painful. I'm determined to get it right, though. A couple of weeks ago, we were in Spain for the weekend, in a house owned by one of my dad's friends, and there I was, in the pool, working on my drop-jump, trying to get it sorted out before going back to work on the Monday. Sure what else would you be doing?

Friday 31 August

UCD

The RaboDirect Pro12 starts tomorrow and we're away at Llanelli, though obviously some of us won't actually be there. The IRFU's player management programme decrees that, because of the New

Zealand tour, I've another couple of weeks to go before I can play again. My season won't start until the trip to Treviso, the third game of our league campaign. It all makes sense – but I'm dying for a game.

When I meet Joe Schmidt, in the corridor, I can tell he's excited to get going again, but also a little apprehensive. The Scarlets have just announced their side and they have most of their big guns involved, whereas we've only a few first-choicers – Isa Nacewa, Richardt Strauss, Jenno. It's the same every season. Joe is used to slow starts, but they don't sit easily with him.

We chat about the Scarlets but I'm more interested in talking about him and his plans. Joe's future with Leinster has been one of the lads' main topics of conversation, whenever he's out of earshot. As things stand, his contract is up at the end of this season, but we know that Mick Dawson has been doing everything in his power to get him to stay for a few more seasons. It's not hard to see why. Joe has led us to two Heineken Cups in two years and we're favourites to complete a hat-trick this season, when the final is to be played at the Aviva.

I've a great relationship with him. I think that was pretty obvious from the pictures that were taken after we beat Clermont in the semi-final in Bordeaux in April. He'd been behind the dead-ball line when Clermont were hammering away at our line and when the final whistle went, we hugged each other like father and son. He's got more of an edge to him than his smile might suggest, but he's a lovely bloke who preaches and practises humility. He also has an incredible rugby brain, and he's great to bounce things off.

I'd plenty to hop off him when we came back from holidays, but he wasn't around that week. The word was that he'd taken his holidays late, but guys were beginning to wonder. We were doing fitness games, the usual pre-season stuff, but it's not the same when Joe's not overseeing things. Guys look forward to him being there. Me especially. I wanted to talk to him about the tour – not for a shoulder to cry on, more to get his opinion on some of the All Blacks' plays and whether we could incorporate them. He tends not to talk about Ireland, except to point out positives. He always seems to find positives in things. When he wasn't there that week, we really noticed it. When he's not reffing those training games, there isn't the same intensity. I found it a bit of an eye-opener. I was thinking, *Christ, is this what it's going to be like when Joe is gone?*

We kind of know that he wants to stay from a work point of view, but there are family considerations. His daughter has returned to New Zealand to go to college, and his youngest kid, nine-year-old Luke, suffers from a severe form of epilepsy, so when it comes to deciding where to live and work, there is plenty to consider. His older son, Tim, is about to start fifth year in Terenure College, so we're hoping that means Joe will sign for at least an additional year, and maybe we'll be able to convince him to stay longer. Leo and I have a cunning plan for Tim, who looks a handy player. At the Rabo awards at the end of last season, we were badgering Phil Orr, who's on the board of the Leinster Academy, telling him that Tim *has* to get a full Leinster contract the minute he leaves school, and that he *must* be made captain of the Leinster 20s. Anything to keep his dad here.

Saturday 1 September

Goatstown

For some reason most of our games are on Saturdays this year, and Saturday games can make a mess of your weekend. So when I get the opportunity to spend a day with Laura, it makes sense to do just that. I should have mentioned that we got engaged six weeks ago. It's not 'out there' yet, although most of our friends and all my team-mates know. They've probably kept it quiet because they know that we like to keep things fairly private. We'd be out and about together all the time, but I have had no media intrusion in my life. We don't do Facebook or Twitter – although the lads are convinced I'll give in, eventually. We don't do openings, or film premieres, or whatever. We haven't even had an engagement party. We'll have a good wedding next summer though, the Saturday after the final Lions Test in Sydney. Sounds like wishful thinking? We had to pick a date that couldn't be changed, so that seemed like a reasonable choice!

It's an exciting time, but you couldn't really call it a whirlwind romance. We've actually known each other since we were twelve or thirteen. Laura went to Loreto on the Green, where she now teaches, and only lived down the road from me in Rathgar. We met at Rathgar Tennis Club, which was behind our house in the village – my dad used to whistle from the back gate when it was time for dinner. I would have spent all day, every day in the club during the summer holidays. We were boyfriend and girlfriend for a while in our early teens, then went our separate ways but remained good friends, and then got back together at fifteen.

It was just around that time that my parents started growing apart, so her friendship was really important. She was the person I confided in most. I hadn't an unhappy upbringing, but it's weird when you start realizing everything isn't right at home and your folks are spending less time together. It was also the time that rugby was getting serious for me, and one of the reasons I loved it was that it was a getaway for me. The other getaway was to hop on the bike and call up to Laura for a chat.

We've been through everything together. Laura has been in my life since I was playing Junior Cup for St Mary's, so she has picked up bits and pieces over the years. She gets slagged about knowing all the terminology. Some of the other guys' girlfriends might only be around for six months or a year and it can take a while to understand the game. They might be up in our apartment in Goatstown, watching us play, and as the chat drifts away from rugby, Laura will still be locked into what's happening on the screen.

'Johnny! What the hell are you doing in the pocket?' she'll gasp.

'Pocket? Whose pocket?' one of the girls will ask.

I've only just turned twenty-seven, but I've known from way back that I'll spend the rest of my life with Laura. The topic of engagement and marriage came up with Eoin Reddan, my most regular room-mate, on one of the first nights in New Zealand. We were up chatting in the middle of the night, struggling with jet lag, despite having taken sleeping tablets. Reddser told me he knew a guy in London who would do a good deal on a ring. Seeing as it was daytime in London, he actually rang the chap there and then, and put me on to him. Yer man says he'll email me the next day with various

designs and price options. Deal almost done. The spooky bit came
the next morning, on our way down to breakfast, when Reddser
asked me if I remembered what we'd done the night before. I hadn't
a clue what he was on about, until he reminded me about the jeweller
in London. Jesus, of course. The ring! Strange the effect jet lag can
have on you.

From that point on, the toughest bit was going to be keeping it a
surprise from Laura before popping the question in Cancún. In the
couple of days between our week in Portugal and Gordon and Aoife's
wedding, I managed to pop over to London, saying I had an appointment at the Adidas shop – which wasn't a lie – but also picking up the
ring from our jeweller friend. Myself and Reddser were all nods and
winks at the wedding. Then off to Mexico.

I reckon Laura knew what was coming, because she knows me
pretty well at this stage. We normally go to Spain or Portugal every
summer but suddenly here I am, booking an expensive holiday much
further afield. It was also a real couples' resort – everyone was either
newly engaged or on honeymoon. At the reception desk, it was,
'Ah, you guys must have just got engaged?' No, no, no, just the room
key, please. So she probably knew what was coming, but she definitely wouldn't have expected me to actually source the ring, buy it
and bring it. She probably expected me to ask the question with some
piece of crap and make her do all the work when it came to getting the
ring. I can be pretty disorganized about certain things – everything
except rugby and study, really – and she says I haven't a romantic
bone in my body. So I was going to shock her on this one. I'd actually
put a bit of thought into it.

The big issue now was hiding the ring from her until fairly late in
the holiday. I wanted to pop the question early and enjoy the break,
but I knew that if I did that Laura would spend the rest of the trip
on the phone to her friends, making arrangements. I had to put it
somewhere clever. I was paranoid about the security standards in
Mexico, and justifiably so – on the journey home, a load of cool Adidas leisure gear was whipped from one of the side pockets in my bag.
And I was paranoid about Laura finding it in the back of the safe in
our hotel room, where I had it hidden in a case for my headphones.

She says she never saw it, but she'd have been snooping around, you can be sure.

Finally, I booked dinner at a restaurant which has this table for two at the end of a pier. You could hear the waiter pushing his trolley all the way out, about a hundred metres. And that's where I showed what a romantic devil I can really be.

Later, I texted the news to my folks, my brothers Mark and Jerry, my sister Gillian, and a few of the Leinster lads that I'm closest to. Laura was in touch with some of her pals too. A day later, I sent a global to everyone in my Leinster address book. By the time I arrived in training the following Monday, a few of them were waiting for me, wearing black armbands. Another man down. There was some serious slagging.

It's not exactly national news, which is grand by me. A couple of weeks after we arrived home, there was a polite enquiry from one newspaper to Platinum One, the agency that represents me, who informed the journalist that they don't comment on players' private lives. So nothing has appeared. Like I said, we didn't have an engagement party. To be honest, I never reckoned we'd have a big wedding. I just thought it would be the two of us going off and getting married by ourselves, and then heading off on honeymoon. When we got engaged, there was talk of a party to celebrate but I wasn't keen. The wedding is enough, thanks. I don't need a pre-wedding too! We simply had a few drinks with my brothers and my uncles in John B. Keane's pub in Listowel, the weekend after we got back from Cancún – I have strong family connections in Kerry. It was all very low-key, which is how both of us like it.

The wedding is still ten months away, so there's no frantic organization just yet and we were able to spend a fairly chilled day today. The evening wasn't quite so relaxing, because I had to sit through the coverage from Llanelli. The Scarlets gave us a right kicking, running seven tries past some pretty flimsy defence. I'm fuming at the scoreline but more at the way we almost accepted them running over us. For one try, one of the Scarlets patted one of our guys on the head just after he touched down, just to rub it in. It's not easy to watch that sort of thing at home, and I was roaring abuse at the TV. You would far rather somebody threw a dig and at least showed some resistance.

I know we're missing a lot of players, but you still don't want to see Leinster being humiliated like this. Words will be had.

Monday 3 September

Team meeting room, UCD

It was George North, actually. And he didn't so much pat Darren Hudson on the head after scoring as pet him on the cheek, which made the lack of retaliation from the lads even more galling to watch again. That's what we did first thing this morning in UCD: trawl through the 'highlights' of Saturday's defeat. It wasn't quite as painful as watching Hamilton last week, because the numbers weren't quite as damning and also because I wasn't actually playing. But it wasn't good.

Like I've said, there's a simple reason why Leinster tend to struggle at the beginning of the season. Our success means we have a lot of players in the Ireland squad, which in turn means we have to be drip-fed back into action. I remember in Joe's first year, when we won only one of our first four games, and lost away to Treviso, there were a few critics questioning his coaching credentials. They'd changed their tune eight months later when we beat Northampton in the Heineken Cup final.

That won't stop us being slow out of the blocks every year. A couple of weeks back, Joe took a very inexperienced side to Northampton for a pre-season friendly and they lost 43–0. It was as if Dylan Hartley and his mates were taking revenge for the 2011 final. Some of those same lads were playing in Llanelli, against a strong Scarlets side, so I wasn't really expecting a Leinster win. I did expect a bit more fight, though, a bit more attitude. We are European champions, after all. These forty-point scorelines don't look great. This was an opportunity for some of the younger lads to stake a claim. Not all of them looked like they were hungry to take it.

Being made to watch it again isn't some form of special punishment devised by Joe. There is always a video review on Monday, so the mood at work will always be defined by the weekend's result and by the quality of the performance. After a victory, especially in the Heineken, guys will really look forward to the video, because Joe knows how to show us something we've done well and extract the maximum benefit from it, either for an individual or for the group. It's not just the feelgood element he's looking for, it's so that we are continually learning. He also knows how to deliver a bollocking, though. You'll rarely hear him using bad language, but somehow that can make his criticism even more pointed.

He gets annoyed more by lack of effort than by someone making a mistake. He'll show individual errors on the screen, which can be pretty embarrassing for the individual involved, but he's not out to humiliate, more to educate, to ensure that the mistake isn't repeated. He also has a nice habit of balancing things up by showing a positive clip by the same individual at some stage in the review session. But simple laziness, he just can't accept, and he'll show you up for it. If you've taken a breather between rucks, or taken your time hauling your sorry ass off the floor after a tackle, he will have spotted it on the day or on the tape and then he will make sure that your sin is highlighted up on the screen, for all to see.

There was a moment in a game in Joe's first season when Leo and the forwards had a quick huddle on the left side of the pitch, having been awarded a penalty, appearing as though they were discussing a lineout call, when I cross-kicked for Isa, trying to catch the defence dozing. The cameraman was briefly caught dozing too so for a few seconds, all you could see on screen was our guys' reaction to the sudden change of plan. It became a race to get to the ruck on the right touchline. Mercilessly, Joe picked on one of the backs and hit him with his laser beam.

'Look, you're in the lead,' he said, before his tone changed.

'Oh, but you've just been passed out. By a front rower. Is he a quicker runner than you?'

It might sound like a mickey-take, but it feels a lot worse than that. And I think that we need more of that sort of straight shooting. One of the main reasons that Leinster turned from being talented underachievers to European champions was because Michael Cheika used to say what needed to be said. He put people on the spot. He mightn't have been everybody's cup of tea and I had a few run-ins with him myself over the years. But he brought the mental toughness that Leinster needed, and still need, if we want to stay ahead of the game.

I feel slightly uncomfortable about taking issue with the lads about Llanelli when I wasn't even playing, but I'm not the only one who feels that something needs to be said. A couple of the senior players say that they felt let down on Saturday. It doesn't matter who's wearing the jersey on the day. They are representing the entire squad, the supporters, the province. As champions, we are up there to be shot down, and everyone has a responsibility to maintain standards. At least most of the lads who played in Llanelli will get a chance to redeem themselves this Saturday, when the Dragons come to the RDS.

As it turns out, Joe didn't need to say very much at today's meeting. I think it suits him to save up the memory of last Saturday for another day – maybe the next time we play the Scarlets in their place, which just happens to be in the Heineken Cup, seven weeks from now.

Wednesday 5 September

The 105 Cafe, Clonskeagh

Wednesday is usually a day off, a chance to get away from rugby and do something completely and utterly unrelated – like kicking. To be honest, we spend so much time doing team-related stuff that you have to make time for individual skills, and given the importance of kicking it's worth setting aside a morning to do some quality work at least once a week.

I work on every type of kick, naturally, but at the moment I'm hot on restarts. This is another direct result of recent experiences in New Zealand, where the All Blacks were so good at this critical part of the game. It wasn't that our restarts were particularly bad, just that we didn't have the precise strategy that they did. Maybe we should have had higher expectations of our restarts. I know we do at Leinster. The key for the shorter ones is that you make the contest at least 50–50 between fetcher and receiver. The kick is only as good as the chase. Carter has outstanding touch and amazing accuracy, but then he has

Kieran Read chasing, who is incredibly effective. Shane Horgan and Rob Kearney are the best I've played with in this regard. With some players you have to get the kick absolutely spot-on. With Kearns, it is a case of putting it into an imaginary ten-metre box with the right trajectory and he'll gobble it up every time. Shaggy was the same.

Now Deccie has asked me to work on short restarts because Ireland will be using them more. Which is good. So that's how I spend a couple of hours in the morning – in UCD with Leinster's kicking coach, Richie Murphy, doing some place-kicks, some tactical kicking, and a lot of restarts. I'm focusing on getting the height and trajectory right for different distances. Because there are so many different options for restarts the technique for each one is slightly different. Some require letting the ball bounce and catching it on the up, rather than on the half-volley, as you would for a drop-goal. Others require a flat trajectory and need to be hit like a low drop-goal. I stand on the touchline at halfway with a bag of balls, and cones spaced at ten, fifteen, twenty and twenty-five metres infield, and try to drop balls into each space, based on Richie's choice – ten metres for the restart to Rob Kearney right up the middle, fifteen for the angle that invites a forward onto the ball at the ten-metre line, twenty-five for a winger, and so on. We've been working hard on them for a few weeks now and I'm happy with the results. I just wish I didn't have to wait another ten days before I get the chance to try one in a competitive situation.

This afternoon I'm meeting some of the lads for lunch in Clonskeagh and then we'll probably spend the afternoon chatting and drinking coffee. My social life isn't very fascinating, to be honest. I still like to hang around with my friends from school but I don't get to see them all that much. A lot are abroad now, many of them in Australia or New Zealand, so I'll only see them at Christmas, and those who are still in Ireland tend to work different hours from me. The time of the week when they're looking for entertainment is usually the time when I'm trying to provide it.

So I end up spending a lot of time with my team-mates. Here, in no particular order, are some of the guys I've spent the most time with, on and off the pitch, at Leinster:

Kevin McLaughlin. We go back to junior school, so Kev is probably my oldest friend. Underrated rugby player, though not by Joe, who usually picks him for big games. Fearless, despite having suffered numerous injuries. Bright lad and a good singer. Someone that you want in your team every week because you know he will give it everything, no matter how big or small the fixture is.

Fergus McFadden. A character. Brilliant story-teller who can lift the mood of the squad. Another player who gives everything – skilful and hard and has a huge heart. The toughest player I have ever played with.

Rob Kearney. Ever since I first met him as an Under-15, when he made the rest of us look like scruffs, he has been immaculate. Always a step ahead – first of our age-group to play for Leinster, Ireland and the Lions. Occasional roomie of mine. He gets awful stick about Isa – we tell him he's the best full-back in Ireland but the second-best in Leinster. Takes it in his stride, like he does with everything.

Leo Cullen. Understated, composed, doesn't say too much but when he does, everyone takes heed. We argue the toss over things on the field but he always has the last word. Dry wit. Everton fan. Out on his own as a three-time Heineken Cup-winning captain. Played a massive part in Leinster's transformation from nearly-men to champions.

Shane Jennings. Leo's second-in-command and another standard-setter who will say what he thinks. Hard-nosed and a great link player. Like Kev, you only know how good he is when you play with him. Great sense of humour, despite the serious exterior. A good St Mary's man.

Brian O'Driscoll. Sometimes you forget that we're privileged to play with someone they'll still be talking about a hundred years from now. Has achieved so much yet is still ridiculously competitive in everything, which means we have the odd bust-up in training, but we have a good relationship. Young at heart and great company. The greatest Irish player ever.

Cian Healy. A freak. The strongest, most explosive, powerful guy I've played with and, with thirty-odd caps before his twenty-fifth birthday, Church should break all propping records. Incredible ball carrier. An unbelievably generous guy who would do anything for you.

Sean O'Brien, aka the Mayor of Tullow. We're convinced Seanie wears the mayoral chain every time he heads home, because he seems to run the town. He's proud of his roots, and that country hardness has been great for Leinster. Never does anything by halves, always in good form. Like Cian, he is a massive ball carrier for us and we always miss him when he is not playing.

Jamie Heaslip. See him an hour before kick-off with his monster headphones on, practising drop-goals from halfway, and you'd think he's not switched on. I don't think I've met a more switched-on rugby player. Along with Brad Thorn, he is easily the most professional guy I have worked with in Leinster.

Luke Fitzgerald. Struggled with injury over the past couple of years, but when fit he is world class and has made a massive contribution to Leinster's success. Good pal and great room-mate. Big character in the squad. Brave and a great guy to have when the going gets tough in big games.

Gordon D'Arcy. One of the nicest guys to me when I first came into the squad. Leinster through and through. Has an incredible partnership with Brian, and I love playing with both of them together. Incredibly professional. Leinster's most capped player – says it all, really.

Isa Nacewa. Along with Brian and Felipe Contepomi he is the best player I have played with. Hard, humble, and doesn't make mistakes – class act.

Mike Ross. Our techie. The most important player in Ireland. Really popular member of the squad.

Richardt Strauss and Sean 'Nugget' Cronin. We're blessed to have these two powerful freaks. Both great characters in totally different ways.

Eoin Reddan. Most regular roomie. Great conversationalist, deep thinker. Plays the markets and studying for a potential career in the world of finance but could be a great coach. One of my closest pals. We have developed a great understanding with each other over the last few years and know each other's games inside out.

This isn't an exclusive gang. In fact there are no cliques. Drico and Reddser are both in their thirties but you'll see them having lunch with some of the younger lads. We like to lunch. And drink coffee. Because we do so much physical work, time off is fairly sedentary. We did go through a phase of playing 'crazy golf' up in Dundrum.

You can picture the scene. In one corner, there's a ten-year-old's birthday party going on. Only a matter of yards away, eight or nine overgrown kids are engaged in serious competition. You'd swear we were playing in the Masters – except that there's no golf etiquette at all. There could be ten balls in play, lads trying to put each other off by all means possible. Very childish, I know. There was usually a big bet or a forfeit at stake, so you can imagine the pressure coming down the last few holes. Losers might have to buy everyone dinner, or hand in their keys, wallet and phone and make their own way home. Professional sport: just a means of delaying the onset of adulthood.

Saturday 8 September

RDS

Leinster's first match of the season at the RDS, on a beautiful late summer's evening in Ballsbridge. The Dragons aren't the best team in the Pro12, but nearly 17,000 punters turn up. We almost take our massive support for granted now, but I'm old enough to remember going to watch Leinster play Heineken Cup games in Donnybrook when the capacity was around 6,000 and it wasn't always full.

I think it was about ten years ago that people began to realize what Leinster could become. I've heard that when they got a home Heineken Cup quarter-final against Biarritz, Matt Williams, the coach, wanted to play the game in Donnybrook because he reckoned the atmosphere there was an advantage that the team couldn't do without. Mick Dawson insisted on moving to Lansdowne Road, because there was the possibility of a much bigger gate. He was probably hoping for Lansdowne to be half full. That day, just over 46,000 people turned up. The atmosphere was like an international, only the crowd was even more one-sided. As I remember it, Leinster only just squeezed home, so maybe the players were more comfortable in Donnybrook. But this was the first clue that Leinster could become something massive, if only they could achieve something on the pitch.

We've done just that, and the result can be seen on evenings like this at the RDS, where we have over 13,000 season-ticket holders. The place has a unique atmosphere, very old-world with all the stables and the picket fences, and also very family-oriented – there are always loads of kids waiting for autographs outside the dressing room after a game. The players' families are looked after, also. Following every game there's some food and a few drinks in one of the function rooms inside the RDS complex, right beside the room where we have our post-match dinners. It was Leo and Jenno who drove this idea when they came back from their time in Leicester, because they'd seen over there how involving players' families can help the squad become more of a family too. Joe reinforced that when he arrived. He's very keen on the idea of us doing things correctly. We have to be in our 'number ones' – suits and ties – and regardless of whether you're involved on match-day, you have to come up and eat with the opposition afterwards, even if they are often in a rush to catch a plane. Joe also pushed to set up the family room next door, and for passes to be provided for brothers, sisters, girlfriends and so on.

Laura comes to the games, usually with Mark, my brother. I'm the eldest of four, with Gillian next, then Mark and finally Jerry, the 6'6" baby of the family. Gillian goes to Ireland games at the Aviva and texts to wish me luck, but she's not really into rugby. I could come home afterwards and she wouldn't even know whether I'd played well or not. That kind of thing helps to keep you sane. The males of the family do know their rugby, though. My uncle, Willie Sexton, played flanker for Garryowen, Munster and three times for Ireland. Dad – Jerry senior – played on the first ever Irish Schools team in 1975. He boarded in Castleknock College, then went to UCD and captained the team that won the Metropolitan Cup, which was a big deal at the time – the plaque is still up on the wall in the family home in Listowel. After UCD, Dad went to Bective Rangers, where he became more of a drinker than a rugby player. He played firsts in Bective, a big scrum-half – I don't think the out-half ever saw the ball.

It's not by accident that you end up playing rugby. Since I was two or three years old, I would have been running around up in Bective. I used to look forward to going to a match every Saturday. While Dad would be out on the pitch, I'd be getting into trouble for smashing lights in the ballroom with a rugby ball. Or I'd be on that patch of green outside the clubhouse that has been tarmacked over, knocking lumps out of my brothers, playing on into the night by the light of the bar, and then returning the next morning to play with the minis, with broken bottles on the grass after Saturday night. Those weekends in Bective were a big part of my upbringing and definitely contributed to my love of rugby.

Both my brothers are good rugby players. Mark's four years younger than me but I played club stuff with him a few times in St Mary's. He's a centre and as good as, if not better than, some of the Leinster Academy lads – I'm pretty sure Connacht had a look at him at one stage last season, and he could have gone over to play Championship rugby in England if he'd fancied it. Basically, he has been really unlucky with injuries. He had a horrible leg break in fifth year at school, snapping both his tibia and fibula. After the op, there were serious complications. He was out of action for twelve months, and only made it back in time for a cup quarter-final, by which stage he was playing with a limp. Critically, he'd missed that window of opportunity when there might have been a slot in the academy or sub-academy. At twenty-four, he's happy to play with St Mary's, although if an opportunity arose I'm sure he'd grab it. Last year he helped them win the Ulster Bank League, scoring two tries against Young Munster in the game that clinched the title.

Meanwhile Jerry's in the Leinster sub-academy and his heart is set on being a professional. He's finding it fairly tough going, though. He's only nineteen, talented enough and big enough with time to fill out, a skilful lineout operator with good hands and a decent place-kicker, which is a bonus for a lock! I advised him to repeat his Leaving Cert as he was young enough to play Irish Schools for a second year, and would have made more of a name for himself. He's too young for the Leinster Under-20s so he's kind of in no-man's land and doesn't really understand yet just what it means to be a professional. I'd love him to spend a week following Leo around to see how he operates, and what it takes. Hopefully it will work out for Jerry. He just needs a break.

My brothers' experiences make me realize how lucky I am to be making a living from rugby. And that's not just some empty line. While I wanted to be a pro from the time I made the Junior Cup team in Mary's, I only fluked my way into the system. I played Leinster Schools in fifth year but chose a disastrous time to be injured and missed out on Irish Schools, despite Mary's winning the cup that year, 2002. In sixth year, I nipped in for the Irish Schools tour to Australia, but didn't get capped, didn't even make the bench. I went off to study chemical engineering – don't ask – in UCD. At the weekends, I played for Mary's and drank pints. I still wanted to be a professional rugby player but didn't have the first notion how to go about it.

Then I got lucky. One day Mary's were playing Dungannon at Templeville Road and, unbeknownst to me, the Ireland Under-21s coach Mark McDermott was at the game, mainly to have a look at my opposite number, Gareth Steenson, now at Exeter. I had a stormer, scored a couple of tries and kicked a load of points, and next thing Macker rings to tell me he's bringing me into the 21s squad. I was in terrible shape, but the 21s had been drawn in the same pool as physically huge teams in that year's World Cup in Scotland – Argentina, France, New Zealand – and Macker wanted guys who had been playing against men in the All Ireland League, not Under-20 interpros. I barely featured at the World Cup, but just being there got me into the academy. It went from there.

So I look at Mark and I realize that I was lucky to get a break. That's only a start, however. From that point, you have to make it count. Which, for young pros, means taking advantage of opportunities, such as tonight's game against the Dragons. In fairness to them, some of the young backs who were humiliated last week started brilliantly – Noel Reid and Brendan Macken combined to set up a try for Andrew Conway that is already a contender for try of the season. Tonight was also an opportunity for Quinn Roux, a horse of a man from Cape Town and only twenty-one, who's our 'project player': a South African who is looking to qualify as Irish by living here for three years, like Richardt Strauss. We're pretty certain Brad Thorn won't be rejoining us this season, so there's a second-row slot up for grabs. Quinn has impressed in training and for his first game he did pretty well.

The 45–20 win is almost a reversal of last week's scoreline, but the concession of three tries to the Dragons' backs is annoying. Two games into the league campaign and we have the worst defence in the league, having leaked ten tries. Next Monday's video review will be a happier experience, but not without the odd stern word from Joe.

Monday 10 September

UCD

Finally, a game to prepare for. I've enjoyed pre-season, worked hard and made gains in the gym, sharpened a few individual skills. Great. But there's nothing like playing. So no more dropping in and out of team sessions, chipping in with suggestions from the side. I'm starting this Saturday, so I'll be calling the shots again, and that starts from today.

There's just one thing I've promised myself for this season – to be a little less narky with my team-mates, to show more self-control, in training and in matches.

I can be a bit hot-headed at times. Rugby's more than a job to me, it's an obsession, so I demand high standards from myself and those around me. If I feel those standards aren't being met, I'll have a go at someone. It's the way I've always been. If things are going well, I'm positive; if they're not, I'm bound to bark. It's something that I am conscious of trying to control, but it's hard. It's in there, and I'd rather be the way I am and try to control it, than be laid back and too cool for school.

My crankiness doesn't go down well with everyone. I thought Brian would like it, given the standards he has set for himself. But no. Occasionally he'll tell me to chill out – which is one way to really make my blood boil. I understand his argument. Having a go at someone can make him tense up, especially a younger player who might not perform to his potential as a result. But I'd like to think I wouldn't have a pop at someone for making a physical mistake. Most of the time it's because someone doesn't know where they are meant to be in a certain move, because they haven't done their homework or they've simply stopped concentrating. This can make everyone look foolish, but especially me, because as the out-half, I'm supposed to be organizing the team.

I don't care if you're nineteen or thirty-four. If you can't handle a fellow professional having a go at you in training, how are you going to be able to handle the pressure of 80,000 people having a go at you when something goes wrong on the big day? Why mollycoddle players? I remember Felipe Contepomi bollocking me on plenty of occasions when I was starting off. Brian too, actually. I got over it.

Maybe it's the way I was brought up. Dad started off his education at a boarding school in Kerry and the priests there would have given him the odd clip. So when I was out of line as a kid, Dad wouldn't say, 'Jonathan, I'm disappointed in you.' He'd bark at me or give me a slap. Maybe it's more a Munster trait. I know that Munster used to have fights all the time in training, especially in the weeks of Heineken Cup matches. That attitude did them no harm, while for years Leinster bottled it on the big days. Perhaps we've been helped recently that we've had a bit of country edge with guys from outside Dublin like Jamie Heaslip and Seanie O'Brien.

Some people encourage me to keep driving standards. Leo loves my narkiness. Maybe it's because that's what he saw working during his time at Leicester. Jenno has no problem with the way I go on. I got on really well with Brad Thorn when he was here last season and he told me never to lose my edginess. Reddser too. He says the best thing about coming to Leinster is that he no longer has to be Mr Cranky, which was the role he played at Wasps. He just lets me take over.

We have ongoing arguments, me and Reddser. That's the way our relationship works. Watch us at training and you'd wonder how we could be room-mates. Sometimes it can get out of hand. There was one team run in the week of a Heineken game where I had a go at him for throwing a poor pass, then bollocked him out of it a few minutes later for ignoring a call. He bided his time and when one of my passes was off-target, he shoulder-charged me on his way to the ruck and hissed at me, 'Look after your own shit!' So I chased him, and took a wild swing and swiped the legs from under him. It's a couple of days before a cup match and we're supposed to be running the show, organizing the team, but instead we're almost coming to blows and shouting abuse at each other. But then afterwards we laughed about it. We're the best of friends and happy to room together even when we have the worst arguments.

My coaches? Joe likes me keeping people on their toes but warns me about going too far sometimes. At first, Deccie thought it was something I needed to control. He'd suggest I stop throwing my hands up in the air and barking, as it only encouraged the opposition to believe they were getting to us. But more recently he suggested I take my Leinster persona into Irish camp with me.

Up until fairly recently, I had almost a split personality. There was Leinster Johnny and there was Ireland Johnny, poles apart. With Ireland, Brian was always saying, 'Get in there and drive us.' And I'd respond angrily, 'I don't even know if I'm going to be playing. How can I drive a meeting on Monday afternoon if Rog's name is going to be called out on the Tuesday morning?'

I never knew if I was in or out. That was half the problem. The other half was not knowing how a Munster lad was going to react if I had a go at him.

So things were tense between myself and Brian for a while, especially during the 2011 Six Nations. There was one balls-up in the first game, in Rome, a game we looked like losing until Rog came off the bench to drop a goal. It was a breakdown in communication and I got the brunt of Drico's anger. He had a right pop at me on the pitch. On the one hand he's telling me to take control of things, on the other he's bawling me out of it in front of everyone. I took it but I bottled it up. I thought, *Right, I'm going to remember that*. Six weeks later, we had an almighty blow-up at the RDS on the Tuesday before the final game, against England. It was literally the two of us going crazy at each other and the rest of the squad watching, half embarrassed.

The problem was that we were both making the backline calls at that stage and it was a recipe for disaster. I said I wanted him either making the calls or shutting up, because it had become a mess. It was either me or him. We got very heated but it helped clear the air and, who knows, maybe it set the tone for the week. We went out and hammered England at the Aviva. I know for a fact that after our stand-up row, the lines of communication were a lot clearer.

Anyway, I've promised myself to be more controlled, to look after my own game a bit more, maybe be a bit more selfish, not fret over everyone else's performance. We'll see. Brian's down to start in Treviso too. I wonder will he notice the new me.

Tuesday 11 September

IRUPA offices, Leeson Street

I'm taking over from Brian as chairman of the Irish Rugby Union Players Association. He was good at it but it took up a fair bit of his time and he wanted to take on a different role, maybe as a mentor. So I was approached by the association's chief executive, Omar Hassanein. He said he was looking for someone a bit younger than Brian, who'd be in the game for at least another five or six years, and had a high profile. Would I be interested?

Omar noticed that I'd been reasonably vocal at IRUPA meetings over the years, certainly one of the younger guys to pipe up and ask questions. For example, it always intrigued me how our win bonus for league matches of €500 was still the same as it was when 2,000 people were turning up at Donnybrook, yet now we were selling out the Aviva for Leinster v. Munster matches. Still, I was a little shocked when he approached me and not sure if I wanted it, because I wasn't sure what people in other provinces would think. But he said he had checked with the likes of Paul O'Connell (Munster), Rory Best (Ulster) and Gavin Duffy (Connacht) and they were happy for me to go ahead. It's not a massive role. It's important to be at the meetings and to help make decisions, but most of the work is done by Omar and we are just there to bounce ideas off. I also think it's important for players to be educated about their welfare and how to prepare for the rugby afterlife.

So I've accepted, and this morning I have to pop into the IRUPA offices for a quick photo and a few words with the media. I have a good bit more time on my hands now, having finally completed my Commerce finals in UCD. I took a long road to get there, ditching that chemical engineering degree, taking the odd year off, resitting the odd exam because of tours, and so on. But I got there in the end and finished up with a 2:1, which I was delighted with.

Getting that out of the way freed me up to do other stuff. I'm on the board of Headstrong, a charity for young people suffering from mental health problems. It's the charity of choice for O2, and I'm one of O2's brand ambassadors, so that's how the connection came about. They were interested in having a twenty-something male involved, as that would be the same age as a lot of the people they're trying to help. So I'm on the board of management and get to go to their meetings. It's really interesting to see how decisions are made and how a board operates. There are a lot of people who aren't directly associated in the charity but bring expertise from their own field – finance, marketing, IT, social media. It's fascinating.

It's the same with IRUPA. It gives me the inside track on all sorts of stuff, and from a selfish point of view it also looks good on my CV to have been part of a body representing all Ireland's professional players. I hope that I can bring something to the party.

'We've been planning for some months to directly involve Johnny in our organization,' Omar told the *Irish Times*. 'He is a very capable individual and is very enthusiastic about the collective player cause. To add to this, he is well respected by the IRFU and the key stakeholders within the game, making him an important cog in the longer term development of our organization.'

I smiled when I read the line about being respected by the IRFU. Through my agent, Fintan Drury, I've been trying to get the Union to sort out my contract, which is up at the end of this season. I'm hoping for a three- or even a four-year deal, just to give me some certainty, some security. It might also help me in my quest for a mortgage. With house prices in Dublin right down, this is a good time to buy, but the banks are impossibly cautious. The Union won't play ball, however. A while back, I asked Leinster manager Guy Easterby to try to apply some pressure, as it's obviously in Leinster's interests to have some certainty when it comes to planning for next season. But the Union refuse to do business until after the November Tests, which means Fintan has been looking into alternatives. The best opportunities are in France. I've no huge interest in leaving Leinster, but we need to have something as leverage when the Union are finally willing to negotiate, so Fintan has been doing some research in France on my behalf.

I was half-thinking that taking the IRUPA role might help to speed up the negotiation process – the association has a fair bit of contact with Maurice Dowling, the Union's director of human resources. No chance. Maybe the Union think that by December, the French clubs will have already finished all their recruitment for next season. Two years ago I considered an offer from Michael Cheika, then at Stade Français, and Fintan made sure that the story found its way into the media, but this didn't impress the Union, which refused to budge on their final offer: €300,000 a year, for two years. We only really came to a solution thanks to the generosity of O2, who made me a brand ambassador and so 'topped up' my salary.

I'm aware this may seem a lot of money for someone approaching his twenty-sixth birthday, as I was then, but I could point out that Stade had been offering me the guts of half a million euro per season. Professional rugby careers are brief, and while most of us try to prepare ourselves for the 'afterlife', we will be entering an unfamiliar job market in our thirties with uncertain prospects. It's also worth saying that I spent the first few years of my career on pretty ordinary money, despite being on the fringes of the Ireland squad. Back in 2008/09, before I was on a central contract, it was just me, arguing my case with Leinster chief executive Mick Dawson that if I was in the squad for Heineken Cup matches and if I had helped win a Magners League title, then I was worth more than €85,000 a season. I may have been third-choice 10 behind Felipe Contepomi and Isa Nacewa at Leinster but I was also third choice for Ireland, behind Ronan O'Gara and Paddy Wallace. Eventually, Leinster upped that to €100,000 for two years, to kick in at the start of the 2009/10 season, by which stage I'd been part of a Churchill Cup-winning side.

Soon I was challenging Rog for a starting place in the national side, but at no stage in those two seasons did the Union, who are basically everyone's paymaster, say, 'Let's renegotiate a fair deal.' My pay was bumped up to €150,000 once I had six international starts, as per my contract, but that seemed pretty ordinary money for some-one who looked like travelling to the World Cup as first-choice out-half. This was around the time – spring of 2011, a month or two before the Heineken Cup final in Cardiff – when I had my first hard negotiation with the Union over a central contract. A solution was found, as I said, but the bottom line is that things have never been easy on the contractual front. I have never really felt I've been paid what I'm worth. I think I know what the Union think: *Johnny will eventually settle for what we're offering him. He's going nowhere.* And that attitude pisses me off. Money is not my driving force, far from it, but at some stage in my career I'm going to get paid what I'm worth. At some stage, I'm going to take a stand.

Friday 14 September

Hotel Boscolo, Treviso

I was pleasantly surprised by the number of Leinster supporters on our flight here this evening, especially for an early-season Rabo game. But then maybe I should know our fans better by now. Treviso is just a half an hour's train ride from Venice and it's around twenty-five degrees here at the moment. There's some fine wining and dining and shopping to be done. *Avanti*, Leinster!

We had a pre-season tour to Treviso four years ago and some of the lads ventured into Venice, but it's out of the question on an in-and-out trip like this. It's late afternoon when we arrive at the team hotel and all we've time for is a stretching session, dinner, a meeting, a snack and then bed. We did our captain's run earlier in the day and that went well, considering this is the first week back for myself, Brian, Jamie, Kev, Ferg, Reddser, Cian and Mike Ross – Joe reckons it's best to throw us all back in together, rather than phase us back in gradually. Time is tight – we have Munster in three weeks' time, and our first Heineken Cup pool game against Exeter is the week after that. We're just fortunate to have drawn Exeter at home as our first game, given we have Clermont in our pool. Speaking of which, where's the logic in that? The two best teams in the Heineken Cup have been pooled together. Crazy.

That's an argument for another day, though. Treviso are a serious side, especially on their own patch. I've only played here once before, on that pre-season tour, and we only squeezed home on that occasion, while they beat us fairly comfortably here in Joe's first year. We know they've over half the Italian national side playing tomorrow. They've already beaten Ospreys here this season, and drew with them in last year's Heineken Cup, when they also did a number on Biarritz. Luckily, we've an evening kick-off tomorrow but it will still be warm. No matter how hard you work in pre-season, nothing prepares you for the aerobic shock of your first game.

The food at our hotel is delicious, but there are very few items on the menu that would correspond with my dietary needs. Food is one of the few areas in life where I wish I was Cian Healy. He has a licence to eat whatever he wants, because he turns everything into muscle. He nearly broke the calorie counter when he was wearing it – something like 10,000 calories in one day. It makes me sick. I find it hard enough to load muscle, and if I overeat I put on flab. It's completely unfair, but then some of us are made differently from others. So I go easy on the pasta dishes in the hotel restaurant and avoid the desserts altogether. At times like this, the best place to be is tucked up in bed.

Saturday 15 September

Stadio Comunale di Monigo (Treviso 18, Leinster 19)

Some nights, this can be the best job in the world. To get the win was sweet, especially after a predictably scrappy performance in testing conditions, but from a personal point of view there is no better feeling than executing a skill under pressure when you've worked bloody hard to be ready for that moment.

As if by design, the result of my first game of the season hinged on our ability to reclaim one of those short restarts. We looked dead and buried when Treviso's replacement scrum-half, Fabio Semanzato, nipped in for a try with three minutes left on the clock, to draw the teams level at 16–16. When Luke McLean knocked over the conversion, around 5,000 Treviso supporters went mental, thinking that they'd turned over the European champions for the second time in three years. In fairness to them, we could have had no complaints if this had happened, because they'd been better than us on a sweltering night. But it didn't happen.

Rushing back up to halfway, I told Devin Toner, all 6'10" of him, that I'd be looking to land the restart just where the ten- and fifteen-metre lines intersected. Dev did brilliantly to reclaim the ball. Once he'd done his bit, we were in with a shout and two or three phases later I slotted a peach of a drop-goal from all of forty-five metres. When you do something like that, you have a feeling that this is going to be a good season.

It was roasting over there. We had our team walk-through a few hours before the game and at that stage, in mid-afternoon, it was nearly thirty degrees. It had cooled considerably when we came back to the stadium but by then the place was swarming with mosquitoes. Naturally, our bagman Johnny O'Hagan had mosquito spray that was four years out of date. Still, I covered myself in it because they love me for some reason. As I was taking kicks, I was trying hard not to inhale mozzies. Add all that to the fact that we aren't match-hardened yet and it wasn't much fun. We were helped by Brian scoring a great try early in the second half after a sweet offload by Damian Browne, which kept us in the game.

Personally, I was really happy with my place-kicking and also with my kicking out of hand. Deccie has asked me to be more aggressive with my line kicks off penalties. I'd been kicking the ball good distances, but being safe enough on my angles. Deccie backed me to go for extra length along the touchline – if I missed the odd touch, well, he was happy to take that gamble. That went well this evening.

The only thing bugging me is that I lost it with Reddser on the pitch – first game as the new me and there I am, bawling him out of it, same as ever. And it was over nothing! Some ridiculously small detail. He was supposed to pick the ball from between Jamie's legs at the scrum, take a step to draw their scrum-half, then feed me behind Ferg, and so on, but he couldn't ferret the ball out. The move didn't work, basically. It wasn't his fault, but I didn't see that. So at the next break in play, I'm abusing him and he's abusing me back. It gets heated. As I walk back to my position, there's Brian, shaking his head, giving me the 'I'm disappointed' look. Brilliant. I feel like telling him to fuck off. I'm trying, right?

Don't get me wrong, I get on really well with Brian. We'd be good friends. I often sit beside him on the way to games and we chat away about all sorts of stuff. Funnily enough, on the bus earlier this afternoon, he'd been telling me about the autobiography he's been working on with Paul Kimmage, the journalist, and how hard he's finding it to write about me and Rog. He says it's difficult for him to compliment me without feeling like he's stabbing Rog in the back and vice versa. He doesn't seem to have any problem going on about Rog having the bottle to kick last-minute match-winning drop-goals or penalties. I mention a big penalty miss in the 2000 Heineken Cup final against Northampton and a couple of misses in the final against Leicester two years later. Overcoming those disappointments was what made Rog as a player, and makes his match-winning moments all the more impressive, I say. And Brian says, 'Yeah, yeah, I never thought about it that way.'

The weird thing is, as I was lining up that late drop-goal against Treviso, my bus conversation with Brian popped into my head. I'm in the pocket setting things up and while I'm picking my spot, I'm also thinking, *Christ, myself and Drico were only talking about this a few hours ago on the bus to the stadium.* It's incredible the things that can pop into your head sometimes. Anyway, I nailed it, and we won. And when the final whistle went, part of me was thinking, *Stick that in your book, Brian.*

I was feeling pretty good about myself as we boarded our charter plane at around eleven o'clock. That was when I heard about Nevin Spence. I can't remember exactly who told me – I think the news broke when one of the younger lads received a text from one of the Ulster guys – but word spread through the cabin with eerie speed. I received a text from my mum. An accident on the family farm. Nevin's brother and father died too. It was only when we touched down in Dublin that some of the gruesome details filtered through – how a dog falling into a slurry pit had led to the deaths of three men. It's too tragic for words.

It always takes me hours to settle after a game, but that night I wasn't rewinding back through various plays. All I could think about was Nevin's sheer vitality and his apparent indestructibility. I didn't know him very well, had played against him once or twice, trained with him at the odd Irish camp. All I really knew was that he was a hard bugger, a great man to take a hard line, to smash someone man and ball. Not a big man but he used every kilo he had. Off the pitch he came across as a really quiet, humble chap. Those are my memories of him. It was too surreal to try to imagine the horrible few moments in which he was taken.

Sunday 16 September

Medical rooms, UCD

There's a grim irony in what we do this morning, heading down for the medical staff to assess the damage we have done to our bodies by flinging them around a rugby pitch, when a fellow professional has been cut down by such a random sequence of events involving the people who meant most to him. Hearing it on the radio on a Sunday morning or reading about it in a newspaper is still shocking, even though it's nearly twelve hours since I first heard the news.

As rugby players have become bigger and more powerful, and the collisions more violent, we must take greater care over how our bodies recover. So we spend the mornings after games moving gingerly from hot baths to cold ones and back again, rather than sleeping off hangovers like previous generations of players might have done. And we do medical examinations, so that by Monday, our busiest day of the week, Joe will have a full run-down on who will be able to do what for the week, and who has been ruled out for the next game.

At Leinster, it's standard procedure that we all do an MSR – a musculoskeletal report. It's an Australian system that Michael Cheika introduced a few years ago, and now Ireland and the other provinces use it as well. You go into the gym with the medical and physio staff and there are various stations set up. You do a sit-and-reach, to measure stiffness in your hamstrings and lower back. You do a 'groin squeeze' using a blood-pressure sleeve and they take a reading from that. And so on.

If you've taken a bang to the head, it's mandatory to do a 'cog' test on one of the computers upstairs. They throw stuff at you, to see how well you can remember pictures, letters, numbers. Your baseline cognizance score is there from the summer, when you've had no collisions for a while, and they measure your responses against that. Even if you haven't taken an obvious bang, there are questions to be answered, again on computer:

How well have you slept since the game?

Have you been sick at all?

Are you worried about non-rugby-related issues?

Have you moved house? (In other words, have you been getting enough rest?)

Have you been studying for exams?

It's very thorough, and the bottom line is that there are any number of issues that can contribute to someone not being in optimal physical condition to play rugby. The medical and S&C staff will have all this info mailed through to Joe by 8.30 on the Monday morning. But there's also a sense that we're being monitored because we're in a dangerous job and they have a duty of care towards us. It's exactly the sort of care and attention Nevin Spence was used to in Ulster. But now he's gone. You wonder how the Ulster lads can even contemplate trying to play rugby again.

Thursday 20 September

UCD

It's Nevin's funeral today. A good few of us had wanted to go up north to express our sympathies to the family and to Ulster, but the family have asked that it remain a funeral for family and friends, rather than a rugby funeral. There's a memorial service in Ravenhill next Monday which some of us will go to, but in the meantime Guy Easterby, our manager, was keen that we find some other way to show our support, apart from wearing an armband in the game against Edinburgh this Saturday at the RDS. In the end, we agreed to wear T-shirts carrying the initials 'NS' while warming up for the game.

Thursday is when we focus on attack. As I've already mentioned, our busiest day is Monday, what with reviews, meetings, gym and a field session. You could be in UCD from 8.30 until 5. In general, the focus on Tuesdays is defence. We get the 'A' team to play the part of Edinburgh. Their backs run Edinburgh plays against us while our forwards will defend Edinburgh lineouts, or whatever. Wednesday is a day off – except for the kickers – and Thursday is attack. We are told our plays on Monday and Joe expects us to have done our homework, so that when we turn up today, we have everything spot-on. There is no Leinster playbook as such, no sheets handed out. You can take notes as he is putting them up on the whiteboard but he refuses to spoon-feed. Joe believes that if you have a sheet, you won't go to the trouble of learning the information properly. And you need to know it properly. While we may walk through moves on Monday, today we do it at full tilt.

Joe is a true all-rounder of a coach who knows his rugby inside out, but I think what defines him is the way that he coaches attack. Maybe it's because he was a winger himself. What we noticed immediately about him was his knowledge of the opposition and the detail he'll go into to ensure a move works. There are times when you might think you have the line-break executed to perfection but he'll insist that it's not precise enough to break the team we're up against next. So we go back and do it again. How many times? Until we get it right. Just when you think we've nailed it, he spots that the blind-side winger wasn't 'animating', or drawing attention to himself, the way Joe wanted. No one is allowed to be redundant. If you're not actively involved in the play, he wants you doing something to make the opposition think that you are.

I love that attention to detail. It gives you greater confidence going to the game. Take that try Brian scored in the quarter-final against Cardiff last season, when there were seven of us involved – Richardt, Leo, Reddser, Jamie, me, Luke Fitzgerald and Brian – and not one Cardiff hand laid on us. We ran that countless times, just to get the timing absolutely on the money – and not just the guys who touched the ball. Watch the replay from behind and you'll see me jumping in the air to celebrate as Drico dots down. That's the joy of seeing something click that you've really rehearsed properly. The funny thing is that we probably didn't run it to Joe's complete satisfaction. By his reckoning, I probably stepped to the right a millisecond too early. Oh, well.

Saturday 22 September

RDS (Leinster 22, Edinburgh 16)

An amazing thing happened at kick-off today. We'd just stood for a minute's silence for Nevin, as happened in grounds all over Ireland and Britain, and as I was waiting for the ref to give me the nod to get the game going, I noticed the crowd was singing a song you don't often hear at the RDS – 'Stand up for the Ulsterman', to the tune of 'Go West' by the Pet Shop Boys. I think it started on the terraces beneath the Anglesea Stand, where the real hard-core Leinster fans congregate, and got louder and louder, even after the game had started. You couldn't have missed it, even if you'd been playing, and it was quite moving. When I got home this evening, I went onto RTE Player just to see how it came across on TV but it wasn't the same. The commentators didn't even mention it. But it was a special moment at the time and fair play to the RDS crowd for reaching out to Ulster in that way.

If that was uplifting, the dressing room was pretty flat afterwards. Edinburgh haven't won in Dublin for seven seasons and shouldn't have even come close tonight but somehow we managed to make things sweaty for ourselves. We're still in the silly season, of course – as Joe pointed out, he's picked something like forty players in four games. But we need to start hitting some form quickly. We have Connacht next week, a game I'll be resting for, then Munster at the Aviva the week after that, and then we're into the Heineken.

Personally, I feel in good nick. All the gym and track work has me feeling sharp, quick, and confident running at defences, and that confidence helped me score an early try. We lost Darce early on but young Brendan Macken took his chance well off the bench, scoring a couple of tries. The second of those came with a quarter of an hour still remaining, when we led 22–9 and looked good for the four-try bonus. Instead, one of their donkeys went over for a try and we ended up defending for our lives, relying on one of the touch judges to spot an Edinburgh knock-on to get us out of jail.

Joe was clearly unhappy with aspects of the performance, and even more so with the fact that eleven of us will be missing on Monday and Tuesday because of an Ireland camp. This means he'll have only one proper session to prepare for next Friday's game away to Connacht, who are always foaming at the mouth whenever we come to Galway. Deccie didn't have a camp in September last year but you get the impression that the IRFU's priorities are shifting more towards the national team. It was fantastic to have ourselves and Ulster contest a Heineken Cup final in Twickenham a few months back, but that result in Hamilton has placed enormous pressure on all of us. It seems like Earlsy's words at the Aviva about putting our country first might have been prophetic.

TWO

Thinking Ahead

Carton House has been our base for this two-day camp and it will be Ireland's centre of operations for the foreseeable future. This was one of the changes that came out of our meeting in the Aviva a few weeks back. We felt it didn't make sense to be skipping from one centre to the next because it meant we weren't getting full value out of our time together. In Limerick, for example, you could spend an hour in traffic just going from the team hotel to the weights room in the university, and another hour back. That's two hours wasted. We have the Springboks in six weeks' time, and Argentina two weeks after that, with World Cup seedings at stake. As things stand, we're ranked seventh in the world, but two defeats could mean slipping to ninth, which in turn could mean we end up with two big guns in our pool in 2015. That would be disastrous.

So Carton is our new home from home, and everything is on site – gym, pool, training pitches, plus two championship golf courses, incidentally. If the facilities are good enough for my beloved Man United, then they're good enough for us too. There are also lots of single rooms available, which suits me just fine, and plenty of space in general.

We'll have two weeks together to prepare for South Africa, but even this far out from the game it's good to get people thinking about how we're going to go about playing them. Already it's pretty obvious the coaches want us to play a territorial game. It seemed like all we've worked on for the last two days has been our kicking plan, with the focus almost entirely on exit strategies from our twenty-two. I was slightly uneasy about this at first, I have to say. With Leinster,

I find it easy to find space to kick into because most of the time the opposition wingers are so worried about us moving the ball that they stay flat, opening up kicking options in the backfield. But if they see you kicking everything, they hang deep, while the guys outside you can switch off from the possibility of moving the ball. Les Kiss gives me some clarity on the strategy, though. He explained that South Africa's entire game-plan is to get into your twenty-two and smother you, so it's imperative that we reduce risk in our own half. Sounds reasonable enough.

We got some good work done over the past couple of days. We spoke at our Aviva meeting about turning up at camp ready to work, and it felt like a day's work – there was no one here carrying knocks or sitting around watching. We're determined to maintain this standard when we come back here in five weeks' time.

Wednesday 26 September

The Goat Bar & Restaurant, Goatstown

Lunch with Fintan. It's a good week to meet him as I'm not playing in Connacht on Friday. He has news: there's going to be a big offer for me from one of the French clubs. Eye-popping money. Around double what I'm on with the Union. It's flattering, I can't deny it.

Not that I can see it ever coming to anything. I'm not really motivated by money, more by success, which is why I can't ever see myself leaving Leinster. But the fact of the matter is I've had no choice but to investigate my options. I've no real interest in playing in England. If I did ever go to France, I'd be testing myself in the best league in the world, learning a new language and a new culture, maybe broadening my options for life after rugby.

It's a fall-back plan. I wanted to thrash out a deal with the Union before the season began. It would have been in both the Union's interest and mine. But negotiations won't begin until after the November Tests, so I have to see what's out there. What if I wait for the Union's offer and it's not good enough? Do I start looking at alternatives then, when some clubs have already made plans for next season? Of course not. I have to start looking now, and that means doing a thorough investigation of clubs that I might join, even if the possibility is minimal. I can't just lob my name into the air and see who responds quickest, as that would give the impression of another Irish player simply looking for the highest bidder, and then using that bid to get a better deal from the Union. This is how we are viewed in France, apparently, seeing as no current Irish international has ever gone there. I needed to make a short-list of clubs where I would want to play, if the worst came to the worst.

So I've been doing a bit of research on the QT. My man in France is Bernard Jackman, the former Leinster and Ireland hooker, who is working in Grenoble as defence coach, and doing pretty well for himself – having been promoted from the French second division, Grenoble were expected to go straight back down from the Top 14 but have got off to a flier. Berch was starting hooker with Leinster when I broke into the side in 2007/08. He was always really good to me, always helpful to younger players, even in his own position. I have a lot to thank him for as he gave me a lot of time when things were not going so well – chatting on the phone till all hours and persuading me to be patient. He also introduced me to Enda McNulty, the former Armagh footballer who's now a sports psychologist and whom I consult from time to time. Berch is also a great man for chat, and is all over French club rugby like a rash, reads every word of *Midiolympique* and *L'Equipe* and keeps up to date with all player and coach movements. I trust his opinion.

He's been keeping me posted on how Matt Giteau has been getting on at Toulon, or Luke McAlister in Toulouse. I'd be interested in this stuff anyway, because I'm a rugby fan. But this is a bit different because I'm looking to see what's out there for me. I've been keeping an eye on Clermont particularly, seeing as we have them in our Heineken Cup pool – again – and because I feel some affinity for them, given that Joe was there for four years and I've also kept in touch with Nathan Hines, who joined them from us. Their Top 14 form has been reasonable but the word is that they're really targeting Europe this year, and are still hurting after losing the semi-final to us in Bordeaux last season.

From what I know of Clermont – their supporters and the resources at their disposal, but especially their ambition and the way they play the game – they had to be included in the short-list. Toulon also have potential, seeing as there's a possibility that Jonny Wilkinson might be in his last season there, and we included Toulouse, as they are still one of French rugby's big guns. Finally, there's Racing Metro. Berch tells me they are hugely ambitious and the club president has the money to back up the ambition. They're building a new stadium, hiring the current coaches at Castres, who are highly rated, and the word is they are signing Jamie Roberts and Dan Lydiate, as well as Brian Mujati and Juandre Kruger from Northampton, though nothing is official yet. With all this happening, Berch reckoned they could be a force in France and England.

Fintan was over meeting with a French agent last week – apparently the clubs over there insist on using an intermediary. If this sounds like we mean business, then that's because we have given that impression, at the very least. Fintan would be thorough like that, anyway. I was introduced to him by Shane Horgan a few years ago and Shaggy is another whose opinion I'd respect. I knew Fintan was a high achiever in the business world whose main sporting interest was soccer but that he had represented a few rugby players, including Shaggy, Darce and Denis Hickie. I was having a few contractual difficulties at the time so I agreed to meet him. What I liked was that there were no big promises. He just said, 'All you need to know is that I will do my best for you.' He also mentioned that the IRFU probably didn't like him very much, which I took as a positive sign, I'll admit. I did like him. He can be abrasive but that's because he's competitive, which I like. And I trust him. The last thing you'd want is to have to go in and argue your own case with the Union, so you need someone who'll go in and battle for you, who won't cut corners.

Fintan is constantly at loggerheads with the Union, but that's part of his job. It would be easy for them to portray him as some sort of threat to Irish rugby, trying to lure players abroad, seeing as a couple of players that he represents have had discussions with French clubs. This ignores the fact that none of Fintan's players has ever left, despite there having been offers. He is merely assessing my options, putting feelers out there. Toulouse have no interest, apparently. Clermont say they'd rather not do anything about it until after we play each other in our back-to-back pool matches in December, which seems reasonable enough, though not very enthusiastic. Toulon are unsure also, because they may want to stick with what they have. Keenest by far are Racing. I don't know how much substance there is to them, but they could make things interesting when the Union finally come to the table in December.

Friday 28 September

Goatstown

There was good news and bad news for J. Sexton on Sky's *Rugby Club* last night. Apparently I'm good enough to make the Lions Test team, but not good enough to take the place-kicks. Four former Lions – Will Greenwood, Ieuan Evans, Scott Hastings and our very own Shane Horgan – picked their Test team to play Australia and it was nice to see all four of them included me. But Evans said that Leigh Halfpenny would have to be picked at 15 to ensure the Lions had a world-class goal-kicker.

So there's suddenly a problem with my goal-kicking? What's this based on? The World Cup? Yes, I had a few problems out there, but that's nearly a year ago and my kicking stats for Ireland have been great since – over 85 per cent, and I've taken on every kick that was within my range, unlike some kickers, who protect their averages by avoiding long-range shots. I've had a 90 per cent success rate in the Heineken Cup for the past two seasons, 80 per cent in the last Six Nations. I rate Halfpenny as a player and as a kicker but I don't like the suggestion that I'm unreliable.

Today I met any number of people who saw the programme and said I must have been delighted to have made everyone's Test team. I played along and smiled and nodded. I didn't tell them that last night

I was cursing at the TV and calling Ieuan Evans all sorts of names. Is this what the Lions do to you?

I know I shouldn't let stuff like this get to me. The Lions don't leave for Australia for another eight months so there's a lot of rugby to be played. But judging by the reaction, everyone is plugged in already. I was talking to Brian about it today and he says that already the hype has gone beyond anything he's known, and he's been on three Lions tours already. He's keen to go on another one too, so he reckons the best thing to do is to avoid watching or reading anything more on the subject. Maybe he's onto something.

The frustrating thing is that most people will take what Ieuan Evans says at face value. Even if Warren Gatland knows better, it might alter his perception too. All I want to do is go out and prove that my goal-kicking is world-class – but of course I'm off this week. I had to sit and watch tonight's game on TV. It didn't do much to improve my mood.

In Galway tonight, Connacht stuffed us, 34–6. A record hiding. Embarrassing. I was at the team meeting yesterday and we talked about how our defence needed serious improvement – Greg Feek has been given responsibility for that area, but the focus of the chat was how we need to take more personal responsibility for defence on the pitch. Then we go out and concede five tries to Connacht.

I'd say Joe is livid. He was already furious about his preparation being disrupted by so many of us being in the Ireland camp on Monday and Tuesday, which meant he only had one proper training session this week with everyone back on board. When they arrived down in Galway, things only got worse. Quinn Roux hurt his shoulder in the warm-up and only lasted ten minutes or so. Darce didn't even last that long – he was gone with bruised ribs after five minutes or so. Connacht were well up for it, of course. They thrive on the notion that they are hard done by, that we nick their best players. Here was a brilliant opportunity for them: the European champions coming down to their patch. They always treat this fixture as a cup final and this time they had the bonus of knowing we weren't properly prepared. They took their chance, in fairness to them, and the good news for Irish rugby is that they have some talented young backs in Tiernan O'Halloran, Dave McSharry and Robbie Henshaw, who's only a year out of school and looks a real talent. But God, it was painful viewing.

The guy I felt sorry for was Rob Kearney, as he took a bad bang in the back during the first half and looks like being out for at least a month. His back has been giving him trouble for a while, since the second half of last season's Heineken Cup semi-final against Clermont, in fact. Not that you'd have known it during his golden ten minutes early in that second half, when he was dropping long-range goals and setting up a brilliant try for Cian. But he wasn't himself on tour in New Zealand and while he hoped the summer's rest would sort things out, he was still struggling a bit in pre-season. Poor guy. With the season that he had last year, it was always going to be hard for him to live up to those standards, even more so when he was struggling with a niggle. Now this.

I don't envy the lads the bus journey back from Galway. At the same time, I'm pissed off. We're one week away from Munster coming to the Aviva, which is always a massive game for us, and then it's Exeter in the Heineken a week after that.

Monday 1 October

Meeting room, UCD

Here we are again in our plush new meeting room, with the smell of newness still in the air – spotless walls and carpets, flat-screen projectors, subtle lighting and sturdy, comfortable chairs. It wasn't like this in Riverview. Most of the chairs in our meeting room were a bit bockety, and the floor was slippery. Every now and again, in the middle of one of Joe's presentations, some seventeen-stone lump would lean back and – *splat!* – the legs of the chair would spread-eagle and the culprit ended up on the deck in an embarrassing heap. Cue uproar. Thirty seconds of guys screaming and shouting abuse at him. Funnily enough, Joe didn't seem to mind. He liked a bit of banter. Some bloke snotting himself in the middle of a meeting? It gave us some light relief.

Now I'm worried some of the younger lads might be too comfortable with things. You wonder what they've done to deserve it all. A little bit of hardship can be a good thing. Maybe this is in the back of my mind as Joe is beginning to talk about how we're going to go about playing Munster next Saturday, how we need to tighten up on our defence, and so on. Because suddenly I can hear my own voice, not his. And it sounds pretty cranky.

I apologize to Joe for interrupting but there's something I need to get off my chest. We have to make a decision as players if we're going to follow through on our commitments. There's nothing worse than the team that talks about doing something and then does the complete opposite – which is what happened last week. I was there when Jenno said he was sick of going to the Sportsgrounds and how it was always their World Cup final and how they beat us up because we were never properly up for it but how this time would be different, this time we'd get stuck in. It never happened, because we defended like amateurs and they gave us an almighty stuffing. In the past, if Jenno or Leo said something around here, it was law. Does it now go in one ear and out the other? Are we getting a little bit too comfortable with each other? When did that happen? Just because there are those three gold stars on the Leinster jersey, signifying three Heineken Cup wins? It should mean the opposite – that we don't accept a slip in standards, no matter what the circumstances.

So I challenge everyone. I say, 'Look, last week we talked about what we would do in Galway and then no one did it. So what about this week? Are we going to do what the coaches and senior players are asking us to do?' There. Said it. Brian backed me up, which was good, and emphasized the bit about our commitment in defence and our defensive system. That afternoon, we beat the lard out of each other during the field session. Lads were flying into contact. It was good.

Tuesday 2 October

Media suite, UCD

It's Munster week, so that means the newspapers have one angle they can rely on: me and Rog. I know the routine by now. On the front of the sports section, they'll put a picture of me on one side and a picture of Rog on the other, and we'll be facing each other, preferably with narky expressions. Our rivalry is meat and drink to TV directors too. Whenever I've been picked ahead of Rog, they'll devote one cameraman just to capture his facial reaction when I'm taking a kick at goal. People ask me if it's distracting when I'm teeing up the ball and this thirty-foot image of Rog's face is popping up on the screen at both ends of the ground. I say I don't notice, but I have noticed it, of course.

In general, you'd try and stay out of the papers on a week like this, to avoid saying anything that the opposition could pin up on their dressing-room wall as motivation. I understand we have to help promote the game, although by this stage, Leinster v. Munster seems to sell itself. But you still have to be diplomatic, especially on the Rog issue. So I tell them it's not about me and Rog, it's about Leinster and Munster. And there's truth in this.

It's made out to be this head-to-head, whereas in fact Rog and I would barely come across each other during the course of a game. You rarely tackle your opposite number and you very rarely run at him. We probably send people charging at each other all day but we very rarely take each other on. And so much of it is out of our hands. Like, he will have a better game than me if the Munster pack outplays the Leinster pack, and vice versa.

There is a personal rivalry there, of course. And there is history. At the start of my involvement with Ireland squads, we didn't really know each other, and because Rog was so nailed on as Ireland's out-half you couldn't have called it a rivalry. This was January 2008, just after a disastrous World Cup, when Eddie O'Sullivan's reign as coach was coming towards an end. I was only twenty-two and hadn't broken into the Leinster starting Heineken Cup team yet. I had huge respect for what Rog had achieved in the game but there was no relationship, as such. It was pleasant, we would say hello to each other but not much more. He wasn't passing on any tips, or anything like that, which I took as a positive sign. Maybe he rated me. Maybe I could be a threat, not now, but down the line. Then we had a game in Thomond Park the following season and that was when it all kicked off.

It's worth remembering our respective places in the rugby universe in April 2009. Munster were reigning European champions, and only a month previously Rog had steered Ireland to our first Grand Slam in sixty-one years. He was about to be selected for his third Lions tour. And me? Even though I started the majority of games in our victorious league campaign, I was still Leinster's second-choice fly-half, behind Felipe Contepomi. I was stroppy and impatient. We were well behind when I came off the bench in the second half at Thomond Park but I was determined to make an impact.

Soon enough, I was involved in an incident with Lifeimi Mafi, Munster's centre, and who should rush in to lend a hand but Rog. He said something like, 'What the fuck are you doing, you eejit?', to which I responded by feigning to throw a punch at him. When he winced, I called him a coward, and that really set him off. 'Call me a coward? You're nothing! You're a nobody!' He was right in many ways, but it got to me.

I bottled it all up until we came across each other in Croke Park a month later, in the Heineken Cup semi-final. I made it onto the field a little earlier that day when Felipe did his cruciate ligament, and as luck would have it we came face to face after Darce scored in the left corner. There's a famous photo, with Rog on one knee and me roaring down at him, with real animosity. I'm not even sure if I actually said anything comprehensible – maybe I was letting him know that I wasn't so useless after all. My expression said all that you needed to know.

I'm not particularly proud of that moment. I was just being myself – stroppy, competitive – but I know there's a way to behave on the rugby pitch. So I went over to Rog after the game and offered my hand. He told me to fuck off. I probably would have done the same in the heat of the moment. Later on, he came into the Leinster dressing room to congratulate Drico and Shaggy on our win and he gave me a dirty look on the way out. So there was a bad vibe between us for a period of time.

This sort of thing can last only so long in the Ireland set-up, though. The slagging would be unmerciful. You'd be sitting having dinner in the team hotel when Rog would walk into the dining room and Donncha O'Callaghan or someone would start shouting, 'Rog! Rog! Look, there's a free spot beside Johnny!' That sort of thing broke the ice a bit. Eventually we had a conversation. He said he thought what I did at Croke Park had been disrespectful. I said this was in response to him calling me a nobody. We shook hands and went from there. Everything that had happened between us in both games happened in the heat of the moment, and I'm glad we patched things up.

We'd no option but to get on. You can't hold a grudge when you're training together regularly, going for kicking sessions on a Wednesday. Our relationship has improved – though as someone said, there was only one direction it could go in. We talk tactics openly and we have a laugh. It's not as though we're sending each other Christmas cards, but I appreciated it when he called me after the 2011 Heineken Cup final to congratulate me on being man of the match. I thought it was a lovely touch. At the same time, I was suspicious, because we had to play Munster in the Magners League final the following Saturday! That's the nature of our relationship.

Drico is always saying how similar we are in terms of temperament and our sense of humour. You see it in strange situations. There was one Sunday afternoon in the team hotel, the day after a game, when Rog was wrecked, having been up all night with his twins, Molly and Rua. The kids were at him for chocolate and he tried to pull a fast one. He said, 'Johnny will give you chocolate,' thinking there was no way I would have any chocolate on me and if I couldn't deliver, this would make me the bad guy. But I knew that there was a stash of mini chocolate eggs in the physio's room, so I ran in and brought them to the kids. I wasn't going to let him get away with anything. The only problem is that every time I see the twins now, they're looking at me expectantly.

I've heard Rog say that the edge between us is a myth, and he has mentioned the fact that I'd been playing with the twins as evidence. But there is an edge, or at least there was. I haven't liked some of the things he's said publicly, such as after the win over Australia at the World Cup, when he basically told the TV cameras that he should have been starting.

I've never heard or read him publicly giving me credit, or saying that I deserved to be picked. I was always brought up to be gracious in victory and defeat. Guys like Joe and Felipe, who have had a big influence on me, are also big on humility. At the same time, there are probably people who think that the way I behaved towards Rog at Croke Park wasn't exactly humble!

It's never going to be completely harmonious, when you have two fiercely competitive guys going for the same slot. And the rivalry was definitely good for me as a player. The uncertainty over my place in the Ireland side has weighed on me, but I've learned how to deal with being dropped. When you've been through that experience, it means you appreciate the good days even more. It just remains to be seen how long the rivalry will continue. Today was the first time in the build-up to a Leinster v. Munster match that I was asked my opinion on who would start at 10 for Munster – Rog or Ian Keatley, his understudy. I've no doubt they'll go for Rog, but the fact that there is some uncertainty suggests that we may be edging towards the end of an era.

Friday 5 October

Goatstown

Newsflash – Joe Schmidt will remain as Leinster coach until the end of next season. Great news, but not really a surprise to the players, to be honest. Most of us have known about it for a while and there has been speculation in the media for weeks. But it's out there now, and the announcement has probably been timed to give us a lift before our first big game of the season.

The rivalry between us and Munster is massive. Ulster making the Heineken final last season changes the dynamic between the provinces and they are becoming a serious force, but there is still something unique about Leinster v. Munster. Every year, our first meeting feels like an official confirmation that the Irish rugby season is well and truly underway. Since it's been moved to the Aviva, it's got even bigger. There are already over 45,000 tickets sold for tomorrow.

It's 'only' a Pro12 game but it will be the noisiest day of the season, bar none. I reckon this is because Leinster supporters still feel they have to match the Munster fans, who earned such a reputation for their loyalty and their faith in their team. They also probably feel that this is their time, when they can enjoy their team's recent success. Even though we've had that success, and even though we've had a clear edge in derby matches in the past few years, we're still motivated by the memory of being second best for most of the noughties. My generation grew up watching Munster dominating Leinster and constantly challenging in Europe.

I've heard it said that Munster blazed a trail for us and it's true, they did set standards. But what used to really annoy Leinster players was when Munster were held up as examples of everything we weren't. They had more bottle than us. We were softies from D4, the posh part of the capital city. Put us in a pressure situation and we hadn't the mental strength or the leadership of the Munster warriors. This was still being said when we lost to them in the Heineken Cup quarter-final in 2006, which was the season I made my Leinster debut. The Leinster Ladyboys. That used to annoy the hell out of some players, especially as it had been coined by a former Leinster player, Neil Francis, who used to take the piss out of us in his newspaper column.

Maybe he was trying to stoke something in us and maybe it worked. I just found it funny to hear him talking about us on Setanta and now he refers to Leinster as 'we' – as if he's proud to proclaim his allegiance now that we're winning things. No matter how successful I am now, I don't think I could ever play for Leinster and then in twenty years' time start calling the Leinster team names. I understand that the media has a job and that it's a fair cop to criticize the team if they don't front up. I just don't like the name-calling, or having a go at a player because of his appearance, as he has done.

Leinster v. Munster has all sorts of special resonances for me. There's a family divide. My mother's a Dub and has become a big Leinster supporter. She owns a hairdressing salon, Rathgar Hair Studio, and on match-days she'll have the place all decked out in blue flags. People know who she is and ask her to get shirts signed, and so on. She loves all that. Dad's from Kerry and his family wouldn't have missed any of Munster's Heineken Cup matches at Thomond Park for years. Dad obviously played in Bective but would never have been a Leinster fan so I'd say it was a bit strange for him when I started making Leinster sides. I remember the build-up to my first start for Leinster, which was in Thomond Park. I received texts from my uncles, which went something along the lines of, 'Best of luck, Jonathan. Hope that you have a great game, score a load of points, get a couple of tries and get the man-of-the-match award . . . but Munster win!'

Tomorrow's game is all the more exciting because Munster have been playing some pretty ambitious rugby under their new coaches, Rob Penney and Simon Mannix. Joe knows Penney well from New Zealand and knows the type of game that has worked for Canterbury in the NPC – lots of pace and lots of width, lots of ball in hand. It isn't exactly the traditional Munster way but it promises to be exciting. All week you've been able to sense Joe is up for this one. He's in direct opposition to two fellow Kiwis. Leinster haven't scored a single try in this fixture for the past three games. We leaked five tries to Connacht last time out. The Heineken Cup is only a week away. But we've been in this situation before and the Munster game at the Aviva sparked our season. We spoke about that in a team meeting today. We could do with something similar happening tomorrow.

Saturday 6 October

Aviva Stadium (Leinster 30, Munster 21)

A weird thing happened during the game tonight. I was standing over a penalty during the first half, all lined up and ready to go, when this thought popped into my head: *Is Warren Gatland watching this kick?*

I call it weird, but then it's not really weird because stuff like this happens fairly regularly. I could be standing over a really important kick and suddenly I imagine Laura or my mum, with their heads in their hands, unable to watch. Then I just snap out of it, and get on with the job. Last season in Montpellier, I had a kick at the death to draw a Heineken Cup game, out on the right touchline, and my mind briefly went back to a kick I'd had from the same spot in an Under-13 league match for Mary's against Belvo out in Cabra. I got the kick, and a few minutes later, when I turned on my phone back in the dressing room, there was a text from my school coach, Richie Hughes:

Just like Belvo!

I texted Richie back to let him know I'd had exactly the same thought.

I kinda hope Gatland was watching because I played well tonight and we won well – just what we needed a week ahead of our first game in Europe. My place-kicking was good enough, too. I got six from eight and the two I missed weren't easy. One of them was ten metres in from touch, forty-five metres out – I actually had to bring it back a bit because the turf in that spot had churned up a lot – something to do with the Lady Gaga concert here three weeks back, supposedly. Anyway, it was a really tough kick and I just shaved the left post. The other one was three metres in from touch on the left-hand side and it hit the left post.

In general, I struck the ball well. The only thing that's bugging me slightly is that everything seems to be going just slightly left of where

I want it. It's something I need to bring up with Dave Alred when he's over in a few weeks' time. Dave is probably the top kicking coach in the world, the guy who helped turn Jonny Wilkinson into a kicking machine, and I work with him as often as his busy schedule allows. Like I said, I'm striking the ball well but I want things to be perfect. Maybe it's something to do with Ieuan Evans and what he said about Leigh Halfpenny.

If you hadn't already guessed it, I get a bit wrapped up in my job. By now, Laura knows I'm best avoided on match-day. She might cook something for me but then she's gone, because she knows she's not going to get much in the way of entertaining conversation. She knows I'll just be sitting on the couch, watching a game or a box-set, or doing a crossword, trying not to think too much about the game – which makes it a long day, when we're not on until 6.30.

I don't suffer from obsessive-compulsive disorder like some players, and I'm not superstitious. But I do like to be organized, professional. I packed my kit-bag on Thursday night, for example. It's something that was recommended to me by Enda McNulty. Moulding a gumshield or running around looking for gear on the day of the game can be a tiny bit stressful and you don't want anything to drain you in the slightest. Enda also got me to devote a certain amount of time on match-day to mental preparation but also to have time when I'm not thinking about the game at all, or at least trying not to.

An hour or two before I leave the apartment to head down to UCD, I go through my notes for the match. I keep them in a hard-back notebook, a two-page spread for each game, with the opposition and the date at the top. Again, I'll have written these up a day or two before the game. On the left-hand side, I'll list our calls and, directly opposite, the part of the pitch where we'll use those plays. I'll have something about restarts, and where we're looking to land them, and write down the steps of my place-kicking routine as it works at any given time – these things tend to change with time. Then sometimes, not always, I'll write in some more personal, emotional stuff, especially if I'm feeling particularly nervous. I remember before the Heineken Cup final against Northampton, I scribbled something down about how I wanted to make a happy memory of the Millennium

Stadium, as my previous time there with Ireland hadn't gone so well. That's one of Enda's big things, to use past experiences to your advantage. If I've had an average game, he might get me to write down some of the best games I've played and we might talk about them for maybe half an hour, not just how I played but how I felt coming into the game or anything that I did which put me in a positive frame of mind. Or he might just tell me to go home and watch clips of those games, of a try or a really good kick.

There's still a fair chunk of time to be killed on match-day and the trick is to switch off, if you can, and not to waste energy worrying too much about certain moves. You'll see some players looking almost zombie-like as they step off the team bus. They'll all have their relaxation techniques, recommended by psychologists and performance analysts, so they could be reading a book up until an hour before kick-off. The thought of playing a game has barely occurred to them. I'd be a bit different. From the minute I wake up in the morning, it's all I'm thinking about. It's partly to do with the position I play, partly to do with my personality. Sometimes I'll use music as a trigger, to get me into the right frame of mind on the bus heading down to the stadium, but only if I feel I need it.

Tonight wasn't one of those nights. It was a cracking game, played at a cracking pace throughout – it's amazing how this fixture always delivers the goods. We set off at a hundred miles an hour. When we're on, there's a pace we can play at, a sort of controlled frenzy, that must make us a nightmare to play against. Tonight was the first time this season we were at that level. We might have been without six front-liners, mainly because of injury – Rob, Darce, Luke, Cian, Leo and Seanie – but we started off at that relentless tempo, hammering away at channels either side of the ruck, and Richardt Strauss got over with only four minutes on the clock. But then Munster responded in kind, moving the ball wide from deep inside their own half and putting real pace on their game and scoring a great try by Peter O'Mahony. We'd known the sort of game they were coming to play, but they still surprised us with their width.

I always reckoned we were in charge, however. Just before half-time, Ian Madigan got in for a try after some ridiculously skilful handling by Straussy, who was playing like someone who was trying to make a point to the national management – he will be a qualified Irishman in time for the Test series next month and, on this form, is in line to make his debut against his native South Africa. Then Drico squeezed in for a third after the break, leaving us just over half an hour to go in search of a bonus point. It didn't quite work out. Drico hurt his ankle and had to go off – I just hope he's OK for the Heineken Cup next week against Exeter. Mike Ross and Isa were replaced also and, in the end, we had to battle to make sure Munster didn't sneak a losing bonus.

It wasn't perfect but it was a big improvement on last week. Having been leaking tries all over the place, we only let Munster in for two and scored three of our own. We showed real spirit despite all the changes at the end, when we had a makeshift back three of Fionn Carr, Mads and John Cooney. The changing room was buzzing afterwards. Joe was beaming. We have injury issues but it felt like our season started tonight. We needed something to pick us up, just in time for Europe.

As usual with these evening kick-offs, my mind is still racing as I'm sitting watching the TV at home at 2.30 a.m. The only thing that's niggling at me is those two missed shots at goal. It's true. I'm never happy.

Sunday 7 October

Killashee House, Naas

Our secret is out. Laura and I have been engaged for eight weeks, so it's a surprise nothing has been in the papers until now. But I'm expecting something in tomorrow's editions after we were rumbled at a charity function this afternoon. I'd kind of wanted to keep it quiet but if the news helps get some publicity for Debra Ireland, then I'm more than happy.

I heard about Debra a few years ago through a St Mary's old boy, Jimmy Fearon. The charity was set up to help sufferers from epidermolysis bullosa (EB), a horrific and incurable skin disease that causes the skin layers and internal body lining to separate and blister at the slightest touch. Through Jimmy, I met Emma Fogarty, a remarkable woman of about my age, who has lived with a severe form of EB since birth. Emma has been an inspiration to me in many ways. Her strength and positivity when things are rough have helped me to put things into perspective at times. It was Emma's idea to open a butterfly garden in the beautiful grounds at Killashee, a sort of sanctuary for EB sufferers and their families, and I'd been invited to do the official opening. Because it was on a Sunday, I was able to bring Laura along. There were some press photographers there and Jimmy let it slip, congratulating us in front of a pile of media. It's a small price to pay.

THREE

Getting Serious

Wednesday 10 October

Kicking practice, RDS

So, Heineken Cup week. We've been made pre-tournament favourites, which is only to be expected, given we've won it the past two seasons and this season's final is to be played at the Aviva. No pressure, then.

The possibility of Leinster becoming the first side to win three European Cups in a row has not been the main talking point, however. The English and French clubs have been threatening to organize a breakaway competition from 2014 because they feel the qualification process for Europe is unfairly weighted towards the Rabo teams – this may have something to do with the fact that ourselves and Munster have won five of the last seven tournaments. Just to stir things up further, Premier Rugby recently announced that they've done a lucrative deal with BT Vision, including Heineken games in England, which clashes with the current arrangement between Sky and ERC (European Rugby Cup Ltd).

I don't think the English and French clubs will ever leave, because they can't afford not to be involved in a Heineken Cup, but as they're so important to the tournament, their complaints can't be ignored. They have a point about the qualification process. Realistically, you should have to earn your place in the premier club competition in the northern hemisphere. As things stand, English and French clubs have to make sure they finish in the top six of extremely competitive leagues (comprising twelve and fourteen clubs, respectively) to be sure of qualification. Meanwhile, Ireland and Wales are guaranteed to have three representatives, while the two Scottish and Italian teams sail into the Heineken every year, regardless of where they finished in the previous season's Pro12. The Heineken is supposed to be a competition between the best teams in Europe, but in terms of quality it's hard to argue that a team like Zebre, who finished last in the Pro12, deserves to be there ahead of London Irish or Stade Français, who finished seventh in their domestic leagues. It's not straightforward when the qualification process involves two single-nation leagues and one incorporating four countries, but maybe instead of ten Pro12 teams qualifying, it could be eight – the best-finishing Irish, Welsh, Scottish and Italian teams, to ensure all four nations have a representative, with the other four getting through on the basis of their final position in the league. That's my suggestion, though you get the feeling there's a fair bit of negotiating to be done before a solution is found.

Leinster's main gripe with the tournament is that we've drawn Clermont in our pool again. There's something wrong with a seeding system that lands the two best teams in last year's tournament together in the same group. Clermont are probably still hurting after we pipped them in Bordeaux in last season's semi and Joe says they are targeting Europe again. He should know, as he spent three seasons there and is in regular contact with their coach, Vern Cotter. It's probably no bad thing that we avoid them until the back-to-back ties in December.

We start against Exeter, who are making their debut in the Heineken, and the game is in Dublin. I don't know too much about them, to be honest. They only earned promotion to the Premiership two seasons ago and surprised a few people by staying there. Now we'll be expected to rack up at least four tries against them but we're still without some first-choice players – Rob, Seanie, Darce and Luke – as well as quality back-up in Eoin O'Malley and Dave Kearney. Mads is going to fill in at full-back again. Brian hasn't been able to train fully either, having picked up a knock against Munster. And Joe has warned us to respect Exeter. Their form in the Premiership has been decent, and last weekend they ran five tries past Harlequins, the English champions, beating them 42–28 at Sandy Park. From what we've seen, they have no real stars but they are well coached and they play for each other. Their out-half Gareth Steenson has done really well for them since arriving from Ulster a few seasons ago. He'll probably be keen to make a point over here.

He'll find that the RDS takes a bit of getting used to if the wind is blowing like it was today. In a way, playing here before a crowd of 18,500 will be a bit of a come-down after playing in front of nearly three times as many people in the Aviva against Munster. We've never been beaten at the Aviva and given the choice we'd play all our big games there, but our arrangement with the RDS is that we play only one pool game at the Aviva, and this season that was always going to be against Clermont in December. The main reason I prefer the Aviva is simple: place-kicking is easier in a more enclosed stadium.

People in the stands at the RDS probably don't realize how tough the wind can be, especially at the city end of the ground. That's the end we kick into every Wednesday, because that's where the wind tends to come from, almost always from the left corner. From the right-hand touchline, you're kicking almost directly into the wind. From the left, you usually have to aim to the left of the posts. There have been times when I've done just that and the wind has died, and the kick has stayed left; on other occasions, the wind has blown so hard that the ball is blown out towards the twenty-two. That wind was wrecking my head today. I'm striking the ball well but I'm convinced I'm tugging the ball left ever so slightly, and then I've got to factor in a wind that's coming strongly left to right. It's not easy, but knowing the RDS should be a massive advantage to us on Saturday.

Saturday 13 October

RDS (Leinster 9, Exeter 6)

For one horrible moment this afternoon, I thought the RDS wind was going to let us down. We were in injury time, leading 9–6, when Ignacio Mieres, Exeter's replacement fly-half, set up a shot at goal after we'd been pinged for not rolling away at the ruck. It was just inside our half, to the right of the posts, and when he signalled towards the posts, I reckoned he hadn't a prayer. The wind had been swirling all day and he was kicking towards the city end. But as soon as he placed the ball on the kicking tee, the wind died, as though someone in the stadium had flicked a switch. Gulp. If he got it, we'd share the points, at home, which would feel like a loss. Thankfully he didn't strike it cleanly and halfway through the ball's journey I knew we were safe.

Safe, but not remotely satisfied. A draw would have been a fair result. They came with a plan to stop us playing and they executed it ruthlessly. We didn't help ourselves by spoiling a few half-chances in attack in the first quarter. Normally we pride ourselves on being clinical in what we call the green zone – inside the opposition twenty-two. The idea is to hold the ball, play at pace and gradually wear them down, but in situations where we closed the deal against Munster last week, we coughed the ball up. You couldn't call them unforced errors because Exeter defended our continuity game really cleverly. They barely contested at the tackle, just stayed on their feet, forming a pink wall in front of us. It was particularly pronounced in their half, with the wingers staying flat, the scrum-half joining the line and the full-back covering the chip-space. It wasn't pretty but it sucked the life out of the crowd, who had probably turned up expecting fireworks. Last season and the one before, we had sunny afternoons like this for our first Heineken game at home and we bagged the four-try bonus point on both occasions. Happy, noisy affairs, both of them. When Steenson kicked a penalty to draw them level at 3–3 on half-time, the only noise you could hear was coming from the travelling fans.

It was more of the same after the break, with Exeter squeezing us off our own park. They may not have any of the star names that you get in some Premiership teams but they seem to love playing for each other. They are fit, too. It felt like mid-July out there this afternoon but they kept going. Even on the rare occasions when we made line-breaks, they would scramble like lunatics and seal off the threat. Rob Baxter, their coach, made the point afterwards that they are probably more battle-hardened than we are. Like us, they'd played six league matches coming into this weekend but would have had a more consistent selection – this was only my fourth game of the season, for example. At certain times of the year, the Irish system has its disadvantages.

Joe probably wasn't sure whether to bollock us or reassure us. I don't think we'd been complacent but at the same time we probably underestimated Exeter. In the end it came down to a place-kicking contest – three out of five for us, two out of five for them. I was happy to nail the winning kick in the final corner but narky about a missed opportunity a little earlier, when I'd pulled the ball to the left – again. Positives? We'd won, which was the primary objective. We'd kept a clean sheet on tries conceded for the first time of the season. Then I came out of the showers to learn that Clermont had put forty-nine points on Scarlets. Six tries. Early days, but advantage Clermont.

Wednesday 17 October

Media suite, UCD

I had agreed with Guy Easterby, our manager, and our media man, Peter Breen, that I wouldn't be doing any interviews this week. This afternoon I get a phone call from Volkswagen, one of our sponsors, to tell me that Gerry Thornley of the *Irish Times* was waiting for me in UCD. Apparently this was organized weeks ago. No way out of it.

I've nothing against Gerry, or the *Times*. It's just that I'd been keen to stay out of the papers this week. We're playing the Scarlets on Saturday, which gives the media a Lions angle, even this early in the season – Sexton versus Priestland, the showdown for the number 10 jersey. I know it's only October and this might seem a bit precious of me. But no matter how diplomatic I am, I know there's a headline-writer out there who'll take something I say and make it look as though I'm bigging myself up. I don't want to give Priestland any extra motivation and I certainly don't want to give the wrong impression to Gatland, who's someone I've never met.

As for newspapers, I understand it's a two-way street. They need us to help sell their product, we need them to sell us – Leinster, Ireland, the players, the entertainment of rugby. I've just tried to avoid reading them for the past few seasons. Enda McNulty was the guy who advised me against them in the first place. It was around the time I was first trying to establish myself in the Ireland team, the 2010/11 season. That Six Nations I was in for two games, out for two, then back for the final game, against England at the Aviva. There was uproar in the papers that Deccie was switching Rog and me in and out. Some people were saying that my running game didn't suit Ireland. You might not agree with what is being said but it still gets into your head. Enda put it pretty simply for me: I wasn't gaining anything from reading the papers except stress, so why not cut them out altogether? So I did, pretty much.

When you start out, you devour every word on the rugby pages. I still like reading newspapers in general. I miss Sunday afternoons where you'd get a pot of tea, clear the decks and read the papers back to front. It's not that I never do it – there are times when you might have a couple of weeks off through injury and you mightn't be featuring much, so you don't mind having a little peek. In camp, there are times when you can't help but see a headline in a sports section that's hanging around the team room. Some lads get inspiration from reading what's being said about us in the papers. Either they feel good when they read something good about themselves, or maybe they are motivated to prove a point when it's the other way around. I just don't need the distraction, especially in the build-up to a Test match or a big Heineken game.

This interview turns out to be fairly soft-focus. Plenty of stuff about my background, about Joe, a bit about getting married, nothing about Priestland. I offer up some platitudes about the Scarlets: 'We know it's going to be bloody tough against these lads. They came out on fire against Clermont and they were well in the game until they got a player sent off. It's going to be as tough a game as it was last week, but hopefully we can look after our performance.' The piece isn't due to appear until Saturday and we have a lunchtime kick-off in Wales. Even if someone in the Scarlets set-up were to read it online, there's nothing that can come back to bite me. Paranoid? Maybe a little.

Saturday 20 October

Parc y Scarlets, Llanelli (Scarlets 13, Leinster 20)

Sunshine – for the second week running. The joy of a dry ball. We're in the lunchtime slot, a 1.35 kick-off at a stadium that's only two-thirds full. Not that we're offended, or demotivated. We're up for this one. We need to send a message out after last week's lame win. Plus there's the small matter of the lads having been bullied and patronized the last time Leinster played here, the first game of the season. We watched a few clips from that in the team meeting last night.

I'm up for this one too, in case you hadn't noticed. And I'm pretty happy with the way that it goes. In fact, for the first fifty minutes or so, it's probably as well as I've played for Leinster. We'd talked about the threat that George North posed with ball in hand but also about how vulnerable he can be on the turn, being such a big lad. Around ten minutes in, we're in their twenty-two and I spot that he has drifted in off his wing. Fortunately, Isa spots it too and I manage to get my choice of club just right. Isa leaps and catches in the in-goal and then has the strength and flexibility to dot down, even while North is trying to hold him up.

Right after the break, I gather a clearance just inside my half, run a few metres and smack – I land a drop-goal from around fifty metres. Sweet. We're 14–0 up and we're motoring. We've created a couple of try-scoring opportunities. This is going really, really well. Then suddenly everything I touch turns to poo. Bizarre.

It starts with a penalty kick, straightforward enough, on the right-hand side, fifteen metres in from touch. Just as I'm about to start my approach, this voice in my head says, *Don't miss left*. Where did that come from? Something like that never pops up before a kick. Naturally, I push the kick right of the posts. I'm furious with myself. A few minutes later, I try to squeeze a punt into the right corner and overcook it by a foot, out on the full. I reckon this is unlucky. But then, when Priestland misses a shot at goal, I put the drop-out into touch on the full. There's loads of space in behind North but I just put too much on it. No excuse.

That ten-minute spell really pissed me off. It also brought the Scarlets back into the game. Their centre, Gareth Maule, surprised Drico by burning him on the outside and then going on to score. Priestland's conversion made it 10–14 and suddenly we were in a game. This was when our pack earned their pay, forcing a couple of kickable penalties, which I got, one of them from long range. This earned us some breathing space, but not much. Mads was binned for challenging Liam Williams in the air and we had to negotiate the last seven minutes with fourteen players, leading by seven. Thankfully, Priestland let us off the hook in the final minute, kicking the ball dead instead of setting up the corner lineout that might have seen them nick a draw.

It probably says something about the quality of our performance that Mike Ross was chosen as man of the match. No offence, Rossy, but props are supposed to know their place! The good news is that, for the second week running, we conceded only one try. Also good is that the Scarlets are now pretty much out of the running in this pool, and we rated them as a team. From a selfish point of view, I was reasonably happy with my performance. This was only my fifth game of the season, but in those first fifty minutes I felt in top form. I scored fifteen points and generally outplayed Priestland. But none of us were singing songs on the bus to the airport, because we're still some way off last year's form. I was sitting beside Brian and he was seething that he'd been caught off balance and left flapping by Maule. He's the best defensive centre in the world and just never makes mistakes like that, so he was pretty sore for it to happen in a game like this, in Wales, with Gatland watching.

Are we down? No. Content? Not quite. We've won our first two cup games. Our hope is that Exeter might do us a favour at home to Clermont, but almost as soon as we touched down in Dublin, the news spread through the plane – Exeter 12, Clermont 46. Six tries. That's the second week in a row they've put forty-odd points on someone. So far, they're the only team with maximum points after two rounds. This could get tricky.

Tuesday 23 October

Ireland squad announcement

Straussy's in the Ireland squad, and in line to make his Ireland debut against South Africa next month. Jamie has been at him: 'Only two weeks to go now, Straussy. How are the Irish lessons coming along?'

Some of the lads have given him a printout of the national anthem, with the words spelled phonetically. Tony Cascarino is supposed to tell a story about how he was convinced for years that the final line had something to do with 'shoving Connie around the field'. So we've been telling Straussy to go with that line.

I'm sure there will be a few negative comments about the fact that Straussy's first language is not even English, but Afrikaans. If he plays against the Springboks – and on current form he has to be involved – he'll be the first 'project' player to play for Ireland, in other words, the first who came here with a specific plan to qualify via the three-year residency rule. I'm just surprised we haven't had more players qualify that way. It's not like other countries are ignoring this option. Straussy deserves it. He has been incredible for us for the past few seasons and was one of our best players in both our back-to-back Heineken Cup victories.

Deccie has named three other uncapped players – Munster's loosehead Dave Kilcoyne, Ulster's twenty-year-old centre Luke Marshall, and another young Ulster bloke in Iain Henderson, a lock who can also play at 6. There are ten players from Ulster in a squad of thirty-one, which is about right: Ulster have set off like a train this season, winning seven on the bounce. The squad looks a little short on full-backs – Rob is due to have an operation on a slipped disc today – and on tightheads, with Rossy the only one listed, but there will be further names added after the Pro12 games this weekend. Between South Africa and Argentina, there's a game against Fiji in Limerick for an 'Ireland XV' which should be something like an 'A' team.

But probably the most interesting news has to do with the make-up of the coaching staff. Anthony Foley is replacing Les Kiss as defence coach, with Les concentrating mainly on attack, and this gives us greater clarity. It's one of the things we spoke about at our meeting in the Aviva in August: the resources that are given towards our attacking game. When Alan Gaffney finished up after the World Cup, Deccie thought that he didn't need to be replaced, that he could get Kissy to double-job on defence and attack, with contributions from Mervyn Murphy, our video analyst, from our kicking coach, Mark Tainton, and from Deccie himself. But the one part of our game that was really struggling was our attack and we said that we needed someone to take ownership of that with clear ideas, someone we could bounce things off.

We haven't always had absolute clarity of information. I know Brian brought this up in a newspaper interview recently – maybe not the ideal way to make a point, but I suppose it shows a degree of frustration. At Leinster, Joe is our point of reference for all things to do with attack and there are no grey areas. If there's the tiniest detail out of place on an attacking move, he'll pull us up on it: 'Why are you here when you're supposed to be there? You should know that. Do it again till we have it spot on.' With Ireland, there have been times when the move has worked in training, but not perfectly, and it would be accepted. There isn't the same rigorous attention to detail. Sure, we mightn't have the same time together as the provincial sides but we're playing at a higher level so you could argue the detail should be even more exact.

So that's probably where Brian is coming from. Now Les is on attack and Axel is on defence. Straight away, it gives clarity. When Les gets up to talk, we know it's going to be about attack. Les is good on attack. It's hard for me to compare him to Joe because I am Joe's biggest fan, but Kissy is a rugby man, he knows his stuff, and he's good to deal with.

Wednesday 24 October

RDS

I wish I'd met Dave Alred when I was sixteen, like Jonny Wilkinson did. It was no fluke that, by twenty-two, Wilkinson was the best place-kicker in the world: he'd had the best coach in the world for six years. I met Dave when I was twenty-three, through Adidas, so to get to my optimum was always going to take a bit longer. Dave is phenomenal. He's brilliant as a technician and as a psychologist. His sessions are always varied and he's a great communicator. Perhaps best of all, he's a great listener.

Meeting him was a massive turning point for me. I had no routine in my practice, no routine in anything, really. I'd just grab a few balls after training and smack a few over. I watched Felipe for years and that was how he did things – a few on Thursday, a few more on Friday, usually from the touchlines. I used to ask him why he didn't practise from other angles and he'd say, 'Hey, if I can get them from out here, I can get them from anywhere.' It sounded reasonable. Then I read about Wilkinson, and when I got involved in the Ireland squad I got to see how much work Rog did. He always said he'd had his eyes opened by Wilkinson's dedication to his craft on the Lions tour to Australia in 2001. Rog couldn't believe how far behind he was.

I might see Dave half a dozen times a season now – we'll plan in advance certain times when he can fly over for a day or two and we can do some quality work one-on-one. He's unselfish in that he lets Leinster's kicking coach Richie Murphy attend the sessions. Richie and I go way back, to my days in the Academy. We have a great relationship and he loves getting to work with Dave too. He will often spot the same things as Dave, which shows how good he is. Joe has a good relationship with Dave and asked if he'd mind Richie coming along because it's important for me that he's up-to-date on everything. I also keep in contact with Dave by phone. If I email him a clip, he'll come back with suggestions.

We worked a fair bit towards the end of last season and he came up with a couple of tweaks to my technique which worked really well. One of them happened almost by accident. For years, I'd walked into the ball for place-kicks, but as part of a warm-up routine Dave had me jogging into the ball and we noticed how straight and how much further the ball was travelling. My misses had invariably been pushes to the right – I'd been dipping my upper body, trying to force the kick, and that's where the push was coming from. Dave spotted that jogging into the ball gave me the momentum to stay tall and follow through. I think that's one sign of a good coach, that he's not rigid in his thinking, that he can spot things and adapt on the run.

I'm especially glad he's in town this week because my brain has been fried over my place-kicking ever since the Munster game, when I missed a couple left. Even a couple of my 'gets' in that game just sneaked inside the left upright. I've been striking the ball well but why isn't every kick flying dead straight? It probably has something to do with that comment by Ieuan Evans on *Rugby Club*. In the search for perfection, I went out and probably worked too hard. When you go into a game with the mindset of trying to fix something, it's usually a disaster.

I've always been a bit of a perfectionist about certain things. Exams, for instance. For my Leaving Cert or in college, I used to panic in the lead-up that I hadn't every angle covered. Golf, too. I'd go in search of a flawless round and lose my cool if I spoiled everything with one loose shot. Basically, I'm driven to succeed at anything that can be measured in numbers. It comes from having parents who are results-driven. Good results guaranteed acknowledgement from them. It crept into my sport from an early age. At ten or eleven, soccer was my sport and one day Dad said he'd give me £20 if I could complete 300 consecutive keepy-uppys in the back garden, and then left me to it. I was out there all afternoon but eventually got there. You can be sure he was counting, too. He wouldn't have handed over the money that easily!

Dave's psychological approach is slightly different from my dad's. Everything with him is positive instruction. Rather than saying 'Don't do x,' he might say, 'Try this angle and stay nice and big.' If it works, he'll ask what feels different from what I was doing previously. He understands the mental side of being a kicker so well. One thing he has told me is that your brain has difficulty processing negative thoughts mid-swing, to borrow a golfing term. If, as you're standing on the tee, you're preoccupied with avoiding water on the left, you'll probably overcompensate and hit the ball right – or else hit left to avoid over-compensation! Think of where you want to hit the ball, rather than where you don't want to hit it, is the idea.

We sat down and went through all my kicks on my laptop and he showed me that I've actually been performing very well. There's an imaginary box on the pitch he likes to call the 'red zone' – ten metres in from touch on either side and from the ten-metre line in – which is your bread-and-butter area. Kick 90 per cent plus in here and you're doing very well. From further out, he says you're going to have to accept that you're going to miss the odd one. All the kicks I've missed this season have been difficult, bar one. Listen, he said, you missed one from forty-eight metres against Munster and you missed another one from the touchline. One hit the post, the other one shaved it. Sometimes you've got to accept that they are not all going to go over, even well-struck kicks. Basically, he told me to stop beating myself up, to stop putting so much pressure on myself. Sounds obvious, but it's something I needed to hear.

Friday 26 October

Captain's run, RDS

Leo did a cool thing this evening. He asked everyone to pick the bloke numbered below him on the team and send him a message before tomorrow night's game against Cardiff – text, email, tweet, whatever – telling the bloke one quality you admire in him. So Mads had to contact Dave Kearney, Dave had to contact Drico, and so on. Not everyone's idea of team bonding but I thought it was a great suggestion.

We need something to perk us up. We've had a lot of injuries and haven't performed as we would have liked. We were excellent for fifty minutes against Munster but should have picked up the bonus.

We've won our first two Heineken games but haven't clicked yet. Guys have been making mistakes in training, coaches have been getting pissed off. During the captain's run, there was even a bit of bickering on the pitch between Dave and Gordon D'Arcy – not usual suspects, by any means. Back in the changing room, Leo reassured us that things would come together. And then he came up with this idea.

It's not really a very Irish way of doing things. We spend most of the time taking the piss out of each other and are generally uncomfortable with open declarations of admiration. I had to write to Reddser, and I tried to be as honest as possible:

You're the best scrum-half that I have played with. I think you've got all the attributes of a great scrum-half, but what I think is your best attribute is that you produce your biggest performances in the biggest games. That's the sign of a brilliant player.

What I didn't expect was for him to have prepared a mini-essay in response for me. Remember, he was only expected to send something to Jamie. What he wrote blew me away. I don't feel comfortable reproducing it here, but it's enough to say he made me feel good about myself as a rugby player but especially as a team-mate and as a friend.

We struck a friendship almost as soon as Reddser arrived in Leinster from Wasps a few seasons ago. We room together a lot and we have similar ideas about how the game should be played. In fact our closeness puts a little bit of pressure on my relationship with Conor Murray, because Conor and I haven't really clicked as a half-back partnership yet. We get on well off the pitch and we're both hopefully going to be around for a while yet. On the pitch, he's still probably getting used to me and vice versa. He's so laid-back that he must wonder when he sees Reddser and me shouting at each other for half the session.

It's great to play with someone who has that understanding with you. There are times – less argumentative times – when we don't have to say very much at all, because there's an instinctive understanding out there. It's pretty easy. Reddser knows what I want and vice versa. We've a pretty good record playing together for Ireland.

We've only started three or four games together – England at home when they were going for the Grand Slam, and Australia in the World Cup. Two big wins for us. Deccie's clearly a big Conor fan, though, and Reddser's getting on a bit. He can get a little down when he's not selected, particularly when he's playing well. I'll be in the room with him and he'll go mad for twenty minutes, venting his frustrations. But then he'll stop and say something like, 'I'm going to have a big impact on this game.' He has great positivity and it's something I've tried to take from him.

Leo is clearly trying to generate some positive energy too. Usually he says relatively little for a captain. His influence is more about his presence around the place and his organization. But he has done something like this before. Three seasons ago we lost our first Heineken Cup pool game at home to London Irish, which meant our season was on the line the following week in Brive. Cheiks spoke to us in the dressing room before the game and then said, 'Skipper, anything?' I was itching to get out and practise my place-kicking but Leo was in no hurry. He went through every one of us one by one and told us what he admired about us. That Saturday, we went out and hammered Brive, got the bonus point and everything. I'm interested to see how the guys respond tomorrow. Already I think it was a brilliant idea. In fact, I emailed Leo to tell him so.

Saturday 27 October

RDS (Leinster 59, Cardiff 22)

We smashed Cardiff tonight. They had four guys in their side who'd fancy themselves as Lions Test hopefuls – Leigh Halfpenny, Alex Cuthbert, Jamie Roberts and Sam Warburton – but we never gave them a sniff and had the bonus point sorted after twenty-five minutes. It's fair to say Leo's exercise had the desired effect. All that man-love made for some awkwardness in the dressing room beforehand – some of us had difficulty making eye contact. But out on the pitch, we were in perfect harmony.

We scored nine tries in total, seven of which I converted. Cardiff have never conceded this many points in the league and we were only three short of our highest score. It was probably our most complete performance of the season so far – just as the international players are about to duck out for a month! The only bum note was losing Drico in the first quarter with a gammy ankle. He'd been playing out of his skin, too. Which is quite a sight. Having been rounded by Maule last weekend, he was out to make a point, and was throwing himself about the place. The injury looks bad, though, and I'd say he might struggle to be ready for the Springboks. Rory Best took a bad knock to his shoulder in Newport tonight also, so we could be down a couple of leaders.

Tuesday 30 October

Marco Pierre White's Steakhouse & Grill

The plan is to train so well this week that we're ready to play the Boks this coming Saturday – seven days ahead of schedule. Deccie was still keen for us to have a night out together, a bonding night, especially as there are quite a few youngsters new to the group. The older guys made just one condition: we choose a decent restaurant. We have some real food snobs in this squad.

In fairness, we deserve a treat. We've worked hard the past couple of days, and trained with real intensity. Axel has made a really positive impression on defence. He has a tough act to follow because of Les's track record and ability to innovate. You could argue that Ireland's Slam four seasons ago was built around the choke tackle because their opponents came up against something they didn't know how to deal with. You can see the impact it had by the number of people who are now trying to do it. The choke was Kissy's thing and everybody bought into it. Axel always struck me as a very intelligent player, so already you know that he understands what he's talking about. You might not always agree 100 per cent with his ideas, but the fact that they are different from Kissy's is refreshing in itself.

Getting clarity on defence is important and it certainly makes my job easier. Les and Axel complement each other. We haven't forgotten what we did with Kissy, and Axel brings his own ideas, very simple and to the point.

This afternoon we had an open session in Donnybrook and there was a great turnout to watch us. I'm happy to report I got a good cheer from the kids when I ran onto the pitch, but they went crazy for Rog. He has a slightly iffy hamstring and when he did a lap of the pitch to warm up, he got a great response. I told him I'd expected him to be booed, seeing as we were on Leinster's turf. I told him as much. It was also the public's first viewing of Michael Bent, who has just arrived from New Zealand to join Leinster, but may well appear for Ireland first. He is an Irish-qualified tighthead who has been going well for Taranaki in the NPC and, seeing as Declan Fitzpatrick was concussed playing for Ulster last week, Rossy is the only fit tighthead in the squad. No doubt there will be complaints about Michael coming straight into an Ireland squad, but it's a problem position for us. He still looks a bit bewildered himself. He only flew in on Sunday, and today he was being asked to pose for photographs holding a hurley.

We're working hard this week, like we said we would, but there's the odd diversion to keep us amused. Tomorrow afternoon a few of Ireland's Olympic boxing team are coming in to spar with us – though I think I'll give that a miss. And this evening we ended up in Kehoe's on South Anne Street, a favourite pub of Ireland teams going back a few years now. There were thirty of us there, plus management, and it definitely helped to break any remaining ice there might have been. I don't drink alcohol often, maybe a handful of times a year. I came to professionalism relatively late in life and so I have a fairly young 'training age'. It also takes me a lot of work in the gym to make small gains, so in general I look after myself and take my recovery from training and playing seriously. At the same time, I love to celebrate success properly. You get a lot of memories from that. It's one thing we've always done at Leinster, to celebrate our Heineken Cup successes. By doing it in style, it kind of makes you want to win again, because of the fun you've had celebrating them in the past.

Tonight was more about integrating some of the younger guys. A couple of them stood out as characters. Simon Zebo and Paddy Jackson had a rap-off which gave us great entertainment. You'd imagine it was no contest, right? Black dude against a pale ginger-haired fella from Belfast. But Zeebs tried this freestyle rap which flopped and Paddy blew him out of the water. It was good crack and had the desired effect. At dinner you might have seen guys sticking to their provincial groups, but by the end of the night there was much more of a mix. We had the option of taking the early bus or the late bus back to Carton. There was really only one bus to be on.

Wednesday 31 October

Goatstown

Fintan brings news from France. Clermont, my favourite French club, have said they are interested, but they don't want to talk until after we play them in the back-to-back games in December. Toulouse aren't interested, Toulon say maybe but it depends on Jonny Wilkinson's plans. Racing are still keen, very keen, and Fintan seems excited by this option. So am I. If I am going to leave Leinster, it is starting to look like it will be to Racing.

His first impression of the club wouldn't have been that hot, but this was last year, when he went on a reconnaissance trip for another player he was representing. Apparently Fintan was less than impressed by Pierre Berbizier, the director of rugby, and by the standard of the facilities. But a lot has changed in twelve months, he says. He met with the two coaches who are taking over next season, Laurent Labit and Laurent Travers, and was especially impressed by the enthusiasm and intelligence of Labit. Fintan was blown away by the new training facilities on the outskirts of Paris, which he says are even better than Leinster's – he took pictures to bring back as proof.

He also met the club's president and financial backer, Jacky Lorenzetti, who means business. He sees the club as a project, apparently, with a new stadium in the city that will double as a concert arena. By his own admission he has spent some money unwisely, but this time he's intent on getting it right. And he wants me to come and play for him. First, however, he wants to meet me face to face – to see the whites of my eyes, is the way it was put by the French agent present at these meetings, Stéphane Dray. He won't make a firm offer until I demonstrate that I see this as a genuine possibility. Fintan said I wouldn't travel until there was a firm offer. That's where they left it, but Fintan thinks that I should go over for a look at some stage. At least we have time on our hands. The Union won't make me an offer until after the November series is over and, as things stand, it looks like we'll have a serious option to throw back at them if their offer isn't up to scratch.

Friday 2 November

Goatstown

I have people texting me asking if I am the new Ireland captain. Brian has been ruled out with his ankle and Besty has a neck issue, so I'm assuming it's Paulie. I know his back has been at him but he looked pretty good in both of Munster's Heineken games so far. But seemingly there's talk it's between myself and Jamie to lead the side against the Springboks. I called the old man about it last night.

Dad always lets me make my own calls on everything but he's great to bounce things off, great for theories, great for trying to predict team selections. In the build-up to a Test match, he'll even go on the website of Inpho, the photographic agency, to search for clues in the shots taken in training – he knows that you can tell a lot from the numbers on people's bibs. Having been a Munster fan for years before I ever started playing, he has watched Deccie's form and reckons he knows the way he thinks. He tells me there has been a lot of speculation in the papers about the captaincy. He reckons he'll talk to me about it but he'll eventually go with Jamie.

I'm not too pushed either way. I know that might sound strange but I've never even captained Leinster and when you think about it, there are very few place-kicking captains, and relatively few captains who are out-halves. It would be a huge honour, obviously, and it's something I'd love to do at some stage, but I'm not sure I fancy some of the extras that go with it. I can imagine trying to finish a place-kicking session on the eve of a Test match, and having the press officer looking nervously at his watch because he needs to drag me up to face the cameras.

Jamie has already captained Leinster – he's next in line whenever Leo isn't playing. He's an unbelievable pro and leads by example on the pitch. While he's laid-back, he's always on top of the game-plan in the build-up to matches and has the habit of producing big performances in big fixtures. Yes, he'd probably have to tweak his routine a bit as captain. There'd be no sneaking off during the post-match dinner, not with a speech to make. He'd have to be a lot more visible in the team hotel, whereas the mere foot soldiers get to do what they want after dinner. But I think he could handle all that, and still be as effective on the pitch as ever.

The captaincy came up for discussion this evening, at a meeting of the main leadership group – Donnacha Ryan, Conor, Earlsy, Tommy Bowe, Reddser, Jamie and myself. Deccie was trying to sort out what qualities we would look for in a captain. This is typical Deccie – getting as many contributions as possible before he ultimately makes a decision.

Deccie takes a bit of getting to know. For my first couple of seasons in the team, when I was in and out, I found it hard to get straight explanations whenever I was dropped. He'd tell me I'd done nothing wrong, he was just rotating because he needed to have two out-halves. As a player, you think there always is a reason for being dropped. You end up second-guessing yourself, or coming to your own conclusions as to what your problem is. Then you go out to fix something or to prove a point about a facet of your game and that's when you can get into trouble. When you are being told nothing, you search for problems that probably don't even exist.

I found the 2011 Six Nations especially difficult. I thought I'd played really well in the first game in Rome and created a lot of try-scoring opportunities. We were winning when I got taken off, but Rog was the hero with that drop-goal at the end. I gave everything against France in the next game. We played great in the first half but didn't convert chances again, and the game got away from us. I was angry when Deccie brought Rog in for Scotland because I felt I had done everything I could have done in the first two games. Sure, there had been a moment in the France game when I moved the ball to an overlap and we turned it over. Was that my fault? The coaches felt I should have kicked for the space in behind, but I was adamant that if there was a five-on-three then I should move it. That's the way I've always tried to play. I felt my decision was being questioned, when what should have been criticized was our execution.

Nearly two years on, I'm not such an angry young man, and I can see that Test rugby is a little different. Sometimes you do have to rein in your attacking instincts. I still have the odd disagreement with Deccie but we always remain on good terms. People might assume we have different rugby philosophies, but the funny thing is he has often backed me when I haven't expected it. In Cardiff that year, I came off the bench and put the ball out on the full, and as a direct result, Mike Phillips scored off an illegal quick throw. My head was wrecked. My instinct had been to move that ball but I got caught in two minds because I felt the coach wanted me to kick more. We got a penalty two minutes later, well inside the red zone, and I'm thinking, *I'll make up for that now*. But I pushed it right of the posts. I reckoned I was in trouble after that game, but instead Deccie told me that bar those two mistakes it had been the best game I had played for Ireland. He'd spotted a couple of nice balls into the corner and seen how I'd set up what should have been a match-winning try. We had England next up and he picked me to start. I owe him a lot for sticking by me on that occasion.

People say he's no technician, but that's not his role. I don't think Clive Woodward coached much when England won the World Cup. He was the big-picture man, the decision-maker. The buck stopped with him. The finer details of a back-row move, he left to his technical staff. Deccie is the same. He sees the big picture, selects the team and manages people. He gets a lot of things right.

Tonight we were discussing the traits that we'd look for in our captain and the suggestions were fairly predictable: composure, intelligence, the ability to lead by example. At one stage, I said I didn't think it mattered who the captain was. The important thing was that we had leaders in every section of the team, which we do. I meant it as a positive statement about the group, rather than to devalue the captaincy role. So just in case I'd created the wrong impression, I clarified things with Deccie afterwards. Then he told me he'd wanted to talk to me about the role anyway!

It was a weird conversation. He asked me if I'd like the job and I said of course I'd like it. But then he told me he was just checking to see if I wanted it, even though he was thinking of going with Jamie if Paul was out. He didn't want to put more pressure on me, given I'd enough responsibility as the playmaker – which is pretty much along the same lines as I'd been thinking anyway.

'Sure I've heard all this already,' I said to him.

'How do you mean?'

'My dad knows you better than you know yourself. He told me this is what you'd say!'

He chuckled at that.

The captaincy will be good for Jamie. He plays better for Leinster when he's captain. I'd like to do it at some stage in my career, but for the time being I think it's nice to have been considered. Twelve months ago at the World Cup, I wasn't even guaranteed to start.

Sunday 4 November

Listowel

Feeling miserable. Have a bug. Sitting in my granny's, smothered in blankets. No central heating but the fire is blazing. Six days out from playing the Springboks, this isn't ideal. In my position, basically running the team, missing training days isn't an option.

This was supposed to be a bit of a getaway for me and Laura. It's nice to come down and see my relations, maybe play a round of golf. My dad has a house down here but I stay with Granny most of the time. She sells kids' clothes. The front room is basically a shop and it's been the same for fifty years. It's old-school. Brenda's remarkable, still running around the place and running a shop in her eighties. She often brings in customers to say hello, when I'm in the back room, watching TV. This is the place I come to get away from everything.

But not today. I'm watching Leinster being beaten 19–10 in Swansea. We're missing lots of front-liners but so are they. Led 10–0 at the break. Beaten by the Ospreys. Again. That's four in a row. Bastards.

Monday 5 November

Carton House

Just heard the team to start against the Boks. Lots to take in. Simon Zebo to start at full-back, even though he's never played there for Munster. It's an exciting selection – he scored a great counter-attacking try against Racing a few weeks back. People may wonder how he'll cope under a bombing, but the word seems to be that the Boks will pick Pat Lambie, who's more of a running out-half than Morne Steyn. Stevie Ferris is out with an ankle injury he picked up on Friday, so Chris Henry comes in. Earlsy at 13, and Straussy to start, as expected. But more surprises on the bench, with youngsters Dave Kilcoyne and Iain Henderson getting the nod. Assuming we all stay fit between now and Saturday, the team will be as follows: Zebo; Bowe, Earls, D'Arcy, Trimble; Sexton, Murray; Healy, Strauss, Ross; Ryan, O'Connell; O'Mahony, Henry, Heaslip. Replacements: Cronin, Kilcoyne, Bent, McCarthy, Henderson, Reddan, O'Gara, McFadden.

I feel sorry for Kev, who has been playing well this season, and for Ferg, who'd been hoping to start. Tom Court is probably feeling a little unloved as he's been a regular member of the squad, but I've been really impressed by Kilcoyne. He's only twenty-three, a bit young for a Test prop, but he scrummaged well against Racing and carries well. But most of all, I feel for Reddser. This evening he gave me a lift back to Goatstown to pick up my car – Laura had dropped me off in Carton from Listowel – and he said he'd been genuinely hopeful of starting this time. He was excellent against Cardiff, when his speed of delivery really made the difference in setting up a try for Drico, and he genuinely believes that together we could really get this Irish team clicking. The great thing about Reddser is that once he's got it off his chest, he becomes the most positive man in the squad again. He always finds ways to contribute to the team. He's unselfish like that. A lot of the time you feel quite bitter about being left out. You spot a problem that should be mentioned for the general good, but you almost feel like not saying it. You almost get angry with the guys who have been selected – as if it was their fault! Not Reddser. He's a model pro.

I'm still feeling ropey but training went well again today and we're where we wanted to be five days out from the game. Paulie played a full part and is looking good. Even psychologically, it will be great to have the guy who captained the Lions against the Boks four seasons ago. It might just take them a while to recognize him in our new change strip – black, with dashes of green here and there. I can't see it catching on.

Tuesday 6 November

Team room, Carton House

It's Tuesday evening so it must be *Geordie Shore*. It's embarrassing to admit, but it's a guilty pleasure for a few of us to watch this so-called reality TV show. It's basically a load of twenty-year-olds from Newcastle who are thrown together in a house and paid to go out to nightclubs and drink as much as they can. The 'entertainment' is to watch what they get up to when they get back to the house in the wee small hours, langers drunk – fighting, roaring and I'll leave the rest up to your imagination. You're almost hoping that the characters' parents aren't watching what their kids are getting up to. But there's something compelling about it. Maybe it's because it's so far removed from our own existence.

I usually watch it with the likes of Andrew Trimble and Stevie Ferris. We have tomorrow off and we're not due back in until the evening. Deccie encourages us to get a night in our own beds, but the northerners are happy not to have to travel two hours up and two hours back. I have kicking tomorrow morning in the Aviva, so it's as easy for me to wait and travel in with Rog and Mark Tainton. After that, it'll be into the Shelbourne Hotel, our base for the rest of the week. I'm looking forward to heading into town. Carton is lovely, but a bit remote. In the Shelbourne, you're in the city centre and you can wander down towards Grafton Street, spend a few hours shooting the breeze over a coffee. Time can move slowly in the week of a big Test match. Distractions are good.

Wednesday 7 November

Shelbourne Hotel

Paulie is out. Big loss in terms of his playing ability, but even more so in terms of his leadership and presence. His back is giving him problems, so Mike McCarthy is in to start. People would probably have expected Deccie to pick Donncha O'Callaghan for the experience he brings, but I think picking Mike is a good call. I really rate him. Leinster chased him hard last year and we almost had him before Connacht got him to reconsider, but hopefully we'll try and get him again. He's only thirty-one, in great nick physically and very switched on, rugby-wise.

That said, it's another blow for us on the injury front – already we're without Seanie and Luke and Rob, then Brian and Rory pull out, then Stevie and now Paulie. That's seven world-class players missing, which loads the pressure on us. We're desperate to atone for the Hamilton scoreline and there's huge pressure on Deccie especially to produce a few results. For one thing, the ten-year tickets at the Aviva are up for sale again next year and the IRFU are heavily reliant on that income. On top of that, we have to stay in the top eight in the world rankings because the pool draw for the 2015 World Cup is next month and if we slip below the water-line, it would mean being pooled with two teams above us, which would make qualification for the quarter-finals even harder than normal.

At least we're not the only team with injury problems – Bryan Habana, Bismarck du Plessis, Frans Steyn, Schalk Burger, Pierre Spies, Heinrich Brussow, Andries Bekker, Juan Smith and others are all unavailable. Their coach, Heyneke Meyer, has tried but failed to get Fourie du Preez released from his contract with a Japanese club, so Ulster's Ruan Pienaar will start at 9. As expected, Pat Lambie gets the nod at 10. Jean de Villiers, formerly of Munster, is captain. Adriaan Strauss is at hooker and will be playing directly opposite his cousin, Richardt! All told, fourteen of their thirty-one-man squad have fewer than ten caps apiece. Are they knackered at the end of a long season? Or just battle-hardened? We'll see Saturday.

Friday 9 November

Shelbourne Hotel

Went for a swim with Earlsy and Peter O'Mahony this evening. I'd normally just lounge around the team room the night before a game but I was happy to break the routine. We all agreed we had a really good feeling about tomorrow. Even though some big names are missing, we feel like a team. We are all really looking forward to it.

Even though I try to avoid the papers, there's no escaping all the talk about the guys who are missing, especially Brian and Paulie. I made a point at a team meeting yesterday: people think this is because those guys have been there and done it in the Ireland jersey for five or even ten years. That's why they have the reputation that they have. We don't, because we haven't done it in a green jersey yet. But they were in our position once. Ten years ago, Brian was like Keith Earls. He had to build a reputation. We have to do that now. Maybe this is the beginning of our time.

I was speaking for the collective but I kind of feel that way about myself, too. I've played for Ireland thirty-two times now and while I've had some great days, I don't feel like I've done myself absolute justice, or really made the number 10 jersey my own. In fact, there have been times after internationals when I've been intensely frustrated about how I've struggled to perform for my country the way I play for Leinster. I've spoken to Enda McNulty on the subject, even to Laura. You hear commentators saying, 'Why can't Sexton play for Ireland like he does for Leinster?' At times I find that sort of talk annoying. Rugby experts should know that there are external factors. As an out-half, when things are going well, it's because guys around you are making your job easy. But there's no escaping the fact that I can look a different player in blue than I do in green. It puzzles me too. I prepare the same way as I do for Leinster but it hasn't clicked. It has been very disheartening at times.

I'm feeling confident this week, though. Sometimes the night before a big Test match, I might ask Mick Kearney if I could have a room to myself, just to have some extra space. I generally share with Rob or Reddser. They're both good friends and, most importantly, neither of them snores – I'm a light sleeper at the best of times. But I'm feeling good tonight. I know sleeping won't be a problem.

Saturday 10 November

Aviva Stadium (Ireland 12, South Africa 16)

I don't think I've ever been in as foul a mood at a post-match meal. Normally a glass of wine and some conversation helps to ease the pain of defeat, but they'd put me sitting directly opposite JP Pietersen, who'd spent the afternoon sledging me and taking cheap shots. I wasn't in the mood for making small talk with him, of all people. Besides, I'm seething about the result. We could and should have won this game, but for a dodgy period in the third quarter.

It was never going to be a great game of rugby to watch. All their coach had talked about in the build-up had been 'northern hemisphere conditions', so it was clear that they were looking to kick for territory. Our game-plan was pretty similar: 1) Don't give them a set piece in our half as they'll overpower us once they get an attacking lineout anywhere from twenty metres in; 2) Keep them in their own half and pressure them with the frenzy and physicality of our defence.

Basically we looked to out-Bok the Boks. And for the first half, it
worked a treat.

We absolutely threw ourselves at them in that first half, with Peter
O'Mahony and Chris Henry superbly committed at the breakdown
and Mike McCarthy really putting himself about. We had them so
rattled that they conceded eleven penalties in forty minutes. It
showed on the scoreboard, too, with me kicking four penalties to
one by Lambie. Trailing 3–12 on the half-hour, their discipline went
altogether, as Pietersen nearly beheaded Chris with a swinging arm
and was sent to the bin.

We were on a roll, then basically lost the match in the remaining ten
minutes before the break and in the ten minutes after it. Looking back,
the time when Pietersen was in the bin was when we needed to really
go after them, do a bit more than just play a pressure game for penalties, maybe be a bit more adventurous. All we managed was to force a
penalty wide on the left, just before the break. I hadn't missed a kick
at that stage and was feeling pretty confident, maybe even a touch
complacent for a kick from that angle. I struck it great and it just
shaved the left post, but when I looked back at the tape it confirmed
what I'd suspected. I hadn't followed exactly the routine I'd agreed
with Dave to try to sort out those misses to the left – three steps back,
three to the left, as always, and then another half step to the left, just
to keep my body at right angles to the target for as long as possible,
only releasing at the last second. At the time, it looked like a great
effort, and what the heck, Ireland are leading South Africa 12–3 at the
break. But what's the point in having a routine if you don't stick to it?

The Boks were always likely to come out all guns blazing after the
break. At this rate, they were in danger of a fourth defeat in their last
five games against Ireland and they would have been crucified at
home for that. We just needed to stick with the game-plan. South
Africa are predictable. We didn't need Gert Smal, our South African
forwards coach, to tell us that if they get a lineout in your half, they're
going to maul it to try to win a penalty, and then they're going to
kick that penalty into your twenty-two for another lineout and
maul again. We allowed them to do just that. There were a couple of
kicks we sent that we should have got back but didn't, and a couple

of kicks they sent that we didn't deal with. Basically, we did everything that we said we wouldn't. They set up camp in our twenty-two, Jamie was yellow-carded for hitting the maul from the side. The next maul opened up a space for Pienaar and he went through it. Suddenly 12–3 is 12–10 and the game has changed.

A really top-quality side might have put us away at this stage, but they were content to eke out a couple of penalties for Lambie as slowly and deliberately as you like. They're not very imaginative, but they are very big, and very powerful. They allowed me just one shot at goal in the entire second half and it was from miles out. I missed. The only other half-chance I remember was when we turned them over in our twenty-two. Had we kicked long and won the foot race, there was the chance of a set piece in their half. But we kicked it out, and gave them another lineout. More pressure, another penalty.

This was death by asphyxiation and it must have been painful to watch. I know it was painful to experience, psychologically and physically. They were out to intimidate us, because that is what South African teams do. You saw it with the Lions a few years back. They just feel they have to intimidate. When they saw that they were playing against such a young Irish team, they probably saw it as an even better opportunity to rattle us, to intimidate us physically and verbally.

As an out-half you expect it, but it barely stopped for the entire eighty minutes. At one stage, I tackled Pietersen and got shoulder charged in the head by one of their props. I was away with the fairies for ten or fifteen minutes. I asked the referee, Wayne Barnes, how he could have missed an eighteen-stone prop going off his feet to bury his shoulder into me. That's what you want from refs, that they look after you. He apologized and said he hadn't seen anything. Any time I got caught in a ruck, it seemed like Pietersen was calling me names or shoving my head into the ground. There's nothing worse than the bloke who's big and tough when things are going well for his side. Looking back, it's kind of funny that we ended up sitting next to each other at the meal in the Shelbourne. But I was still fired up and wanted nothing to do with any of them. Another game that got away from us. Same old story. Are we ever going to turn this around?

Wednesday 14 November

Carton House

When does a professional sportsman get to watch twelve hours of *Breaking Bad* in less than a week? When he has the sort of injury that requires mainly rest. It's nothing too serious, a minor abrasion on my hip cartilage, right up underneath my groin – my kicking muscle, basically. I've had it for years and it just flares up every now and again. I jarred it with fifteen minutes to go last Saturday and so I've been taking it easy for the past few days. I'm still expecting to be on the bench against Fiji this Saturday, so I've been going to team meetings. But for hours at a stretch, I've also been in the world of drug cartels and undercover police operations in New Mexico.

The Fiji game is uncapped, and gives Deccie an opportunity to look at some of the younger players. In some ways, it's a bit of light relief before the serious business of Argentina next week. Losing to the Boks means we have dropped to eighth in the world rankings, which means we can't afford to slip up against the Pumas. Not that this has darkened the mood here. Far from it. The video review of the Boks game was quite positive, despite the result. We saw how we got the game-plan spot on in the first half, and could have won but for ten or fifteen minutes after the break when we went off script. Basically, the game came down to three or four small moments, and especially a couple of contestable balls in the air which we failed to snaffle, which in turn allowed them into the game.

The other thing that has lifted the mood has been the younger guys stepping centre stage over the past few days. It's like they've taken ownership of the side for the week. A guy like Craig Gilroy brings so much energy and enthusiasm that the effect just has to be positive. You see it in his work off the ball. For an out-half, there's nothing worse than finding grass with one of your kicks but then their full-back gets to rifle the ball back under no pressure because your winger was too lazy to chase properly. Gilly's the opposite. He can turn an ordinary kick into a decent one just by chasing like a madman.

So if you were hanging around Carton House these days, you wouldn't guess that we were under enormous pressure to win next week. Argentina have already had a great start to the month by beating Wales 26–12. Unfortunately, Felipe did his knee early in the game, ruling out the possibility that his final game for the Pumas would be at the Aviva, which would have been a nice send-off in many ways. I texted him to commiserate that his international career has ended in this way – he is thirty-five now, and has a medical career on hold. But typically, he pretended to take offence: 'What makes you so sure this is the end of my Test career?'

Felipe's a great guy and an amazing competitor. I know he mightn't be the most popular bloke in Munster, but secretly their supporters must have admired his commitment and his passion. He can be so calm in the build-up to a game but once he gets on the pitch, he can be a lunatic. It's like someone presses a button. He starts blabbering and cursing in Spanish, waving his hands around the place, losing it. Sometimes it's perceived that he's lost his head – and on occasions he has – but most of the time he's just wearing his heart on his sleeve. I've always admired that in him, even when I was younger, sitting on the bench, wondering if or when I was going to get a run.

In fact I know that Munster supporters have admired him, even when he's had a bad day, like the first Heineken semi between Leinster and Munster in 2006. Denis Leamy succeeded in getting under his skin that day and he had a nightmare with his place-kicks. But I'll always remember my dad – a massive Munster fan – making the point that Felipe had never given up. It was O'Gara's day and Munster ended up miles ahead on the scoreboard. But Felipe never stopped trying things. He chipped and chased and regathered. He was in private battles all over the field till the end. And then afterwards, he came out and faced the cameras. He never hid, on or off the pitch. I really respected that about him.

We keep in touch. Before big games, I might get the odd text from him. He's a gentleman. Laura bumped into him on the street in Bordeaux last year before the semi-final against Clermont. He walked to the stadium with her and chatted away. There were times when he gave me an earful on the pitch but he has always spoken really positively about me, not just in the press but to other people. He is one of the nice guys in rugby, really. He's going to the game next week, so we'll catch up afterwards.

I had a job shaking off that cold from Listowel, so these three days off my feet have been welcome in some ways. I had a bit of exercise today, a boxing session with our doc, Eanna Falvey. He's a former Irish super-heavyweight champion, but fortunately he's just holding pads for me. After that it was back up to the room for more *Breaking Bad*. It's addictive. Walter White is a chemistry teacher who discovers he's dying from cancer and turns to cooking and selling vast quantities of crystal meth to provide for his family after he's gone, and gets drawn into a criminal underworld. I'm just coming to the end of Season 4. It's really clever, with brilliantly drawn characters and sharp dialogue. And thankfully, it makes the hours spin by a little quicker.

Saturday 17 November

Thomond Park (Ireland 53, Fiji 0)

Turns out the IRFU got it right when they didn't award caps for this game. Fiji were rubbish and they got the hammering they deserved. They didn't look anything like the team that reached the quarter-finals of the World Cup five years ago – which was beyond Ireland – and that's because they were missing a lot of players and looked short on morale. In the second half, they resorted to taking cheap shots at Paddy Jackson – late hits, high hits and so on. The final whistle couldn't come quickly enough for them.

Not that Paddy looked too put out. He was enjoying himself and rightly so. He got loads of front-foot ball and used it well. It was a day for the young guys.

Gilly scored a hat-trick, including one from eighty metres. Luke Marshall was lively and showed that he has nice passing skills. Iain Henderson was lively too. He is one of those players that you wouldn't notice in training, but in games he really puts himself about – carry, hit, ruck, tackle, non-stop. The interesting thing will be to see whether Deccie brings in any of these guys against Argentina. It would send out a very positive message about developing young talent if he were to select Gilly. At the same time, Ferg scored a couple of tries on the other wing and must fancy his chances also.

I played no part in the end. I trained and kicked on Thursday and Friday but my groin was at me this morning. I suspect it's actually a tiny labral irritation in my hip, which has happened before – often what happens is that pain in the hip is referred to the groin. It didn't feel like anything major until I tried to do the warm-up and everything tightened up. I was ruled out and Earlsy came onto the bench in my place. I'll get an anti-inflammatory jab in the morning, and a scan if needs be. It's a problem that I've overcome in the past but it just means I'll have to take it handy next week. I mightn't train until Thursday, but it's worth being cautious. There's a fair bit at stake.

Samoa did us a favour by beating Wales on Friday night, bumping us up to seventh in the rankings, but from what the numbers men are telling me we still have to beat Argentina to stay in the top eight. More than that, we need to beat them for ourselves, to prove that we're heading in the right direction. The mood in the camp these past three weeks has been excellent, as good as I've known it. Today's result might not be hugely relevant, but the performance helped to keep a smile on everyone's face.

Wednesday 21 November

Aviva Stadium

Officially, I'm not supposed to test my groin until tomorrow, but seeing as the kicking crew were heading to the Aviva for the regular Wednesday pre-Test session, I went along for the ride. I had a bit of a light run-out, chanced a few kicks and everything felt good. Result.

It's nice to be able to report some good news because the pressure on the team feels intense. Already people are calling Saturday a cup final. To me, it feels more like the week of the final pool games in the Heineken Cup, with plenty of talk about points and permutations.

We got a brief run-down from Deccie on Monday evening, just so that everyone is clued in on what it would mean if Tonga were to beat Scotland, or whatever. In reality, though, the maths is pretty simple. If we beat Argentina, we will stay in the top eight and remain in the second band of seeds for the World Cup pool draw in a couple of weeks' time. It would also go a long way towards a pretty decent November series, and be a launch-pad for the Six Nations.

I don't need to read the papers to know the negativity that's out there. We've lost five in a row, and won only two out of nine this year. Lose this one, and Deccie will be under enormous pressure. They'll be talking up the Pumas, who started pretty well against France last week before falling away. And it's true, they look a much improved side for having played in the southern hemisphere's Rugby Championship this summer, with more of a varied attacking game and loads of gas out wide. Because of the history between us, they always see this as a grudge match. It's their last match of what has been their longest ever Test season, but they'll always be up for a scrap against us.

I got a sense of the mood outside the camp from a radio interview I did with *Newstalk* this evening. They were keen to talk about my relationship with Conor Murray, and whether I'd be happier playing with Reddser. I knew what the interviewer was up to, and it's an interesting question: how do I feel about playing outside Conor for Ireland, when I'm obviously such good friends with Reddser and look so comfortable playing outside him at provincial level? What do you say? I couldn't bullshit on about what a brilliant understanding I have built up with Conor because that's simply not true. We're still getting to know each other in rugby terms, whereas Reddser and I have played together so often that we know each other inside out.

So I said that Conor is exceptionally talented but that we are still trying to find out what works for us. It might not have been the answer that Deccie would like me to have given but it's the truth. Conor and I have had some good chats recently, about little things to look for. For example, I like to make a call on the way to a ruck, not when the scrum-half gets there. That way, the 9 has a clearer picture of what's coming next and can set himself up accordingly. Little things like that. We get on really well and are determined to click. We've spent a lot of extra time together this week.

I guess that because our results have been so poor, people are going to assume it's an unhappy camp. In fact, we couldn't be tighter. Partly it's out of adversity. We know it's been a bad year for results but we also feel we've had very little rub of the green. The Six Nations game against Wales could easily have gone our way, so too the draw in Paris. In Christchurch, we were a poor refereeing decision away from drawing with the All Blacks, if not beating them. For this, the last game of the calendar year, we're missing six world-class players, two of whom have been Ireland's most charismatic figures for the past decade – Paul O'Connell and Brian O'Driscoll. But in their absence, the next generation have no option but to take ownership. It's a collaborative thing. Because Jamie is relatively new to captaincy, other people have been making plenty of contributions – myself, Donnacha Ryan, Earlsy, Peter O'Mahony and others.

I know there's a big performance in us because training has been excellent. I'd just like to have a proper crack at Argentina with ball in hand. We barely fired a shot in attack against the Boks, mainly because we were geared up to play a territorial game against them. I look at our outside backs: Earls, Zebo, Bowe and now Gilroy, who'll be making his Test debut – a good call, because it taps into the energy and enthusiasm that the youngsters have brought. Look at that quartet. You'd be mad not to get them involved as often as possible. If only it would stay dry. The forecast for Saturday is crap – freezing rain, maybe even snow. Give us a break!

Saturday 24 November

Aviva Stadium (Ireland 46, Argentina 24)

Nothing beats the atmosphere of a dressing room after a big win, and that's probably the reason I'm usually the last to leave. You put in so much work during the week and then the game itself is so hugely stressful – physically, mentally, emotionally – that you need an hour to come down. It's a precious time, because it's when bonds are formed. At some point, however, it's nice to turn on your mobile phone and feel the flood of good will coming your way from family and friends.

There are lots of reasons for people to send congratulations. Our spot in the top eight of the IRB rankings is secured, and we did it in style, with seven tries and a record margin over Argentina – and people had predicted another ugly arm-wrestle against the Pumas. There was just a small point that some people wanted clarification on. Why had I absolutely buried Craig Gilroy with a tackle after he had scored a try on his international debut?

Look back at the clip and you'll see it was a proper hit. Just as Gilly is getting to his feet, I mow him down from behind. Afterwards, I told Gilly that I was angry that he hadn't hit me on the inside after stepping so electrically past three defenders off his right foot. Why did he have to run away from the posts, leaving me with one of those awkward conversions that are supposedly impossible to miss for the right-footer – ten or fifteen metres to the left of the posts? Of course, there was nothing deliberate in what I did. It was just the release of stress from the build-up but also an expression of how happy the camp has been for the past few weeks. At that moment, we looked like a bunch of ten-year-olds, unbelievably pleased with ourselves.

Finally, we had a day when a couple of things went our way. A key moment came last night, when Deccie sat down for the standard pre-match chat with the referee – Jaco Peyper, from South Africa. At that stage, our video analyst Mervyn Murphy had already told Deccie that 80 per cent of the penalties that Peyper awards at the breakdown go in favour of the attacking team, and what Peyper said only encouraged our coaches further. It was something along the lines of, 'You know how I ref. I want an open game. I want it to go well for myself because I want to be involved in the Six Nations.' So before the game, we were essentially told that if we were good with the ball, we'd be rewarded. We were encouraged to go out and play. So we did. Our other stroke of good fortune was the weather, and the early kick-off time. Rain was forecast for later in the afternoon but we got dry conditions and we made the most of them.

Apparently I looked very animated in the huddle before kick-off.

We wouldn't usually have a huddle after the anthems but I noticed the Pumas had gone into one, and I didn't want them to gain even the slightest psychological edge, so I called everyone in. What did I say? Something about making the country proud of us. About how we've had a great three weeks together and that for the first time in my international career, we have really felt like a team, but that none of that would count for anything unless we won this game.

It was kind of dangerous for me to be getting too excited this close to kick-off. Usually I get my talking out of the way earlier in the week. Seconds before kick-off, I should be focusing on that first strike, on landing the ball exactly where I intend it. Sure enough, I was too fired up, and my kick-off went out on the full. I barked at Gilly for not making more of an effort to keep it in play but really I was angry at myself. Luckily it came to nothing. Imagine if the Pumas had won a penalty off the scrum and had gone 3–0 up only a minute in? Would things have turned out differently?

Somehow I doubt it. Sparked by Gilly's running, and given the licence to play, we took the Pumas apart. It's great when things you have worked on in training come good. We reckoned we could exploit them down the short side and that's the way it turned out. It's not that they were lazy in defence – the opposite, in fact. They're so proud to play for their country that at times they work too hard to make the tackle and over-chase. We knew that if our forwards worked hard coming 'around the corner', then they would match us for numbers at the ruck. I was able to sit in behind and read the situation. If I saw them over-fold, we could sweep back to the short side. We set up a lineout try for Straussy that way, and I managed to work another short-side opening for Zeebs.

From a personal point of view, it was the most enjoyable game I've played in a long time. I worked hard on my footwork, strength and power over the summer, and I've got all my scores written down, all the gains that I made in pre-season. It's great when that work pays off in a big game. I had the power and the step to get past a couple of tacklers for a couple of tries – I'd only scored one in my previous thirty-three Tests! It probably helped that Conor and I really clicked for the first time.

Dad tells me that before the game I was getting stick from the

RTE panel about the fact that we hadn't managed any line-breaks against South Africa. Apparently it was all my fault – I'd been standing so deep that it was impossible to get a backline moving. 'Why can't he stand flat for Ireland like he does for Leinster?' I'm surprised to hear that from Conor O'Shea, who knows so much about the game. Surely he could explain to the viewers how reliant the out-half is on the speed of ball and how the opposition are defending.

Whenever I've run flat onto the ball for Leinster – or for Ireland – it's because the team has allowed me to play like that. The forwards have given me the front-foot ball we need. The out-half relies so much on the people around him to make him look good. People talk about how Dan Carter plays so flat to the gain-line, but it's easier when your pack is giving you an armchair ride. Does he play that flat against the Springboks? Not always, because they don't let you. They'll pressurize you at the lineout so you rarely get clean possession, and they'll slow down your ruck ball. It's fairly simple. If the ball is fast, you're flat, if it's medium-paced, you stand at a medium angle, and if it's slow, you stand deep because you have to have the option to kick, or, if you are passing, you have to hit the guys outside you early so they have enough time on the ball. We generally got scrappy set-piece ball against the Springboks, and slow ruck ball, so I couldn't take the ball to the line and try and send someone through a hole if he was going to get smashed. We were up against a brick wall. Against Argentina, it was easy. We got quick, quality ball and we made hay.

It can be very annoying when you hear some of the things that have been spouted on TV, because a lot of sports fans will take it as gospel. My folks only told me this time because they knew I was in a good place, and because I'd emphatically answered the pre-match criticism about our attacking play.

Maybe some of the Pumas had half an eye on their holidays, because they've been going hard at it since June. But I don't think anyone could argue with the quality of our performance. We can now look back on the November series as a success – a narrow defeat by South Africa in a game that we should have won, comprehensive victories over Fiji and Argentina, plus we finished the month sixth in the world rankings and safe in World Cup band 2, which was our main goal. I had a chat with Deccie in the changing room and congratulated him. I said it was great that he had given us the licence to go out and play, even though he had been under so much pressure himself, which can often cause a coach to go conservative on the game-plan.

We'll look back fondly on this month. We got to where we needed to be without Brian and Paul and other established players, so new leaders have stepped forward. Donnacha Ryan has been immense, so too Peter O'Mahony, Chris Henry and Mike McCarthy. What happens when Stevie Ferris and Sean O'Brien are fit, come the Six Nations? Deccie also has big decisions to make elsewhere. Earlsy, Gilroy and Zebo have all looked the part, so what happens when Drico and Rob come back? Who does he pick at hooker? But that's what we want – competition for places. I said it to him in the changing room: 'Good luck on picking a team for the Six Nations opener!' He laughed.

We celebrated hard. There was so much relief in the squad. We'd felt the pressure all week but we'd played with such freedom. We were a little bit shocked, to be honest. Not in our wildest dreams did we think we would score seven tries against Argentina. New Zealand had only scored four against them. We just stayed in the hotel after the banquet and looked after the guys who had won new caps. Old-fashioned stuff – everyone who has made their debut this month has to have a drink with every team-mate. We've had five or six newcomers so five or six drinks get the evening started properly.

At one stage a message came through from Shaggy, congratulating me on the win, and on my tries, but especially on my tackle on Gilly. I showed Gilly the text and he thought it was cool – that Shane Horgan, a player he'd admired for years, was talking about a try he had scored for Ireland. But that was the thing about today. It felt like the start of something new.

FOUR

Transfer Speculation

Today Fintan had a meeting with Maurice Dowling, the IRFU's human resources director and their negotiator on player contracts. My current retainer with the Union, agreed two years ago, is decent, but it was negotiated on the basis that myself and Rog were 50/50 as first-choice out-half for Ireland. I know that the figures that we deal in are huge in comparison with the average working wage, but I'm at the top of my profession and, like I said before, this is a short career. That retainer was signed when I hadn't established myself as Ireland's starting 10, so the timing of these negotiations should be pretty good from my point of view. My game's in good nick. I feel I present opposing teams with more of a threat with ball in hand, I've been getting greater distance in my punting, and my place-kicking has gone well – four misses in two games but all of those from the edge of my range, plus I accepted those misses better than I might have done in the past. People are talking about me as a probable Lion. But is any of this reflected in the Union's offer? Er, no.

They've come up with two options – an increase of five grand a year with the same match bonuses, or a twenty-five-grand increase with no bonuses. They are also only offering a two-year deal, when I'd been hoping for three or four, in the interests of security. Not so long ago they were trying to tie their best players down on long-term deals. Maybe they just don't value me in the same bracket as other players. Am I offended? Yes. They are taking the piss. But am I surprised? Not really. I actually had a €20 bet with Fintan about this. He said they wouldn't dare offer me any less than €400,000, because he knows that only a couple of years ago they agreed a retainer of

€450,000 with another player, which amounted to the best deal in Ireland. I was surprised when I heard that figure but Fintan knows it's accurate, because he did the deal himself.

At least I won the €20.

I know from previous experience how the Union operate. Having bided their time, they eventually make an initial offer, what in gambling terms would be called a low-ball. The player can come back with what he sees as a fair ask, to which the Union respond with a final offer, take it or leave it, and if you leave it too long, it will be taken off the table after a few weeks.

Fintan is dumbfounded that the Union still view the players as annoying expenses, rather than as their primary assets. He says that if I was a footballer at one of the bigger European clubs – which is what Leinster is in rugby terms, of course – the club would have ripped up my contract at the start of this season and looked to nail me down for as long as possible with a new, improved offer. He even said this to Maurice last May, and predicted that, sooner or later, I'd be offered a big contract by one of the French clubs, given what I'd achieved with Leinster in the past two seasons. Why wouldn't the Union make a pre-emptive strike to protect their asset? Maurice explained that they just don't do business that way.

All I'm looking for is a fair offer. I don't expect the Union to compete with the top French salaries. I just think it's fair to expect that I get the top rate in Ireland. So I'm annoyed at this offer, and I know Fintan relayed that message when he met Maurice today. He wanted to know how the Union could offer me at least €100,000 less than what they have agreed with other players in the past – especially when they're aware that Fintan knows those figures. Apparently Maurice found it irritating that Fintan should bring this up. He explained that the economic climate has changed and that the Union have had to tighten their belt. I wanted to know if Fintan had mentioned what we'd been offered by Racing, but he said we couldn't show our hand until that offer was concrete. A couple of players have been stung in the past. Last season a Leinster player rejected the Union's offer only to be left hanging by a French club. When he went back with his tail between his legs, looking to sign the original deal, it was reduced massively, and then was removed altogether. Basically, if I'm going to threaten to leave, I'd better be certain I have somewhere to go.

We supposedly have to get back with our counter-offer by the end of the month. I still feel they should have come to me with a fair offer at the start. Given that they did not, I'm not really in any mood to let them dictate the course of the negotiation. I still don't want to leave Ireland, and I've no interest in cashing in. I would have left long ago if that was the case. I'm interested in winning things and I'm interested in playing good rugby. There's also the Joe Schmidt aspect to consider. Is he with Leinster for just one more year or might he stay longer? In short, if I was offered what other Irish players have been offered in the past and are currently earning, I would gladly stay. We wanted this done before the season started, but if the Union aren't willing to do a fair deal, then I'll go if I have to. You might think they'd be afraid of losing someone in my position, but then you hear about how Tommy Bowe used to be the IRFU's favourite player, while he was at Ospreys. Why? Because someone else was paying his salary. While Tommy was based in Wales, all the Union had to pay him were relatively small appearance fees and win bonuses, whereas everyone else's salaries were coming from central coffers. But Tommy was still scoring tries for Ireland. Maybe they want a few more Tommys?

For the time being, I have to convince people in France that I mean business. Clermont don't want to negotiate until after the back-to-back Heineken Cup games against us are out of the way. The first one is over there next Sunday week. But from what I hear, they aren't convinced that I would ever leave Leinster. The French clubs have seen the likes of Drico coming down to spend the weekend in Biarritz, posing for the cameras, but then going back to Leinster. They reckon Irish players just use French clubs as a means of getting better deals out of the Union. And that's why the Racing president, Jacky Lorenzetti, won't make a firm offer until I come over and meet them. But when? I'm kinda busy right now.

I see decisions are made more snappily in Scotland. Barely had the referee blown the final whistle on their defeat by Tonga last Saturday than Andy Robinson had resigned as coach. I admire him for that. There are obviously problems there but he could have hung around and looked to squeeze the biggest pay-off from the SRU. Maybe there was an agreement and a pay-off, I don't know, but at least the cut was quick and it was clean. It will be interesting to see how things work out for Deccie, Les, Gert and the lads. Their contracts are up in June but will there be change, even if we go well in the Six Nations? Thankfully I don't have to make those decisions!

Saturday 1 December

RDS (Leinster 37, Zebre 7)

There was an amazing result today, but it wasn't ours. England beat the All Blacks 38–21. I got to see a good bit of it before heading down to the RDS, but I was still amazed when I heard that final scoreline. I expected New Zealand to thump England, especially given it was a dry day. The only person who gave England a chance was Leo. The bookies had the Kiwis as seventeen-point winners, so yesterday afternoon after the captain's run, when Leo said he reckoned it would be a close-run thing, he had loads of fellas throwing bets at him. We couldn't believe what he was saying. Leo doesn't gamble on rugby, more on the financial markets, but he's a good judge. Maybe he factored in fatigue. This was the All Blacks' last game of a long season. Richie McCaw is about to take six months off just to recharge the batteries.

Who was I up for? New Zealand, because they play technically excellent rugby. But you couldn't help but be inspired by how England got into them. They were just really well organized defensively. It was great to see how ordinary Carter looks when he's going backwards and not getting the ball he wants and guys around him are making mistakes. In a strange way, therefore, today was encouraging. When you are striving to reach the standards of a guy like Carter, it's reassuring to see him struggle.

I watched the first half in the apartment, then went to have a shower and go through a few things in my notebook. It was 15–14 when I left and I'm thinking, *Here we go, the Blacks are going to smash England now.* I watched the rest of it tonight, after our game. I was really impressed by Manu Tuilagi. He is just a phenomenal athlete. Combine this with his great offloading skills and he packs some punch. I'm trying not to get drawn into the Lions hype, but the mid-field permutations are beginning to look fascinating. I reckon Jamie Roberts and Jonathan Davies are definitely going, but can you afford to bring another bosher like Tuilagi? What about Brian? Or Earlsy? Where do they fit in? I know Gatland likes a big backline but will he go for all-out bulk?

Today was another good result for Owen Farrell, only a few days after he was nominated for the IRB Player of the Year award. Some people expected me to be annoyed by the news that he'd been included but the bloke has taken so much stick about it that I almost feel sorry for him. It's not his fault that the shortlist is based on man-of-the-match awards. Fair play to him, I thought. A great achievement.

I really enjoyed the first half of tonight's game. I set up one try for Isa and scored another myself – quite the try-poacher these days, so I am – and kicked three from three to give us a 17–0 lead, but when I came into the changing room Joe says, 'You're off.' Apparently, it had been planned that I'd only play forty to reintegrate, same as Seanie, who is just back from injury, having made his comeback against Glasgow last week. Joe pulled Isa and Darce early also, because we just can't afford another backline injury – we're going to Clermont without Rob, Brian or Luke, with Darce playing 13 alongside Andrew Goodman, who's only just arrived from the Tasman Makos. Andrew's big, strong and solid and did well tonight, but facing Wesley Fofana and Aurélien Rougerie will be a different story. He gave me a few strange looks tonight, because I mixed up Ireland and Leinster calls a few times, but I have another week to get fully back on the Leinster wavelength.

Even with all those changes, we still got the bonus-point win against Zebre. Later I watched the rest of that England game, plus a fair chunk of Clermont's 22–30 defeat by Toulouse. It's hard to read too much into the result because they didn't have their first-choice team out – it says something about how seriously they're taking the Heineken that they would rest their first-choice front row and Brock James for a game against Toulouse. A couple of years ago, the bonus point we nicked in Clermont made all the difference in qualifying. This time around they have two points on us, so we need to be aiming to beat them in their place, where they haven't lost for a couple of years. Given their quality, that would be our biggest ever win, I reckon. Thinking about this would keep you awake at night. Or maybe it's the caffeine tablets we take. Trying to get to sleep the night you've played a game can be a bitch.

Monday 3 December

Goatstown

Brian was over in London for the 2015 World Cup draw today. He was in UCD briefly this morning, in his number ones, all dolled up to travel as our representative. 'I'm going over to get you a decent draw for *your* World Cup,' he says, laughing, as if he's definitely going to retire before 2015. I'll believe it when I see it.

He got us a good draw, as promised. The most important thing was to avoid getting Wales as the third team in our pool, but they're with England and Australia – quite a pool for the host nation, that. We would have been in Wales's position had we lost to Argentina, so that's how much there was at stake. We're with France and Italy. I'm not saying it's an easy draw, but it's manageable. While we have an abysmal record against France, we haven't lost to Italy since 1997. There is a huge incentive to beat France and top the pool because if we come second, we'd be more or less guaranteed to meet New Zealand in the quarter-final.

So it's a decent draw, better than what we could have got, certainly. The long and the short of it is that we didn't want Wales, and we didn't get them. Result.

Thursday 6 December

Goatstown

You've gotta love Nathan Hines. The back-to-back Heineken games can be ridiculously tense, and usually in the build-up players are falling over themselves to say nice things about their opposite number. Not Hinesy. Word is that he's slagged Leo off in *Midiolympique*. For his looks! Something like, the reason he doesn't get penalized more for offside by referees is that they take pity on him for being so ugly. Not that Leo will be offended. They've won a Heineken Cup together, so there's a licence to abuse one another. Hinesy's a great bloke and he keeps in touch with quite a few of us. I texted him a few weeks back when he picked up a six-week suspension for stamping one of the Scarlets players, half to commiserate, half to slag him for standing on people's heads. He joked that the commissioner had wanted to give him just two weeks but that he'd asked for six, so that he could be fresh for our arrival in Clermont.

It was strange to play against him in last season's semi, but games against Clermont must be even stranger for Joe. He spent longer with them than he's been with us, and went through a lot of disappointments with them before they finally won the Bouclier de Brennus in 2010. I know he's in regular contact with their coach, Vern Cotter, and they'll probably meet up the night before the game. Joe is different in the weeks leading up to games against Clermont. You can tell it means more to him. He's a bit more animated. He might go on a little bit longer in team meetings, show a few more clips. It's like he wants to make absolutely sure we know how good they are.

Joe has been brilliant this week. We've done a lot of hard work, especially on video analysis. He reckons we can hurt them with an inside-pass play, a bit like the one that led to Cian's try against them in Bordeaux, but off third phase and moving towards the right half of the pitch. Joe has spotted how their pillar – the man defending the space to the side of the ruck – tends to chase the ball a little early once it's been passed, so if we can get a good clean-out on the right side of the ruck, there's a massive hole to be exploited with a well-timed inside pass. This is a try – if we get it absolutely right. We'll only get one shot at it because they won't make the same mistake twice, and we haven't been able to run it in a game as that would be to show our hand.

Saturday 8 December

Team room, Holiday Inn Garden Court, Clermont-Ferrand

This is where Rossy comes into his own. We're in a hotel in the Massif Central on a Saturday evening and we need to watch a match in Limerick, between Munster and Saracens, that isn't being shown on French TV. Our video analyst Emmet Farrell has set up the projector and a screen, the lights in the team room are off, and around twenty of us are ready and waiting. Rossy is hunched over his laptop in deep concentration, ignoring the abuse. Sort it out, Rossy! What's the story, you useless lump? But all of a sudden, Rog's face is up on the screen and the dulcet tones of Sky Sports commentator Mark Robson fill the room. Cue applause for our resident technician. Rossy never fails us.

Were we rooting for Munster? No. You tend not to root for either side in these situations, unless it has a direct benefit to us. The only chat you'll hear is individual slags. If Conor Murray does something particularly well, one of us will gush in earshot of Reddser, 'Well done, Murray! Gosh, he's so strong, isn't he? So quick and strong and *so* big!' Or Mike Sherry might deliver a beautiful throw to the tail of the lineout and if Sean Cronin is about, it's 'Jeez, yer man Sherry must be pushing for the Six Nations.' Childish stuff, but it helps to pass the time.

Naturally if Rog lands a penalty, I get plenty of it. And Rog was on form tonight. Five kicks out of five, whereas Owen Farrell managed only three out of seven. I felt for him watching it, as a couple of kicks were from distance and fell just short. And that was the winning and losing of the game – Munster 15, Saracens 9. An awful game to watch but a good night's work for Rog ahead of the Six Nations. There has been speculation about a new out-half being brought into the squad for the upcoming campaign, but Rog showed how important he still is.

Ulster were brilliant on Friday, smashing Northampton 25–6 away from home and grabbing the four-try bonus as well. Paddy had a good game overall, setting up a try for Trimby with a neat chip and defending really well. He had a tough time off the kicking tee but statistics don't show where the kicks were from. He had a lot of tricky ones on what looked like a breezy night in Franklin's Gardens. Jared Payne seems to make a massive difference for Ulster. He's like Isa in that he doesn't make mistakes and seems to choose the right option every time. I see Connacht also won, beating Biarritz 22–14 in Galway. That's three out of three for the provinces so far this weekend. How sweet it would be to complete the set, and to break Clermont's winning sequence at home. They've gone fifty-one games without losing at the Stade Michelin. An advantage or just more pressure on their shoulders?

Sunday 9 December

Stade Marcel Michelin (Clermont Auvergne 15, Leinster 12)

Our best performance of the season by a distance, and when we walked into the post-match reception an hour after the final whistle, the locals gave us a standing ovation. The Clermont supporters are brilliant, mad about their own team but also willing to appreciate good rugby when they see it. It's an intimidating venue, but even on a freezing day like today it is full of warmth. They even applauded us onto the pitch for the warm-up. When I hit the post with practice kicks from the corner, they shouted 'Bravo!' There is no badness in the air. I noticed during the game that when Morgan Parra was approaching his place-kicks, they kicked up a serious din with their yellow bats, but when I was setting up for a shot at goal, it was a lot quieter, as if to respect Irish traditions. You don't often get that in France.

They obviously still love Joe, too. He may have coached the team that beat them by a whisker in last year's semi-final but they appreciate what he did for them, too. On the pitch beforehand, the announcer calls out the players by their first names, allowing the supporters to bellow the surname: 'Numéro neuf, Morgan ... PARRA!!!' At the end of the Leinster team announcement, it was: 'Entraineur, Joe ... SCHMEEEDT!!!' And a massive cheer to follow.

It's nice to be appreciated but it's even nicer to win. And we could have won this game. There were two or three half-chances in the entire eighty minutes and we created all of them, but finished none. People can talk all they like about moral victories and how a losing bonus keeps us in the hunt. The bottom line is that we went into this game two points behind Clermont and we're now five points back.

That said, I think Joe is proud of our effort today. You could tell during the build-up how special this was for him. Usually we meet four hours before kick-off, either in the hotel car park or a conference room, just to walk through a couple of moves, but this time he asked us to assemble ten minutes earlier in the team room, where he showed us a collection of clips, four or five of each player, focusing on what he considered to be our respective strengths. You feel your heart swell when he does this kind of thing. Maybe he was aware he had spoken so much about Clermont during the week. It was as if he was saying, 'OK, we've spoken about them, this is what *you* can do.'

The changing-room scene was a bit different from usual, too. Ordinarily, everything is very focused on performance, on accuracy of execution. We sit in our spots and Joe goes through four or five technical or strategic points. But this time, out of nowhere, he asks us all to stand up and link arms. He's never done this before. 'Boys, this is where you need to step up physically.' A lot of what we speak about is mental and getting your execution right. But this time it's also about heart. I don't think we let him down.

I just look back on a few key moments and regret our failure to be clinical. That inside-pass play almost worked a treat, with only five minutes on the clock – imagine the pressure on Clermont if we could have put seven points on the board at that stage. It went just as Joe had predicted. Midfield ruck, a defender following Isaac Boss as he passes flat to Jamie and loops around, only for Jamie to hit Mads coming at full tilt on the inside. Mads hits me to the outside with only their winger, Napolioni Nalaga, as the last line of defence, ten metres from their try-line. Everything is falling into place – except the last part, which has someone following on my outside, flooding through. I look and there's no one there! Seanie was blocked trying to get through, which probably made the difference, but we couldn't afford to be 90 per cent accurate today. Everything had to be spot on.

They went in 15–9 up, four penalties to three plus a Brock James drop-goal, but we had momentum after the break when I kicked a penalty to make it 15–12. People are asking why I cross-kicked a penalty for Fergus early in the second half, when I had the chance to level the scores. For one thing, the turf was all churned up where the penalty had been given wide on the left – my one gripe with the stadium was the quality of the pitch. For another, we'd agreed that Nalaga was ordinary enough with the ball in the air – a freak going forward, unbelievably powerful, but not great in the air. I was getting screams from my right that he was infield a bit, so I said what the hell, it's a 50–50. I might have put an extra metre of distance to give Ferg a better chance of catching the ball. But I didn't, and he didn't, and the opportunity was lost. I wouldn't blame the defeat on that, though, and neither did Joe. We felt worse about messing up an attacking lineout near the end, or not finishing that line-break earlier on.

I felt pretty sore afterwards, physically and mentally. We'd really wanted to take that home record off Clermont. In previous years, they've always had an excuse for losing to us. It was either James missing a load of kicks at the RDS, or Fofana dropping the ball over the line in Bordeaux. I wanted to beat them on their patch, no ifs or buts. The Clermont supporters wouldn't let us feel too disappointed, however. They were very chatty. 'Johnny, you come and play for us next year, yes?' We only had an hour or so before the coach took us off to catch our charter flight, but the hospitality was brilliant – even if none of the Clermont players were to be seen. I heard they had a team meeting. Intense or what?

Tuesday 11 December

Goatstown

Rhys Priestland's season is more or less over. He ruptured his Achilles playing against Exeter on Sunday and the word is he's out of the Six Nations and may struggle to get back playing until next season. I barely know the guy but I feel for him. People might assume that I'd be relieved to see a Lions rival out of the running, almost happy to see him injured, but it's not like that at all. Yes, he's a quality player and he's obviously someone that Warren Gatland rates highly. But you don't like to see other professionals suffer serious injuries like that. Besides, if I am lucky enough to be picked for the Lions, I want to have earned it, by being one of the two or three best out-halves in Ireland, England, Scotland and Wales.

Rhys is twenty-six, a year younger than me, so hopefully he'll get the opportunity to tour with the Lions again. Right now, I'd say he's very low. I got his number from Brad Harrington, the Scarlets' fitness coach who used to be with Leinster, and sent him a text to wish him all the best.

Wednesday 12 December

UCD

Joe called me a skinny little prick today. Charming! The lads have had a field day. They know I think the world of Joe, and they know that he rarely uses bad language – he's so articulate that he doesn't need to curse. Plus they know I've worked really hard in the gym to put some muscle on a pretty narrow frame. But it's official. I'm a skunny luttle pruck, to use the Kiwi pronunciation.

I should explain that Joe wasn't calling me this directly. It came up as he was showing us a move which he's sure will open Clermont up, and it involves me 'showing out the back' – in other words, looping behind the ball-carrier on a decoy run. Joe explained, 'Hines and

Cudmore will say, "There's that skinny little prick, let's get him." '
It's grown legs now. It's skinny this and skinny that.

I couldn't believe some of the messing Hinesy got up to on Sunday. We know what he's like, but still. In the semi-final last season, he stamped on Leo's ankle at a ruck. They would have been good pals when Hinesy was at Leinster, soldiering together in the second row. Leo looks at him and says, 'What are you doing?' And Hinesy says, 'Sorry, I didn't know it was you.' So Leo asks him, 'Which one of us *would* you have done it to?' Judging by the video sequence Emmet put together for us from last Sunday, Hinesy isn't too picky about who he clips. He dropped a knee into Kev at one restart and another into Rossy later on. You could say there's no malice involved, but it depends on your definition of malice. As Joe says, we all love him as a character but this is what he did to us. Are we going to let him get away with this sort of rubbish on our patch? It's weird when you play against a former colleague. The things we used to love him for are driving us mad!

Clermont have played six games on Irish soil and lost them all. Meanwhile, we haven't been beaten in seven games at the Aviva and we tend to play well there. Joe has picked Reddser and Jenno, so the idea is to run them off the park.

Saturday 15 December

Aviva Stadium (Leinster 21, Clermont 28)

I don't think I've ever been angrier after a game than I was after this one. In the changing room afterwards, Joe told us to hold our heads high and to bounce back, but I don't want to hear it. I feel like having a pop at someone. Maybe it's because I've never lost a game of this magnitude for Leinster, not since I've properly broken into the side. Maybe it's because I thought a few people could have fought a bit harder when we were in the shit. I looked for the spirit of the Northampton final two years ago, and it wasn't there to anything like the same extent – even if we did nick a bonus point at the death.

Actually, I did have a pop at someone, just after the final whistle. Hinesy. During the second half, just as I was pulling my hand out of a ruck, his boot comes down on my arm. I said, 'Hinesy, you prick.' Then at another ruck, he turns me over and lays on my head. Bastard. On the final whistle, just after I've slapped a conversion attempt horribly wide, he's coming over to me with this dopey grin on his face. I lost it – half out of frustration from the defeat, half blood boiling because Hinesy has got us again, even after we'd been shown clips of how he operates. So I let fly at him.

'That's not on, you prick!'

'Are you being serious?'

'You stood all over my fucking arm!'

I can't remember his response because we were pushing and shoving and people were trying to break us up. It was a pretty silly thing for me to do, just after the final whistle. But at the time, I was furious. I shouldn't have lost it at a good mate, especially after the match was over. What happens on the pitch should stay on the pitch and I was wrong in that regard. I'm glad we patched it up later in the changing room, after I had finally calmed down.

It had been a special day on a personal level, as Leo asked me to lead the team out onto the pitch for my hundredth Leinster cap – actually, my hundredth was last week but he deliberately waited until we were in front of our own crowd. I didn't expect it. It's a big honour, a big highlight in my career. I haven't led a team out since St Mary's SCT at Donnybrook, ten years ago. For Leo to remember that and to let me do it was great. That's another reason for being so upset at the end of it. I wanted it to be a day to remember.

Looking back, I don't think we were where we needed to be mentally for this one. What we did last Sunday was brilliant, especially with the team that we had out. But everyone was slapping us on the back and telling us what a great performance it was, how we outplayed them, how we should have won. Maybe we bought into this too much. We even said some of those things publicly and Clermont probably picked up on this idea: Leinster are saying they should have taken away our proud home record. Their team talk was practically written for them.

Two years ago, we clung on for a bonus point over there and really revved it up the following week at the Aviva, ripped into them. Maybe we thought the same thing would happen just as a matter of course. We were found out. Against a team of their quality and depth, we actually needed to go up a level from last week, but the extra oomph just wasn't there. As for Clermont, the pressure was off them. They knew they could come over here and throw the ball around. Even if they lost, they still only had to beat Scarlets away and Exeter at home to qualify. They were relaxed.

They were also helped by the ref. Every time we got into their twenty-two, they killed the ball and Wayne Barnes let them get away with it. The annoying thing is that we knew they'd do this. Joe and Vern Cotter are best pals and they talk pretty openly about their respective teams, before and after games. Before this one, the line from Vern was how hard it is to get the ball from us when we're on the attack. Clearly he instructed his players to give away three, rather than seven. Certainly there were moments today when we would usually have scored tries, or had an opponent sin-binned. But not this time. They just killed the ball, blatantly, and weren't punished appropriately.

In fairness to them, they attacked brilliantly for Fofana's try, and the timing of it, just before half-time, was a killer. When Seanie was binned in the third quarter we were staring down the barrel. So we did pretty well to take anything from the game. With fifteen on the clock, we were trailing 9–25 but scored two tries, including a great effort from deep with the final play of the game, finished off by Ferg. The bottom line is that Clermont are going to top the pool, but that bonus point gives us a precious lifeline. If we can get our injured players back in time for the last two pool games, a final tally of twenty points is well within range and that's been enough to get sides through in the past. We are sore, grumpy, but still alive.

Wednesday 19 December

Ranelagh

Breakfast with Leo. We're talking transfer speculation – it's that time of year – and I mention that I think Racing are going to come in with a big offer for me. I guess I'm looking for his advice, as he's someone whose opinion I respect enormously. If there is one person in the squad whose respect I value, it's him, and I want him to know what's going on. I explain my situation and where I stand. As usual he is brilliant. He says, 'Listen, I wouldn't have a problem with you going. If they make you the right offer, take it.'

He's speaking as someone who left Leinster for a couple of years and came back a better player. He reckons the couple of years in Leicester were the making of him, just in terms of experience, and getting a different perspective. The same goes for Jenno, and ultimately Leinster were the beneficiaries of that experience. The two of them returning was probably the biggest catalyst in us winning the Heineken in 2009. Food for thought.

If I am going to France, it won't be to Clermont. As agreed, Fintan spoke with them now that the back-to-back pool games are done and dusted, and Monsieur le Président says he won't be making us an offer as he doesn't believe I will ever leave Leinster. In fairness, that's the way I feel myself. Most of the time.

Thursday 20 December

UCD

As part of the player-management programme I'm on a two-week break from playing – five days of strength and conditioning this week and next week off. It means I won't be travelling to Ravenhill tomorrow or playing Connacht the week after that. Nice Christmas break? No. I wanted to keep playing. Just when I feel I'm beginning to motor, I have to turn the engine off for a couple of weeks. The deal is I play six games for Leinster between the November Tests and the Six Nations and the half I played against Zebre counts as one, apparently. I've spoken to Deccie about it so I know the logic. This is the last break I'm scheduled to get for the rest of the season, so I'll benefit in the long run. It just doesn't feel very beneficial right now.

Joe obviously picked up on my mood when I met him today. 'Listen,' he says, 'we're not out of the Heineken yet, we need to be a bit more positive with our body language.' Later on, I texted him: *If you want a cranky, skinny waterboy tomorrow, just let me know.* I think he was delighted that I volunteered to travel.

Friday 21 December

Ravenhill (Ulster 27, Leinster 19)

Now Joe's the cranky one. I've seen him get angry in team meetings but I'd never seen the look that was in his eyes after tonight's game. That's three in a row we've lost now and it leaves us sixteen points behind Ulster in the league table, so we're under a bit of pressure in both competitions. I'm sure he didn't appreciate having to make changes for this game, especially when Ulster were at full strength and looking for revenge after what we did to them in the Heineken final. He was raging in the changing room. It was almost refreshing to see. At times I wish some of the players were more pissed off.

I must have been the most animated waterboy they've seen in Ravenhill. We were 6–0 up, pretty much in control, before we gifted them some points with some silly errors at the back which wouldn't have happened had Rob been there. Then, just before half-time, George Clancy awarded Ulster a penalty try at the scrum – the first time it went down! Yes, they got the nudge on us but we'd already won a scrum penalty at the other end earlier in the game, so to hand them seven points, for what might have been just a slip, was ridiculous. You could live with the odd mistake if Irish refs like Clancy and Peter Fitzgibbon weren't so arrogant in their dealings with the players, especially with internationals. You'd think that they might want to have a rapport with the top Irish players. Both sides could benefit from a healthy, friendly interaction. But they're above all that. It drives me up the wall.

Ferg scored a try at the death but we didn't even get a losing bonus, so it was a fairly subdued bus home. We have our Christmas party tomorrow, which is probably just as well. It's time to let the horses loose.

Sunday 23 December

Goatstown

Woke up feeling slightly tender this morning. Yesterday was a long old day, and fairly wild. No go-karting or paintballing, just a good old-fashioned pub crawl. We divided into teams, to give it a twist. A few 'captains' had already met and drawn names out of a hat, so on Saturday morning you got a text telling you which pub to be at, wearing a Christmas jumper, the uniform for the day. Our team met in O'Shea's of Clonskeagh around lunchtime, and from there we bussed to the Boat, down on the quays, then to the Bath on Bath Avenue and finally on to Kiely's in Donnybrook, where all the teams converged, by various means of transport: Hummer, limo, party bus. It was a riot, and exactly what we needed. You got to spend time with a few fellas you didn't know that well – guys like Tom Denton and Quinn Roux, who started their pre-season earlier than the international players, or Andrew Goodman and Michael Bent, who arrived mid-season. And as a group, I think we needed to let off some steam.

I didn't stay out too late as I'd a busy day today, too. First there was a Christmas lunch in Town Bar & Grill with my friends from school, an annual event that can become a little rowdy. I took it easy as I was due in RTE tonight for the Sports Awards – Rob was the rugby nominee. No major surprise that Katie Taylor won sportsperson of the year. The only surprise was how tiny she is when you're standing next to her. Still, wouldn't fancy getting into an argument with her!

Monday 24 December

UCD

Sean O'Brien keeps coming in handy for all sorts of reasons, but this week he is our poulterer *par excellence*. He's left a turkey for me to collect from UCD, which will go down well with my mum. Naturally it's pretty quiet at HQ but Joe is in his office, preparing a few things for our game against Connacht on Saturday. A quick hello turns into a cards-on-the-table type of chat. We both have a few things on our minds.

Life hasn't been easy for Joe recently, and I'm not just talking about Leinster losing three games in a row. There was a burglary, and also a health scare with his son Luke's epilepsy. Luke has had a tough week but thankfully he is recovering and out of hospital. While Joe is already locked into another season at Leinster, he is understandably keen to learn about my own plans. He needs to know, because if I'm leaving he doesn't want to leave it late to start looking for a replacement.

I feel awkward talking contracts and money at the best of times. That's why I have an agent. But I know I can trust Joe to keep things under his hat. In fact, I'm happy to talk things through with someone whose opinion I value. The bottom line, I tell him, is that I love working with him and I love being at Leinster. I love the staff, and the players are not only great colleagues – they are great friends, too. But I also feel I need to be paid what's fair, simple as that. I tell him about the Union's disappointing opening offer, about the fact that it's only for two years when I thought they would offer me a longer term. I'm surprised and annoyed by that, because I thought they would want to tie me down, given the age I'm at. I'd like something longer-term, if only for my own sanity and not having to go through this bloody thing again for a few years.

I also tell Joe about the big offer from Racing that I'm expecting. I've consulted with my family and we've agreed that I can't ask the Union to compete with those numbers, but at the same time I'm only being reasonable to expect the same deal as the best-paid player in the country. I want to be here. I have aspirations to have good days and to take a leadership role with Ireland. I suppose going abroad could undermine that. On the other hand, this is my living, my opportunity to build for the future, provide for my family. I'm not interested in buying myself flash stuff. I just want what I consider is fair. It is a short career.

It was good to come clean with Joe. He seems delighted to hear that his future with Leinster is a big factor in my plans. He's also keen for us to keep working together. Depending on his family, there's a possibility he may stay in Dublin longer than just one more season, which is interesting. The reason he only signed a one-year extension is because his eldest son is finishing school in eighteen months' time so he needs some flexibility of movement, but he is keen to stay if possible. I ask him about the rumours that Isa is retiring at the end of the season and he admits that it's looking that way – Isa's body is showing signs of all the wear and tear and his wife Simone is a little homesick for New Zealand. But Joe is looking at players of the calibre of Adam Ashley-Cooper and Drew Mitchell as replacements. I tell him we'd need both of them to make up for losing Isa. He's been that good for us.

I tell Joe that I should be able to give him news on my plans within a couple of weeks, though he says it would be nice to get it out of the way before the final two Heineken pool games. Fintan says there is no way Jacky Lorenzetti will give me a concrete offer without meeting me first. This would be a good time to go, when I've some time off, but Lorenzetti is away right now. Tricky.

I load the turkey into the car and drop it off at Mum's. One positive thing about having a two-week break from playing is that this will be an old-fashioned Christmas. I'll drop Laura to her folks' house, go to Mass and then spend the day at my mum's. I'm looking forward to it. The whole family will be together, plus a few guests – my brother Mark's girlfriend from Venezuela will be joining us for the first time – and a traditional Christmas dinner. No calorie-counter tomorrow.

Saturday 29 December

RDS (Leinster 17, Connacht 0)

Another interpro where I'm a mere bystander, this time in the stand wearing a suit, and nowhere as agitated as in Belfast last week. It might have something to do with the fact that we won what had been billed as a grudge match. Connacht are pretty miffed that we've signed Mike McCarthy for next season and their chief executive has been shooting his mouth off in the press about how we 'target' their best players. We won well, too, despite having a very young side out, and the victory puts us back to fifth in the league table. Mads filled in at out-half and scored a typically opportunistic try. His place-kicking was decent too.

I'm in a good mood because the national squad had two good days in Carton on Thursday and Friday, where we got some decent prep done for the Wales game, which is only five weeks away. I was insistent with Deccie that we keep shooting straight with each other as a group, to maintain the standards that were there in November. We got some good work done on the pitch as well, mainly on how we're going to deal with Wales's kicking game – they love to kick long down the middle, to force you to run back at them, and to deny you lineouts where possible. We looked at when to kick back and when to counter, that sort of stuff.

Earlier in the week, I forced myself to take the rugby head off for a few hours here and there. I'm reading *The Secret Race* by Tyler Hamilton – topical, given that Lance Armstrong has been revealed as a cheat and a fraud – and it's a shocking insight into how the doping culture took over professional cycling. Thankfully, there just isn't a doping culture in rugby, or at least not in my experience. One night Laura and I went to see *The Impossible*, an astonishing movie about the 2004 tsunami in South East Asia and how it affected one family. The special effects were incredible – you're bracing yourself every time the wave rushes in, in flashbacks and in dreams – and it was a real tear-jerker of a plot.

I'm also lashing through *Love/Hate*, the drama series about gangland crime in Dublin. Laura gave me the first three series on box-set as a Christmas present and I find it addictive. Most of the Leinster squad have got into it too, except maybe Dave Kearney. He got done in a game of 'roll the dice' and his preordained punishment was to shave his head with blade 1. He's now known as Nidge, after one of the scarier thugs in *Love/Hate* who smashes in the face of one his mates with a five iron. Dave's normally immaculately groomed, so he's a bit grumpy about this.

New Year's Eve? We're having dinner with Kev McLaughlin and Ross McCarron and their girlfriends – Ross is a former Leinster player whom I became good friends with in the Leinster academy and played with a lot at various underage levels. Don't ask me about resolutions. I've enough on my plate with this Racing deal. The Union have been chasing Fintan for our response to their offer. They can chase all they want. I'm not playing the 'counter-offer' game and I've let that be known myself, via the Ireland management – make me a proper offer, based on what they have paid other players, or I'll go. The delay suits, though, because we still haven't nailed a meeting with Monsieur Lorenzetti.

Friday 4 January 2013

Murrayfield (Edinburgh 16, Leinster 31)

A four-try win moves us back into the top four, and also sets us up nicely for our final two pool games against Scarlets and Exeter, when we'll need bonus points – and wins, of course. Brian and Rob both returned successfully to action but the story of the evening is really Luke Fitzgerald, who was making his first appearance in eight months and must have been nervous after recovering from neck surgery. You wouldn't have known it from the way he flung himself into contact. I was delighted for him. On his day, he's one of the best wings in Europe. Deccie now has some serious calls to make in the back three, even allowing for the fact that Tommy Bowe will miss the Six

Nations after wrecking his knee a couple of weeks back – Zeebs, Rob, Trimble, Gilly, Ferg, maybe Earlsy if he isn't picked at 13.

I was pretty rusty out there tonight after my two weeks off but physically I felt brilliant, which was the whole idea of the break, I suppose. I'll be sore tomorrow, though. It's an occupational hazard of playing 10 that the opposition back row will be out to put some pain on you, but the Edinburgh lads seemed like they were interested in nothing else. I'll get no lie-in, either. The late kick-off means I won't get home until 2 a.m., and I'm being collected at seven. I have to spend the entire day kicking rugby balls around a field.

Saturday 5 January

Guinness Estate, Luggala, Co. Wicklow

This is as close as I'll get to being in the movies. I'm a brand ambassador for O2 and we're down here to shoot a TV ad to be screened around the time of the Six Nations – myself and a crew of around two hundred people on this beautiful patch of land in the middle of nowhere. It's incredible the number of people and the amount of equipment needed to make a forty-five-second ad. They wanted me down early to catch the misty morning light, but we ended up spending eight hours in the field. And I'll be back tomorrow.

The idea of the ad is that when you place the ball down on the kicking tee, the kicker goes into a quiet, peaceful world of his own and blocks out the crowd. There's a spot in the Guinness Estate where the tree-line dips to create a shape like the O'Connell Gardens end of the Aviva, so I'm kicking towards that 'end'. (*Silence. You could hear a pin drop.*) But when the kick is good and the trees morph into the stadium and I return to reality, I'm inspired by the roar of the crowd. (*And then you're back.*) Cue shots of the crowd celebrating – *They could be the difference. Hearing that and seeing the green. They can change a game.* Then the other players materialize in the background – Brian, Mike, Zeebs, Peter O'Mahony, Trimby – although they won't be coming down until tomorrow's shoot.

I had to do a lot of standing around, and a lot of kicking. I was petrified that I was going to do a quad or a groin, especially on a January morning after playing a game. So I did a good warm-up, and got one of the crew to kick balls back to me. As with anything to do with O2, it was really well organized and they had nice food, warm clothes, anything you could possibly need. I have a lot to thank them for in general, as it's really only down to them that I re-signed for Leinster this time two years ago.

There's a certain irony in me spending today fulfilling my role as brand ambassador for one of the Union's main sponsors while there's still this stand-off on my contract. There's a time element now, as we have to get it sorted out in the next week or two, at a time when I'm trying to help Leinster qualify from our pool. It's doing my head in. Fintan has us booked on a flight to Paris next Sunday to finally meet Lorenzetti.

Doing the O2 ad-shoot may feel like being in the movies but my contract is turning into a soap opera.

Monday 7 January

Johnstown House Hotel, Enfield, Co. Meath

Leinster's season pretty much rests on the next two weekends – Scarlets at home and Exeter away – so Joe decided having a mini-camp in Enfield would help to set the tone. In training, he got our 'A' team to wear red like the Scarlets and obviously revved them up because what had been listed as a 50 per cent contact session turned into a full-scale war, with fights breaking out everywhere. They flew into us, which was great, just to get us going.

The senior players met in the evening, followed by a general meeting. We've got a pretty clear focus. Clermont already have eighteen points and are likely to end up on twenty-eight, so we're looking to qualify as one of the two best runners-up, which will probably be impossible unless we finish on twenty points – which means getting bonus-point victories from these last two games. The likelihood is that we'll be up against Munster for the eighth qualifying spot, and they have a few advantages over us. They have eleven match points to our ten and eight tries to our measly three – try-count is what separates teams in different pools who finish on the same number of points. Also, both of Munster's final two pool games are on Sundays, so they will have the advantage of knowing their requirements before going on the pitch. We just have to convince ourselves that if we get to twenty, we'll go through and get ourselves an away quarter-final against someone like Harlequins, Toulon, Sarries, Ulster or, God forbid, Clermont.

We aren't going to kick penalty goals because tries are everything. Get to four, go looking for number five. Get to five, go looking for six – that's our mantra. Any penalty in their half is going into the corner. We're practising loads of lineout moves, plenty of catch-and-drive. The old wisdom on this is that you build a lead before you start turning down shots at goal and going for the corner. Go into the corner early and fail to score, and your opponents gain a moral victory. But a victory without a bonus point is probably useless, so into the corner we will go. I have only been practising conversions of tries, across the twenty-two-metre line, basically, because I won't be kicking penalties at goal.

The point was made at the meeting that we've already been written off by some people, and that to fight our way out of this corner would probably beat anything we've achieved in the past. There was plenty of positive energy around the place this evening – except for the fitness doubts over Seanie and Drico. Brian strained a groin today and will struggle to train for the rest of the week, while Seanie hurt his calf in training. Kev got a bad bang on the ribs in Edinburgh, so we could be a bit thin in the back row. It's the story of our season.

Saturday 12 January

RDS (Leinster 33, Scarlets 14)

Mission accomplished. Bonus-point victory in the bag, show still on the road. But are we completely happy? Not really. As planned, we ignored all potential shots at goal and had the bonus point sewn up five minutes after the break, when Rob went in under the sticks. But if this comes down to try-count – as it surely will – then we might regret the fact that we only scored one more, when Mads skipped over off an attacking scrum at the death.

We've got to give the Scarlets some credit. They came here with nothing to play for except pride, and maybe to prove that they can be physical when they want to be. Their number 6, Sione Timani, was after me all night and left his mark – I had to go off with around ten minutes remaining because I was away with the fairies. I'm all aches and bruises.

We missed Seanie's ball-carrying, but Cian and Jamie were out-standing in the first half especially, and I expected the Scarlets to eventually roll over in the final quarter. It never happened. They know us pretty well from the Rabo and they gave us nothing. I still thought we lacked a bit of the killer instinct we needed. We've kept ourselves in contention, though. Munster go to Murrayfield tomorrow. Maybe Edinburgh can do us a favour. I'll have to record it; I'm sneaking off to Paris with Fintan in the morning.

Sunday 13 January

Le Plessis-Robinson, Paris

I'm not exactly travelling incognito, but I did keep the head down as much as possible in Dublin Airport this morning and wore a beanie just in case. How could I explain taking an Air France flight out of Dublin in early January? I can just imagine the chat if I'm spotted and then we don't get what we need in Exeter on Saturday. Sure, yer man

Sexton was over in Paris talking to Racing Metro last Sunday. How could he have had his mind properly on the job?

I don't like doing this at this time of the season, but there is no option. I can't consider joining a club if I haven't seen the facilities and met the people involved, and besides, Monsieur Lorenzetti wants to meet me in person before he'll make a cast-iron offer. So here we are, myself and Fintan, being picked up by Yoann, a French agent employed by Racing, and driven to Le Plessis-Robinson, a pleasant suburb ten kilometres from the centre of Paris where Racing's training centre is situated.

Fintan was right about this place. It *is* impressive, a vast complex that cost €12 million to build and that puts the Leinster set-up in the shade. There's a huge training facility for Racing's professional squad and their 'live-in' academy, with a sprawling gym, a swimming pool and hydrotherapy area, a huge players' room, swanky restaurants and immaculate pitches outside. It was empty today but we were shown around by the two Laurents, Labit and Travers, the incoming coaches, who had travelled up from Castres especially to meet me. They say that Racing have under-performed hugely in the last couple of years, given the budget at their disposal, but they spoke passionately about the players they are signing and the vision they have for the club.

They showed me around the area where most of the players live, near the training centre, which is suburban and spacious, with plenty of parks. Then we went to the president's house for lunch. He made his billions mainly in property, so it's a nice place, as you'd expect – we were given a brief tour of his wine cellar. Yoann acted as interpreter over dinner, as my Leaving Cert French is a little rusty. Monsieur Lorenzetti's English is good enough for him to make his point clearly. He would like me to be Racing's number 10 next season. He's honest enough to admit that Dan Carter was top of his shopping list, but Dan wants to continue as an All Black and the NZRFU won't pick him if he goes overseas. He says he has also spoken with Toby Flood, but whether this is a ploy to hurry me along, I can't be sure. Either way, he is going to discuss terms with Fintan tomorrow.

I've always thought that I would be with Leinster for my whole career and I still hope that will be the case. But I can see the attraction in a change of scene, and I can tell this is a club which means business. Leo and Jenno say that they loved their time in Leicester, just to experience a different culture. I know Shaggy, Denis and Darce have told Fintan that a small part of them sometimes regrets not having tried playing somewhere else for a year or two. Either way, Racing have made a big impression on me. Just to top it off, they're flying me home in the president's private jet tomorrow morning at the crack of dawn so that I can be back in time for Monday training. This is what it must feel like to cheat on your girlfriend.

Tuesday 15 January

UCD

It's out. A French flag was hanging at my spot in the changing room when I came in for training this morning and a few of the lads started humming the Marseillaise as I walked in. All good-natured stuff, and only to be expected with some of the stories that have been in the media. The *Sunday Times* has mentioned the interest from Racing and warned the IRFU to look after its top players. Yesterday, *Midi-olympique* reported the offer in hard figures – €750,000–800,000 a year – and this morning's *Irish Times* picked up on the story. The figures are not entirely accurate but they are not a million miles away. The lads had a field day with it, because obviously they think we put it out there to give the Union the hurry-up. 'Nice one, Sexto. Love those numbers!' I just have to suck it up.

The leaks obviously came from France – one thing I insisted on with Fintan from the beginning was that we wouldn't use the media to negotiate a deal. But there's no point in me trying to convince the guys of this. I can't turn around and say, 'Actually, those figures are fairly accurate and, as things stand, the odds are on me leaving.' But that's the way it's looking.

Fintan's message to the IRFU went like this: 1) We have had a generous offer from Racing, which 2) we don't expect you to match, but 3) we know what the best-paid player in Ireland is earning, so 4) give us your best shot. Fintan tells me he's meeting them on Thursday but I won't be speaking with him again until Sunday, after the game in Exeter. I feel like turning my phone off until then.

I'm generally pretty good at switching into rugby mode and blocking out all distractions when needs be, but I'm pissed off that this should come out in such an important week. Joe asked about the elephant in the room today and I explained to him that I had nothing to do with the story being in the papers. It was leaked in France and I gave him my word I would never release something like that, especially the week of such a big game. At the same time, my trip to Paris meant there was always a danger of something getting out and I feel guilty about that. I guess there's an extra pressure on me to perform on Saturday.

Jenno obviously picked up on my anxiety because he tried to put my mind at rest. He told me not to worry, that he knew I hadn't put this out there. He said that if the figures reported were accurate, then I should be proud that a club would consider me so valuable. I made it clear that I wanted to stay with Leinster, but, like Leo, he pointed out that this was a great opportunity for me. 'Johnny, never feel that your loyalty has been called into question,' he said. 'We know the type of lad that you are. You have to do what's right for you.' Coming from Shane, who has been around the block, who has left Leinster and returned, this meant a lot to me.

Thursday 16 January

Goatstown

It's all happening this week. Jamie has replaced Brian as Ireland captain and they can talk about nothing else in the media. No harm, from my point of view! The two lads were getting all the slagging in training today. As ever, Joe knew what to do and paired them in a game of 'partner touch' – a variation on British Bulldog, where they have to link arms and try to touch the rest of us as we run from the

twenty-two to the goal-line and back again, and any captives join
their defensive chain. It was a good laugh and shattered the possibility of any awkwardness arising between the two of them.

Deccie had called me on Monday night to tell me he was sticking
with Jamie as skipper – a nice touch by him to let me know, and I
thanked him for it. There was a lot of negative reaction to the news,
about how this was a terrible way to treat Ireland's greatest ever
player. I agree that Drico is our greatest player but I couldn't see what
all the fuss was about. Jamie had done well in November and it was
the right thing to do at this stage of the team's development. Make
Brian captain and people will find another reason to complain: why
keep him in charge when he's not going to be around for the next
World Cup? Besides, Brian's only played one and a half games since
coming back from injury. This will allow him to concentrate on his
own game, and Brian the player is more important than Brian the
captain. I understand the captaincy was a big part of his life and that
he is disappointed, but it's not as though he's going to go into his
shell. He's not that type of bloke. He'll still be a leader and I'm sure
he'll help Jamie.

It's nice to have someone else in the spotlight but that hasn't made
it any easier for me to park the contractual issue, especially when I
know that it will be sorted one way or the other next week. I've set
that deadline because even though Racing have given me some lee-
way, I can't allow this to drag into the Six Nations, which is just over
two weeks away. What happens if I pick up a bad injury? Or have a
sudden run of bad form? I don't want to have the contract playing on
my mind.

It turns out Monsieur Lorenzetti has added another layer of
intrigue by saying publicly that he doesn't believe I will come to
Racing, and that the Irish are home birds in general. He even denied
having contacted me. It looks to me like he's trying to dupe the
Union into believing this, and it's certainly what they would like to
believe – that none of the top players will ever leave because of the
loyalty they feel to their provinces. We'll see if it works.

I'm finding it a hard subject to discuss with anybody, especially
now that the figures are out there. I feel uncomfortable talking to my

parents about it, as it's more money than they'll ever earn, or to my brothers – Jerry is a student who is currently earning €10 an hour in Superquinn. The entire country is in economic turmoil. My mum doesn't want me to go because she's a Dub and a massive Leinster fan, who puts blue flags outside her hair salon every time we have a game, the proud mum who loves it when people come in asking to get jerseys autographed. Dad just sees it as a brilliant opportunity for me, plus he doesn't like the Union's attitude towards me and believes in giving players what they deserve. My brothers, too, think that it's too good an experience to turn down.

But what about Laura, the woman I'm marrying in around six months' time? She says she's never seen as many fathers dropping their kids to school as there have been the last couple of days, and they all want to ask the same question. She's a bit like me. Sometimes she says it's a brilliant opportunity and other times she says she just doesn't want to leave.

She feels she will miss her twin, Cathy. They are seriously tight. She also loves her job teaching in Loreto. Never mind her friends and family. She has become close with a good few of the Leinster wives and girlfriends also. Despite all of this, she has said she will support me whatever decision I make. It is pretty unbelievable of her to just give up her life in Dublin at the drop of a hat. Her head is wrecked with all her friends asking her about whether or not she's off to Paris. I tried to calm her, saying that if we do go, it's only an hour and a half away. I don't think she bought it, though.

Friday 18 January

Exeter

There was a terrible weather forecast for Exeter, so Joe decided to have our captain's run at the RDS before departure, just in case they tried to keep us off the pitch at Sandy Park. I still insisted on getting some kicking practice on it this evening. I haven't played here since the Churchill Cup a few years back and that was in June. The ground is wide open at both ends and not far from the coast, so the wind will be a big factor.

Like last week, we have no interest in anything other than tries. My place-kicking routine started the same as last week – just across the twenty-two, in preparation for conversions only. We're looking for at least four tries and preferably six or seven, in winter conditions, when we didn't manage a single try against Exeter back in October at the RDS. That's one of the reasons we're in this pickle now. The other is that Exeter are a bloody good side, and especially proud of their home patch. They are out of the running for qualification but they can still leave their mark by beating the reigning European champions.

The last qualifying spot is basically down to ourselves and Munster now. Toulon could do us a big favour by winning in Montpellier but they are already qualified and won't have the same motivation as Montpellier, who will qualify as one of the best runners-up if they win. So we need to score a heap of tries and hope that Racing can deny Munster the bonus point on Sunday in Limerick. It's no harm that Rog has been suspended for a week for kicking – sorry, tripping – one of the Edinburgh locks, who had blocked him off the ball. Not one of Rog's finest moments on a rugby pitch but hilarious in its own way. He'll get some slagging in camp over that. But Munster are clear favourites to go through – already one ahead of us on try-count, playing at home and probably against a second-string Racing side. And when they run out they'll know exactly what they need to achieve.

There's still a good buzz amongst the lads, though, something to do with the now-or-never aspect to the game. I could tell from early in the week that everyone is switched on. It was in everyone's body language, you could just sense it. Leo says the same thing. Sometimes one of us has to start a fight with someone in training, just to liven things up, but not on weeks like this. The atmosphere is really good. I'm still getting plenty of stick about my 'bluffing' with the IRFU. If only they knew.

At the back of the bus on the way to Dublin Airport, the lads are giving it loads.

'I'd say you weren't happy with Lorenzetti coming out and saying you wouldn't leave, eh Jonno?' says Drico, the arch-bluffer himself.

'Yeah, you'd know all about bluffing, eh Drico?' I counter. At least I didn't have my photograph taken with the club president before the start of a Top 14 game!

Before I finished my place-kicking session with Richie, I practised a few shots from around the ten-metre line, just in case. We're going out to score tries, but so will Exeter, so there could be a bit of traffic in both directions. Imagine scoring six tries but it still comes down to a penalty shot to win the game in the final minute? And I miss? No, got to keep thinking positively.

Saturday 19 January

Sandy Park (Exeter 20, Leinster 29)

Funnily enough, I did end up having to kick a penalty to ensure the win, just as I'd suspected, but it wasn't the comic-book finish I'd day-dreamed about. Yes, we got our win and our bonus point, but we only scored four tries, despite the fact that Jamie got the fourth in the fifty-third minute and we had a gale at our backs in the second half. I was fuming afterwards. It will be a miracle if we qualify now.

At the beginning, it felt like we were going to run riot. I don't know if it was an Exeter tactic or not, but while we were warming up, they showed Montpellier giving Toulon a hammering on the screens around the ground. That result confirmed that we were fighting with Munster for the last quarter-final spot. To give ourselves a realistic chance, we'd need to score a lot of tries.

We certainly started the right way. Only three minutes gone and Darce was in at the right corner after the forwards had softened Exeter up. Around the half-hour, we showed nice hands to get Rob over in the same corner, Brian in at first receiver and me looping behind him to flick it on. We'd blown the same move against Scarlets the previous Saturday but practised it hard during the week, so to execute it was very pleasing.

But Exeter had scored a try of their own in between our two and now they came back again through their maul, and Romain Poite was kind enough to award them a penalty try. We actually trailed 12–17 at the break, but then we turned predators again. Leo offloads to Drico: 19–17. Jamie scores off the scrum: 26–17. With nearly half an hour left, I'm thinking we could get eight or nine here, if we get another one quickly. We didn't. We started doing stupid stuff instead. Crazy things, like quick throw-ins in our own twenty-two, with a greasy ball and a big wind behind us. Huh? Silly penalties conceded. We allowed them possession in our half, while precious minutes slipped agonizingly by. In the end, I had to take that insurance penalty, just to keep them more than a converted try away. I wanted to go for the try, seeing as they had just lost a man to the bin, but the order had come in from Joe – take the points. Very frustrating.

You've got to keep the faith, but you could sense afterwards that everyone knows it. We're goosed.

Sunday 20 January

Carton House

Bloody UPC. I'm all set up in the apartment to watch Racing perform miracles in Limerick, only to find out that it's a 'red button' game and only available to Sky subscribers. I'm stuck with Saracens beating the lard out of Edinburgh and text updates from Mark, who's watching Munster in the pub with Dad. As soon as I hear that Wayne Barnes has sent off one of the Racing players after only five minutes, I'm only half paying attention. I knew it was a long shot once Racing had rested top players like Dimitri Szarzewski and Fabrice Estebanez. Sure enough, Zeebs runs in a hat-trick as Munster score five tries and make it through to face Harlequins at the Stoop. Of all the away quarter-finals, I think Munster got a pretty good draw.

And Leinster? We have Wasps away in the Amlin Challenge Cup – a strange state of affairs after what we've achieved in the last few years. On this day, the final pool Sunday, we've normally had qualification secured, and been out for a few beers to celebrate, waiting to see the quarter-final draw before breaking up and going into Six Nations mode. We saw each other this evening as the Ireland squad assembled but couldn't really talk about it. We just congratulated the Ulster and Munster guys and wished them all the best. Rog was loving it. He was at it as soon as he walked into the team room in Carton. Good luck in the Amlin, lads! Madman. If there is one guy who can get away with this slagging, it's Rog. He has a knack of mentioning the elephant in the room, but in a funny way. It's in good spirits and breaks the ice straight away. I suppose you'd worry if he said nothing.

No word back from Fintan must mean no word back from the Union. Hopefully there will be something tomorrow, so we can make a decision one way or the other. I just want to get this done and dusted.

FIVE

Breaking Up

Monday 21 January

Carton House

An IRFU letter arrived under my door this morning. I'm convinced they send this stuff to me directly to bypass Fintan because they feel he is a bad influence! Do they think I don't know my own mind? Anyway, it's not the letter I'd been hoping for. It's an expression of regret from the IRFU that they haven't received a counter-offer, also some stuff about the economic climate and tough business decisions. I ring Fintan and he assures me there will be a resolution either way by the end of this week.

Training goes well. As in November, we've set ourselves the target of being Test-ready by the end of this first week together. Our entire season hangs on Cardiff. Lose the first game, like we did last year, and you can write off a Grand Slam, a Triple Crown, a championship. So there is nothing half-hearted about training. The energy is good.

More contract talk in the evening – but not mine. John Herlihy, head of Google Ireland, came to Carton to give us a chat. Thanks to team manager Mick Kearney, we've had a few businessmen in to talk to us over the past year or so, including Denis O'Brien and Ben Dunne, and it's a welcome diversion. John was particularly interesting on the cut-throat atmosphere in his chosen game, where people are hired on three-month contracts and penalized if they are even 1 per cent off their projected targets. I suppose I'm lucky that I'm not told I'll be cut if I don't hit 80 per cent minimum with my place-kicks, though sport can be just as ruthless in its own way. It's interesting to hear about what's going on in the real world. I've been living in a world of my own for the past while.

At one stage, John asked us who we reckoned was the most-googled individual in our squad over the past few days, and Reddser wasted no time in suggesting my name due to the column inches this bloody contract negotiation has been getting. Rog, as ever, is ready with a response. 'When you're as famous as me or Drico, people don't need to google you,' he says. No arguing with that, is there?

Thursday 24 January

Goatstown

D-Day. The Union have made their 'final offer'. The letter was couriered to the apartment yesterday and there was a copy sent to my room in Carton. If they'd come to me with this offer last summer, I would have grabbed it. Why did they wait so long? Why insult me with the first offer and get negotiations off to a bad start? I still don't think this is their best shot. I know of two players who have had significantly better deals than this over the past few years. I have taken a stance with the Union: I said I would leave if they didn't put me on a par with the best. If I back down now, then they will never take me seriously again.

So my first instinct is to reject their offer, and go to Racing. That was certainly the way I was feeling while speaking to Dad on the phone while I was driving back to Carton last night. Dad reckons the Union's initial offer was a bit of an insult, so they should be taught a lesson not to take people for granted. My brothers are both encouraging me to leave, too, on the basis that everything about the Racing opportunity is too good to turn down.

That's the way I've been thinking today, when we're not training, or in the gym, or eating. What an adventure it would be to live and play in France! I've canvassed opinions on this before and even someone like Paulie, who is dyed-in-the-wool Munster, has admitted to me that he's occasionally wished he'd taken the plunge, if only for a season. Besides, if I accept considerably less than what one of my team-mates is being paid, it's like I've backed down, and the

Union has 'won'. What happens when all this starts again in sixteen months' time, and no French club will even look at me, seeing as I'm a confirmed home bird? Will the Union pay me what I'm worth then?

But then I have doubts. It's a decent offer in the current climate. Throw in an O2 deal and the sportsman's tax rebate, plus incentives, and it's even better. Paris would be an adventure, but how adventurous am I, really? Life would be far less complicated if I stayed. Leinster is such a brilliant set-up and I love my life here. It would just make things easier to swallow if only they'd make the gesture of offering me the same as the top-paid player.

In the end, I call Philip Browne, the Union's chief executive. I'm intending to tell him that I can't accept the offer but hoping that I can make him see what I need them to do. But I get his voicemail. So I phone Joe instead, in the hope that he'll have a solution, like he normally does. I'm struggling to hold back the tears when I tell him that I'm about to make the toughest decision of my career, to leave Leinster. But the more we talk, the more he can tell this is not a decision I want to make, that I will stay if the Union will budge. Forty minutes later, he asks me to give him twenty-four hours. 'Sign nothing,' he says. I agree, though it's unfair on everyone for this to drag on any longer. We're only eight days from Cardiff and here I am, sitting in the foyer at Carton House with Fintan, still talking contracts.

Bizarrely, as we're sitting there, I get a call from Hinesy, who wants to know if he can give my number to Vern Cotter, his coach at Clermont. The word is out in France that I haven't been bluffing. A few minutes later, Fintan and Vern are chatting away. It turns out Vern would like me to join them the season after next, but when he hears the Racing situation he realizes he has missed the boat. Out of curiosity, he asks about my deal with Racing, and Fintan tells him. Vern's advice is, 'Tell Johnny to grab it.' If only Joe knew what his old pal was saying behind his back! But somehow, I reckon Joe is going to get this little issue sorted out.

Friday 25 January

Goatstown

I don't know if Joe ever got to make the call. He would have had to be out of the blocks pretty quickly this morning because everything was done and dusted by about nine o'clock. Word was out on the street by 9.30 and there was an official IRFU press release before lunchtime, almost as if they'd had one prepared in advance: *Jonathan Sexton will not be playing his rugby full-time in Ireland from next season.* Predictably enough, the spin was that they couldn't compete with the money that was on offer in France.

I'd had another phone conversation with Philip Browne at around 8.30, and it was obvious almost immediately that the Union wouldn't be budging from their final offer. Business decision, economic climate and so on. When I put it to Philip that I might deserve the same retainer as a couple of other players, he argued that the match-fee incentive scheme would bring me close to that number. He wasn't going to be moved on the basic salary. He expressed his disappointment, wished me the best of luck, and off I went to my nine o'clock weights session.

Two hours later, as I headed to a field session, I was still half-hoping for the cavalry to appear over the hill. But it was at this point that Mick Kearney approached me and asked if I wanted to see the Union's statement before it went out, or if I wanted to add anything to it. I told him I wanted nothing to do with it. After training, Mick told me that the statement had gone out. But it was only after I did some kicking, and turned on my mobile to see a stream of disbelieving texts, that it finally registered with me. This is actually happening. I went to my room, locked the door, lay on the bed and cried.

I needed to be alone because there were people I needed to inform, out of courtesy – sponsors like Volkswagen and Adidas. I had given O2 a heads-up before training, just in case, still believing at that stage that things would be sorted. But I also needed to be alone because I just couldn't face the lads. For an hour or so I ignored their phone calls because I literally couldn't talk to them. I basically felt guilty.

We are a tight bunch. In many ways, these guys are my best friends. We celebrate together when we win and we share the depression of defeat. I've been playing with guys like Rob since I was fifteen, when we were called into Leinster underage camps in the summer holidays. I played Under-20s with guys like Sean O'Brien, Fergus McFadden and Devin Toner. I go even further back with Kev. It feels like I am breaking up the group. I can tell from Rob's voicemail that he is particularly pissed off. His contract is up too and we've been keeping each other updated, but I don't think he really thought I'd ever leave. I'm not sure I really thought I'd ever leave, either.

But now it's going to happen and the stark reality of it comes as a shock. Today was tough for me, and it was tough for Laura too. She's going to take a three-year leave of absence, as my contract is for two years with the option of a third. It's handy that she's able to do this, and hopefully we'll still get to spend time at home in November and during the Six Nations, if I get picked for Ireland. Dublin is only an hour and a half by air from Paris. But in another sense, it's a world away, and I know she's struggling to get her head around this. She's disappointed to be leaving her work, her friends, her life. She's also very sad because she has grown close to a lot of the girlfriends and wives. Like me, she spends much of today welded to her phone.

I've kept quite a few of the texts that I received.

Kev:

> Is it true?

Jamie:

> Sorry to hear you are leaving, Rat. You know how much we would have liked you to stay but we understand why you are going. One thing i can say is look after yourself in the business side of things, as nobody else will.

Ferg:

> Was calling in some hope that it wasn't true. Am so shocked. You're a top man and a friend. Can't describe the sort of loss you will be to Leinster and to me off the pitch,

> personally. I respect your decision. It took balls to do it.
> I hope you are okay. Give me a shout over the weekend
> at any stage.

And so on. I gave various responses to the lads but this text is typical. Me:

> Can't believe it happened. Thought it was going to get
> sorted last night. Pretty upset that I had to make this
> decision but I took a stance with the union and in the end
> had to stick by it. Talk to you another time. Hopefully we
> will finish on a high.

It was reassuring to get messages of support from former internationals like Mick Quinn, Tony Ward, Rodney O'Donnell or Donal Lenihan. And Joe, of course. I felt rotten that everything happened so quickly in the end.

Joe:

> Johnny, hope things are going okay. Disappointed for
> Leinster but generally happy for you and Laura heading to
> Paris. Good luck in the Six Nations. At least you can
> prepare with a clear head now that the decision is made.
> Looking forward to catching up and finishing off on a high.
> All the best, Joe.

It would have been easier if he'd sent me a snotty message. We've been building something together for the last two and a half seasons but now the bond has been snapped – with one phone call, it seems. I'm sure Leinster are furious because now they have to go and find another out-half and at this stage of the year most people have their plans sorted. As for Joe, I don't know whether I'll work with him again. It looks like he'll head back to New Zealand after next season. Even the rest of this season will be difficult, because our relationship will be different.

I couldn't face talking to him today, or to anyone in Leinster. Not just yet – even though Guy Easterby and Mick Dawson sent texts which I thought were very thoughtful and understanding. I'll get back to them over the weekend. But this was what I texted back to Joe, eventually:

> Sorry I haven't been in touch, Joe. Do you have an email address you could send me? I'll be in touch with you soon when I can talk without crying like a baby. Cheers, Johnny.

Saturday 26 January

RDS

Dave Alred is over for a couple of days, which is a good thing. The narrow focus of repeatedly kicking a rugby ball between two uprights is a great distraction from The Contract. Even better, I'm absolutely crushing my place-kicks. It's typically blustery down at the Anglesea Road end but my kicks are flying dead straight into the wind. I've never felt in such good kicking form coming into a Six Nations.

We talk about the c-word afterwards, naturally, but I find that Dave is good to talk to about all sorts of stuff. He provides a fresh perspective and knows something of what I've been going through from his close relationship with Jonny Wilkinson, who was also a one-club man for most of his career. He reassures me that I've made the right decision, that new challenges will make me a better player.

Funny thing, though, as I was getting togged out beforehand I had second thoughts about wearing my Leinster gear at the RDS. I know that I'm still a Leinster player until the end of the season and they will always be my province. But what will it be like playing for them now? How will I be able to keep bossing people about when I'm cashing out? (I'm sure that's how it will be described.) The stands and the terraces are empty and there's no one here but me and Dave, but still I feel guilty, an impostor, so I throw on some Adidas kit instead.

I'm due to meet Monsieur Lorenzetti at Dublin Airport this evening with Fintan, to sign contracts. To kill time in between, I head up to St Mary's. Jerry is playing against Cork Con. I don't really want to be in a crowd but I don't want to be alone either. I'm on safe ground here. I'm barely watching the game, just going through some voice messages, when I come across one from last night from Gerry Thornley of the *Irish Times*, telling me he's running a story quoting Jacky Lorenzetti, apparently denying that I'm coming to Racing because I am 'too expensive'. Then Dad calls, asking if I've seen this story in the paper. I tell him no, but that it's sorted.

'But have you actually signed anything with Racing?'

'No.'

'For Christ's sake. Why not? What if he now offers you less, seeing as he knows you can't go back to the Union?'

Now I'm panicking, but Fintan puts my mind at rest. He explains Lorenzetti's media tactics. He has a squad of players that he needs to keep motivated for the rest of this season. He especially doesn't need his fly-halves reading about me coming on a big contract for next season. Besides, there's a regulation in France which says you can't announce any new players for the following season until April. It's supposedly to prevent players being 'tapped up', and if a club contravenes it they can be fined.

Sure enough, Monsieur Lorenzetti is a man of his word. He flies into Dublin in his six-seater jet, as arranged, and we sign contracts in a hotel at the airport. There are a few details to be ironed out, about things like release for Ireland camps next season – I may miss a couple of days here and there, but not many; this is something we'd agreed upon when I was over in Paris. And then he leaves and it's done and I can now get on with playing rugby for Ireland in the Six Nations. I used to think that this coming week was the craziest few days in the season, with all the hype and anticipation. After the last couple of weeks, it will seem almost relaxing.

Tuesday 29 January

Carton House

Rugby would be such a simple job if it was just about rugby. Thankfully, the past couple of days have been almost completely about rugby. About perfecting plays that will help us to get outside Jonathan Davies's rush defence. About crowding the big Welsh backs for space when they have the ball, and flat-footing them when we have it. About how to react when they kick the ball long, as they invariably do. Basically, about doing to them what they have done to us in our last three meetings. Christ, do we owe them one.

Naturally, I've had some explaining to do. The whole contract issue impinges on everyone who is either in negotiations with the Union or will be again at some time in the future. So I had to do a bit of clearing the air in the team room. I'm not going to do any media stuff this week, because all I'd be asked about would be the Paris move, which would be a distraction from what is Ireland's biggest game of the season. But I've had to explain to my team-mates why this has happened, so that we could move on quickly. I've also contacted anyone in Leinster who I reckon might feel let down, just to tell my side of the story. It will be interesting to see what sort of a reaction there is when I return after the Six Nations, but the immediate comments have all been supportive. People say they understand my reasons for leaving.

With Ireland, we'd already moved on to the banter stage this morning. It's '*Passez le ketchup, Johnny, s'il vous plaît,*' at the dinner table. Obvious stuff. Drico tweeted a picture of a sign outside a cafe in Ballsbridge saying 'Free coffee for Johnny Sexton – if he'll stay.' Apparently it's been retweeted over a thousand times. The slagging isn't only one-way. When the Union release a statement proudly announcing contract extensions for Church and Rossy, I tell the lads that I've probably got them a better deal, seeing as the Union can't afford any more defections.

The mood is good because everyone can feel that we are better prepared than we were this time last year, even if we've had to train in diabolical conditions for the past couple of days, with rain and high winds. In fact, we couldn't have prepared better. Everyone is clued in to our game-plan and we've most of the hard work done. It's no harm that Wales are missing my clubmate-to-be, Dan Lydiate, who chopped us out of the World Cup – so much of their defensive game-plan off lineouts and mauls is about forcing runners inside towards Lydiate's channel. We thought they might go with two open-sides in Sam Warburton and Justin Tipuric, but they've picked Aaron Shingler at 6 and left Tipuric on the bench. We have Gilly, Zeebs and Mike McCarthy making their Six Nations debuts and each of them brings a certain energy. We've no Paulie or Stevie Ferris, but we have Rob and Seanie back. Two world-class players. And Drico. His presence makes such a difference, whether he's captain or not.

For me, it doesn't really feel like a Test week because I'm strangely relaxed. No nerves. Should I worry? It's a massive game for Ireland, and also for anyone with Lions aspirations. Gatland has stood back and allowed Rob Howley to take charge of Wales for the Six Nations, but Gatland will be at the Millennium, naturally, and there will be more live candidates in action than at any other game in the championship. The contract stuff should put even more pressure on me, but I'm feeling strong and the mood is good. I've been impressed by Brian, who spoke really well this evening about the need to 'out-physical' Wales. He's sending out the message that he's still a leader, even if Jamie's captain, yet at the same time he's not stepping on Jamie's toes. He says we all have to be leaders on Saturday. And he's right. I love Brian when he gets in this frame of mind. He has a point to prove on a number of fronts. Not being captain. In front of Gatland, against one of his main rivals for the Lions jersey. I can tell by his face and the way he is talking that he is going to have one of those games.

Saturday 2 February

Millennium Stadium (Wales 22, Ireland 30)

I've mixed memories of this place. Two years ago was a bit of a nightmare, what with Mike Phillips's try and my missed penalty. It got even worse after the game when I learned that Joe Nolan had died. Joe was one of my dad's Bective friends, the club president that year and my first mini-rugby coach. As he was coming out of the stadium, he collapsed on the street with a heart attack and died immediately.

Very sad. A group from Bective are over tomorrow to lay flowers and say a few prayers, just before the game. We're in the Hilton, right in the centre of town, but it's too close to kick-off for me to make an appearance, which is a pity. Dad understands.

A couple of months after Joe's death, I was back at the Millennium for a much happier day with Leinster – the 'comeback' final against Northampton. And it's those happier memories that are in the forefront as I'm out on the pitch beforehand. The scene is slightly different as the roof is open today, and there is warmth in the spring sunshine as we prepare for a one o'clock kick-off. I like an early kick-off. No hanging around all day at the hotel. Just breakfast, a few more inspirational words, especially from Brian, and here we are.

My confidence is high. I have barely missed a kick all week in practice, and I nail twenty out of twenty place-kicks in the warm-up. Back in Carton, I was practising in winds of 40 or 50 kph, getting lads to hold the ball still on the tee for me. This feels a doddle. That's one of Alred's theories – you should practise ugly, or in ugly conditions, because when you kick in a stadium like the Millennium, knocking them over from the touchline is easy compared to a twenty-metre kick in gusting winds.

Twelfth minute – Wales 0, Ireland 7 (Zebo try, Sexton conversion)

There's nothing quite like the feeling of transferring something you've practised onto the big stage. This was a rehearsed three-phase play, moving right to left, designed to release Brian behind Rob, who ran a decoy line up front to sit down Jonathan Davies. It worked almost exactly as we had planned, and the slight deviation from the script was where Brian's genius took over. Because the ruck ball wasn't quite as quick as we'd have liked, he had to throw a weighted pass into the space behind Alex Cuthbert. It was a great pass, but Simon also did really well to read what was happening and close the deal. I converted and soon kicked a penalty, to give us a 10–0 lead and an excellent start to the Six Nations – highly unusual for us.

Twenty-fourth minute – Wales 0, Ireland 17 (Healy try, Sexton conversion)

In years to come, will this be remembered as Church's try, or for Zebo's magic flick? Maybe it should be remembered for Jamie's crap pass, for if the ball hadn't been thrown so off-target, Simon wouldn't have been able to produce the moment of sublime skill that got thousands of hits on YouTube. Only kidding, Jamie! The score can really be traced back to Besty's block on Dan Biggar's kick, of course. He wasn't somebody we'd targeted as particularly slow to get the ball from hand to foot – Merv had warned us more about Phillips's tendency to dummy the box-kick. Rory just saw an opportunity and took it. It was a big moment in the game. Gilly should also get credit for keeping the ball alive despite being too tight to the right touch-line, before Church used his power to get over. Once again, I converted and then added a penalty. No one predicted we'd start with twenty unanswered points at the Millennium.

Forty-third minute – Wales 3, Ireland 30 (O'Driscoll try, Sexton conversion)

An even crazier scoreline. Wales had their purple patch before the break but only took three points from a period of concerted pressure, as we defended brilliantly. Even better, we snuck those three points back on the stroke of half-time, to give ourselves another psychological boost. However, in the dressing room I made the point that the key to winning was to score first in the second half, as we knew from the Heineken final against Northampton. Brian did the needful, nipping in at the side of the ruck for a trademark two-footer. If Northampton had scored first in the second half against Leinster here two years ago, it was game over. Here, we gave ourselves twenty-seven insurance points, which was enough.

Seventy-sixth minute – Wales 22, Ireland 30

Well, just about enough. Once you get far ahead, it doesn't matter how much you say you're not going to shut up shop – to some extent, you do. On the one hand, there is no real excuse to stop playing, because this is a tournament that can be decided by points difference; on the other, we were conscious of not showing too much of our attacking playbook. Besides, Wales gave it a good old crack, in fairness to them. When you allow them to run at you, as we did, and when their crowd get behind them, they can be almost irresistible. We were unlucky to lose Darce to a calf injury, for Cuthbert scored before Earlsy had had a chance to settle in at centre, and the way they built on that momentum was scary.

If the first half had been a dream, the last thirty-five minutes were nightmarish. We made an incredible number of tackles – Seanie made twenty-three all by himself! I put a few in myself. I remember at one stage shooting out of the line to hit Sam Warburton, and about ten seconds later I was holding down Jamie Roberts on the other side of the pitch. All hands on deck. Losing Besty and Conor to the bin didn't help, obviously. Usually, when you're a man down, you can come up with ways to run down the clock – let's run a set play to get back into the game and hold on to possession. But when it's your hooker who is missing, and then your scrum-half, that complicates things in a big way. At one stage we had Seanie throwing lineouts and Drico box-kicking from scrum-half. Plus we invited Wales to attack by kicking poorly. Our back three probably needed to get the ball off the park as much as possible, but we kept kicking long, and against Wales that is asking for trouble.

There were still twenty minutes left when Leigh Halfpenny scored to make it 15–30, but only four on the clock when Craig Mitchell plunged over for their third try and the sixth of an incredible match. Not that I was enjoying myself. We held on for those four minutes but we were barely able to celebrate, we were so knackered.

It was only in the dressing room that I got to really enjoy the win. That time is the best part of the job. It's still work in a sense, because recovery and rehab is such an important part of the game, especially in a condensed period of intense work like the Six Nations. We get massages, put on compression garments to improve blood circulation and eat as much as possible – the immediate post-match is a good time to load up, according to the nutritionists. And ice, of course. A pain, but it's a lot easier sitting in a giant tub of freezing water with a team-mate if you've won. You have to stay in there, up to your neck, for three minutes. Seanie likes to count down the seconds as a game – you say 180, I'll say 179, you say 178, and so on. He can be quite childlike at times, our Seanie. But his game works a treat and makes time go so much quicker.

We've a good hour and a half to kill in the dressing room, because we have to wait for the guys who are chosen to talk to the media in the mixed zone – most guys will do whatever they can to avoid this.

I managed to avoid media duty, which means I can get dressed into my dinner suit at my leisure, grab a cup of tea, and then sit back and watch England give Scotland a good shoeing in the second game of the day, at Twickenham. Already I can see people calling next Sunday's game at the Aviva as a Grand Slam decider. And already I can see people tipping us as favourites. I've no problem with that. I reckon we're the better team, and we owe them one from Twickenham last season. I will say that they do look like a team, though, very well organized defensively, very hard-working.

The beauty of our early kick-off is that we'll get home tonight. The post-match dinner is more of a buffet, not the formal dicky-bow deal, but still enough of an affair to have some crack with the lads, and also a friendly enough chat with both Maurice Dowling and some of the IRFU committee-men, who kindly shook my hand and wished me all the best in France. Some of them seem to have the impression that Fintan has driven this whole thing, which shows that they don't really know me that well, but there was no ill-feeling.

In fact, it was a very happy bus that ferried us all out to Cardiff Airport, partly because of the result, but also because Rog has been appointed new toastmaster. He's lethal with a microphone in his hand up the front of the bus, although most of it is fairly harmless stuff. We had a song from the guys making their Six Nations debut, and even a song from Mike McCarthy's girlfriend, who's a proud Geordie lass. Then that old Francophile Rog gives us a rendition of the Marseillaise. Soon the whole bus is singing the French national anthem and I'm happily joining in until I realize that, of course, the joke is on me. Touché, Rog. He hauls me up, takes the piss out of me in front of everyone and then forces me to sing a song. Luckily I've anticipated this might happen and I've something appropriate prepared: 'Don't Look Back in Anger'. Oasis – a song for every occasion!

Tuesday 5 February

Carton House

I don't need to pick up the newspapers in the team room to see that already they're setting up Sunday as the Johnny v. Owen show. It's the Slam decider too, of course, especially seeing as France lost in Rome on Sunday – what a result, what a performance by Italy! But I'd kind of known all along that the England game was going to be a duel of sorts between myself and Owen Farrell. So be it. I won't be saying anything about it, that's for sure.

I doubt he'll say anything in the build-up himself. We had a few words on the pitch in Twickenham last year but I don't think it will be an issue in the build-up to this one. They were riled up, probably sick to death of Irish teams coming over and out-emotioning them on Paddy's weekend in Twickenham. He held me down on the ground a few times and had a go – I told him that just because his old man was a hard man, that didn't make him one too. In fairness, he came into our changing room afterwards, shook hands and swapped jerseys. Sometimes you say things in the heat of battle that you wish you hadn't.

I'd be surprised if he was a bad guy, given who his dad is. I don't know Andy Farrell, but growing up I was a big fan. He was a hard bastard and a seriously good player. He played on a successful Wigan team with some fantastic players, but they never seemed to get ahead of themselves. Stuart Lancaster seems a solid individual too, with good values. So England don't seem the sort of group that fits the 'arrogant English' stereotype. It would be easier if they did. I don't think they're going to be coming over here cocky, like they might have been a couple of years ago. They seem to have changed their personality. Their captain, Chris Robshaw, comes across as down-to-earth. They're a bit humble, which is a little annoying, to be honest. You want to hate them!

Actually, that sounds wrong. I don't want to beat England because of the old 800-years-of-oppression stuff, which got quite a bit of an airing in the lead-up to the famous game in Croke Park in 2007. Any game between England and Ireland is special because of the history between the countries, but that won't enter my head on Sunday. I want to beat them because we are motivated by being successful.

Thursday 7 February

Shelbourne Hotel

Bit of a scare this morning. Seanie accidentally stood over my right ankle during a training run, bruising it badly. I felt the need to try some kicks after training, even though I was in a bit of pain, and now I'm icing the hell out of it all evening. It will be OK, but it's not ideal.

The good news is that Darce has recovered, so we are unchanged from Cardiff. England have made just one change, with James Haskell coming into the back row, and Manu Tuilagi is back on the bench. Like us, they had a great finish to the autumn games, beating the All Blacks, and now have momentum. They have a big midfield, with Billy Twelvetrees and Brad Barritt both strong in defence, but with the right ball I reckon we have the moves to get around them. I'm just praying for decent weather. The forecast for Sunday is crap, with heavy rain on the way in the afternoon. But they've got it wrong before. Here's hoping.

Sunday 10 February

Aviva Stadium (Ireland 6, England 12)

Did my hammy.

Nightmare.

First time ever.

Grade two tear.

Four to six weeks.

Might make it back for France.

Slam gone.
The good news?
There isn't any.

Monday 11 February

Goatstown

Apologies if I was a bit short on detail yesterday but I wasn't feeling particularly chatty. Professional sportspeople are self-absorbed at the best of times, but when something like this happens we can go into ourselves a bit.

The frustrating part is that it was one of those stupid freak injuries. I went to fly-hack the ball but got pushed and missed it completely and stubbed my foot off the ground instead. All the force went through my hamstring, which went into spasm immediately. This was a new sensation for me, an injury I've never had before, but I knew it was bad. My immediate thought was, *That's my Six Nations over*. When the doc arrived, he tried to make me test the muscle but I told him no, it's gone. Get Rog ready.

It was Farrell who nudged me – not that I hold it against him. He was just challenging for the ball. He actually came into the dressing room after the game to see how I was, which was decent of him. At that stage, I was waiting to be taken out to the sports injury clinic in Santry for a scan. There were a few of us on that bus, unfortunately. Zeebs has a broken bone in his foot and will miss the rest of the Six Nations. Darce has a foot problem too and Mike McCarthy has done his knee. From my point of view, the news could have been worse. I didn't rip the tendon and the muscle isn't totally ruptured – I'm told I'm lucky I wasn't moving at full pace. However, there is a substantial tear, not that deep but long, so knitting the muscle fibres together will be a job of work. Now, it's just a race against time. I'll miss the Scotland match, and the medics are saying that to play against France might be rushing it – that game is just under four weeks away. But that's my target.

It might sound selfish, but when you injure yourself during a game, you kind of distance yourself from the events of that game. We were 6–0 down when I got injured and I was in an ice bath when the lads came in at half-time. I could have contributed, but what was the point? It was their game now. I got my leg strapped up and hobbled out on crutches to watch the rest of the game. Rog had just kicked us level at 6–6 and they had just lost Haskell to the bin. Happy days. Or maybe not.

I've since had a chance to watch the whole game. If we had our chance back, maybe we'd have concentrated more on what we needed to do to dog out a win. Yes, we'd seen the long-range forecasts but I think people were still hoping we'd be lucky with the weather and get to play some rugby against them. It turned out to be the opposite of the Wales week, when we trained in crap conditions and played in sunshine. To pull back the curtains in the Shelbourne and see dirty skies yesterday morning was a real downer. We had such good attacking plays ready to go but they were now all redundant because of the pissing rain and the howling wind.

So it was a day for discipline, for defence, for kick-chase and kick-chess. A boring game to watch but still a good one to win. They did all of those things better than us, so fair play to them. They are very well organized and well coached and seem to have a great spirit. But I still think they did very little to win the game, whereas we did everything to lose it. Like, if you look at all twelve of their points, they were more donated than really earned. I think it's ironic that we've beaten Wales and lost to England because if it came down to a shoot-out between the two of them, I'd be backing Wales, big-time.

Even though we played badly and made so many mistakes, it was still there for the taking at 12–6, with ten minutes left. We had a penalty maybe thirty-five metres out and around twelve in from touch: bread-and-butter for Rog, even in those conditions, but I still think we should have knocked it into the corner. With so little time available to us, I'm not sure 12–9 was enough of an improvement on 12–6. He had the angle to get it right into the corner and our maul was one aspect of our game that was going well. Wet conditions, guys sliding low for the try-line around the fringes. It was the aggressive option. Instead Jamie and Brian decided to go for goal – and Rog missed. It looked as though he didn't agree with the decision to go for goal himself, which isn't ideal preparation for a kick. You can be standing over a ball thinking, *We shouldn't be going for this!*

The lads are already thinking about bouncing back in Edinburgh. For me, it's just about getting this hamstring right, and staying positive. I'm confident that my kicking won't be compromised by the injury. There are kickers who take short backswings and a big follow-through who do place a big strain on their hammy, but my quad takes most of the stress. Once I'm back running, I'll be back kicking. It's a race against time.

There's one side of me that says I have to get back for the France and Italy games. We can still win the championship. But what if I rush back and do the hammer properly and rule myself out of Lions contention? I know if Joe was Lions coach, he'd just tell me to get myself right and worry about nothing else. That's what Dad is saying to me, and my brothers: 'Listen, you don't need to play any more in the Six Nations to be picked for the tour.' But you can't get picked if you're not fit. And Joe isn't picking the squad, nor is Dad or Mark or Jerry. I don't know Gatland from Adam, don't know if he rates me, don't know if he feels he needs to see me play as many big games as possible. I'm also aware that Farrell did himself no harm yesterday – man of the match again, even though he missed a couple of kicks.

So I'm just going to do everything I can to get 100 per cent fixed as soon as possible. This part of the recovery process is the most frustrating because there is so little you can do in the days immediately after the injury. You can ice it, and you can stretch the muscles around the hamstring to help the healing process, but you can't stretch the hamstring itself. I'll get physio in camp, but our guys have a whole squad to look after and I want intensive treatment. I'll go to see Mike Carswell, a physical therapist with magical hands who I see at least once a week anyway – his speciality is breaking down scar tissue. I'll work during the day with the Irish physios, and then go and see Mike two or three evenings a week for the next three weeks. I might look at acupuncture and reflexology, anything that could possibly help. I'll sleep as much as possible, and eat as well as possible, whatever it takes to get back in time for France.

Saturday 16 February

Adare Manor, Co. Limerick

Laura and I are in Limerick – to see Ger Hartmann, another top-of-the-range physical therapist, and to meet the folks at Adare Manor to discuss the arrangements for our wedding here in July. It's good to have some company, because rehabbing from injury can be a lonely business. I've been in Carton all week for treatment, but not really feeling part of the set-up, not attending meetings. It's not much fun.

Basically, I wanted to make sure I was doing all I could to accelerate my rehab, and Ger has helped athletes from all over the world. He specializes in soft-tissue injuries like torn hamstrings. He also complements what Mike 'the Bull' Carswell and the Irish medical team have been doing during the week. I know Deccie's medical staff would prefer me to put my feet up for the weekend rather than travel to Limerick but I don't see taking a weekend off as being an option. I'll let them know out of courtesy, of course. I don't want to burn any bridges. I'm sure they'll realize I'm doing it for the right reasons. I'm just doing everything I can.

I'm beginning to get an idea of how much goes into organizing a wedding. Thankfully, Laura is doing most of the work – correction, all of the work. I sit in on the meeting with the hotel manager, but keep excusing myself, supposedly to visit the loo, but really to swing on my crutches back to our room and get some ice on my hammy. At this stage of the recovery process, you're supposed to ice it for ten minutes of every hour, and I'm sticking religiously to the routine. The hotel staff are doing a great job keeping us well stocked with ice, all evening. The plan had been to go out for dinner, but I don't want to break my hourly routine. It's just as well Laura loves me.

Deccie has a decision to make at out-half, obviously. Everyone is taking it for granted that he will pick Rog for Edinburgh, but he's not in great form.

Paddy Jackson played against Fiji and has trained with us all along, but Ulster's coach Mark Anscombe didn't do him any favours by giving

The home match against Munster at the Aviva is a huge fixture for Leinster every autumn. This season we beat them 30–21 in a cracking game of rugby (*Dan Sheridan / Inpho*)

Brian O'Driscoll sometimes has to tell me to chill out – but he's great company, and it's a privilege to play with him (*Lorraine O'Sullivan / Inpho*)

After a disappointing loss to South Africa, we cut loose with seven tries against Argentina. We needed the win in order to hold on to a second-seed spot in the World Cup draw (*Dan Sheridan / Inpho*)

With Rog after the Argentina match. Our relationship got off to a testy start, and the media have made the most of the rivalry between us, but we are good friends now, and the rivalry made me a better player (*Lorraine O'Sullivan / Inpho*)

The loss in the home Heineken Cup group game against Clermont was the most significant of my Leinster career. Nathan Hines, an ex-teammate and a great bloke, got up to some naughty stuff in rucks, and I had a pop at him at full-time – but we patched it up later (*Billy Stickland / Inpho*)

In the Six Nations opener, we ran roughshod over Wales in the first half, then held on in the second for a great win. But the two nations' championships went in dramatically different directions thereafter (*James Crombie / Inpho*)

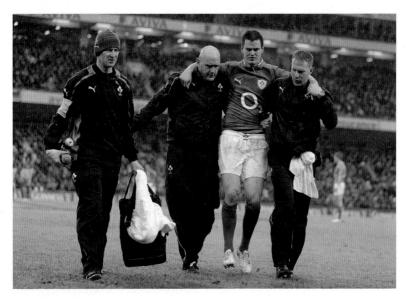

I tore my hamstring in a dreary defeat to England, ending my Six Nations (*Dan Sheridan / Inpho*)

After beating Stade Français in the final of the Amlin Challenge Cup, it was great to lift the trophy with Isa Nacewa, who was in his last season with Leinster ... (*Dan Sheridan / Inpho*)

... and it was even better to win the Pro12 after so many near misses in recent years, and to salute Joe Schmidt, under whom we won four trophies in three seasons, as he prepared to take over as national coach (*Billy Stickland / Inpho*)

The Lions sleep tonight: myself and Jamie Roberts on the flight to Hong Kong, where the first tour match was played (*Dan Sheridan / Inpho*)

Owen Farrell and I made the quick British and Irish Lions transition from rivals to friends on the tour, and spent many hours at kicking practice with Neil Jenkins and Leigh Halfpenny, separate from the rest of the squad (*Dan Sheridan / Inpho*)

Before the tour match against the Waratahs in Sydney, wise words from Warren Gatland (*top*) and Brian O'Driscoll (*both photos Dan Sheridan / Inpho*)

The Lions sleep tonight: myself and Jamie Roberts on the flight to Hong Kong, where the first tour match was played (*Dan Sheridan / Inpho*)

Owen Farrell and I made the quick British and Irish Lions transition from rivals to friends on the tour, and spent many hours at kicking practice with Neil Jenkins and Leigh Halfpenny, separate from the rest of the squad (*Dan Sheridan / Inpho*)

Before the tour match against the Waratahs in Sydney, wise words from Warren Gatland (*top*) and Brian O'Driscoll (*both photos Dan Sheridan / Inpho*)

I said a few words in the huddle before the first Test against Australia, in Brisbane, which we won very narrowly (*Billy Stickland / Inpho*)

You'd have no trouble guessing who won the second Test from this shot of George North (*centre*), Jonathan Davies and myself in the dressing room afterwards (*Dan Sheridan / Inpho*)

My try in the third
Test, after a move
involving Tommy
Bowe, Jonathan
Davies and Leigh
Halfpenny, opened
the floodgates for
what became a
crushing win
(*Dan Sheridan /
Inpho*)

Fighting over a Welsh flag afterwards
with Mike Phillips – one of ten
Welshmen in the team that started
the third Test. On the bus I sang
'Bread of Heaven'
(*Dan Sheridan / Inpho*)

Six days after the third
Test, Laura and I tied the
knot on a beautiful day in
Adare. Then it was a quick
honeymoon in Vegas,
and a move to Paris …
(*Trish Fitzpatrick*)

the place-kicking duties to Ruan Pienaar for last night's game against Zebre. There were further twists this evening. Leinster's game against Treviso wasn't televised but I followed on Twitter – I don't need to have an account to use it as a news source! I could tell from the updates that Mads had a stormer and also place-kicked well. Meanwhile, Rog looked completely out of sorts in Llanelli, and missed a few penalty kicks he'd normally kick in his sleep. He looked rattled, short on confidence, which was strange to see, but I'm convinced he'll still start at Murrayfield. He always seems to bounce back from any poor performance.

Tuesday 19 February

Team room, Carton House

Walk in on the players immediately after a team has been announced and you can get a good idea of the line-up just by the body language. I wasn't at the meeting this evening as I'd been doing some work in the gym, but as soon as I walk into the team room I can tell something's up. Rog and Paddy are sitting there with bemused looks on their faces.

'You missed it, boy!' says Rog. 'The biggest team announcement of the year. He's tricked us all!'

And he's right, it's sensational news. Rog is on the bench and Paddy is starting. In other words, Deccie has overlooked the bloke whose career has been intertwined with his going way back more than twenty years to Pres Cork, and picked a kid who is only just twenty-one to make his international debut in a game that could be a banana skin – Scotland are feeling a lot better about themselves having beaten Italy 34–10 in Edinburgh last week. And Deccie's supposed to be a conservative coach?

Admittedly, he's pulled a few surprises in the past. Everyone expected him to pick Rog to play South Africa in November 2009, but he gave me the nod only a week after I'd made my debut against Fiji. I remember he picked Tomás O'Leary for a Heineken Cup quarter-final away to Gloucester when Peter Stringer was the safer, more experienced option. But this is different. I think Paddy is a talented young player with a lot going for him, but he hasn't been place-kicking for a while and it's a huge responsibility to have on your debut. Ruan Pienaar has been kicking for Ulster since Paddy had a couple of bad days out before Christmas, and although he kicked for the Wolfhounds last month, he's had ankle problems which have prevented him from working on that part of his game, even in practice.

I'd thought the only way Deccie would pick Paddy was if he picked Ferg as well to take the goal-kicks. I'd even said it to Ferg over the weekend, that he should practise as much as possible, just in case he got in for Darce or Zeebs, both of whom are injured. That's the other news, incidentally. Luke Marshall, another twenty-one-year-old, comes in at 12, with Earlsy filling in on the left wing. Drico is feeling very much the senior citizen in midfield. The other change is Tom Court coming in at loosehead for Cian, who has been suspended for three weeks after stamping on Dan Cole in the England game – Cole was up to no good and obstructing Conor at the base of the ruck, but what Cian did looked bad so he was always going to miss one match at least.

I commiserate with Rog and congratulate Paddy. 'I'm just sitting there in the meeting and suddenly I hear my name being called out!' he says. 'I'm as surprised as anyone.' In fairness to him, he has a fairly old head on his shoulders and seems very relaxed. He must be wondering, though. I watched training today and when they were doing ball-work, Rog ran nearly every rep, and when that happens early in Test week, everyone knows who's starting at the weekend. They were wrong this time.

Sunday 24 February

Goatstown

I'm watching the game from Murrayfield on the couch in my apartment, and it feels odd. Then, up pops a shot of Warren Gatland sitting in the stand and you think, *Damn. I wish I was playing.*

You're in a weird place when you're injured. You want the team to do well, so that when France come to Dublin in a fortnight's time, the championship is still on the table. You want Paddy to do well too. He's a good young player and a very likeable bloke. We have become good pals over the past few months. I just don't want him to do *too* well. I'd be lying if I said otherwise. There's this part of you that wants people to appreciate what you bring to the team. You want people to say, 'Pity that Johnny wasn't playing.' I feel slightly ashamed to think this way because it goes against the whole team ethos. But I've spoken to people about it and everyone is the same. It's human nature.

A few of us still laugh about the time, back at the end of 2008, when myself, Kev and Ross McCarron were almost rooting for Wasps to beat Leinster in a Heineken Cup match at Twickenham. At that stage, the word was that if Leinster didn't make it through to the quarters of the Heineken, Cheiks would get the bullet. The three of us were bitter we weren't involved, and if he got the bullet it wouldn't have been the worst thing for us as individuals. We were convinced that he gave preferential treatment to the older lads and we were never going to get a look-in. So there we were, watching the game on telly at my place, half hoping that Wasps would deny Leinster a losing bonus, which would have done the trick. Wasps had a penalty coming towards the end, and if they'd kicked it that would have put us out of bonus territory. Instead, they put it in the corner and we're there, shouting at the telly, 'NO! For Christ's sake! What are you doing?' We weren't really serious, of course. We still have a laugh about it amongst ourselves, and exaggerate the details – how we were sitting there with the Wasps jerseys on, and the black and yellow face paint.

I suppose the point is that sports people are selfish. Ask Rob Kearney what it was like to have to watch Isa Nacewa light up the Heineken Cup in 2010/11 when he spent most of the season injured. Rob got a medal because he played some part, but it would have meant very little to him. He would have said polite things about Isa in public because he had no option. He would have wanted us to win because we are his friends, but at the same time he didn't want us to experience it without him. And you could tell when he came back the following year that he wanted to prove a point, which he did. He was European Player of the Year.

It's a little different with me and Paddy. I'm confident in my form and my ability and I reckon as soon as I'm fit, I'll be back in. There's just a hint of doubt there, though. Deccie slagged me about it when I was leaving camp on Friday. When I wished him good luck, he said, 'You'd better hope yer man doesn't have a blinder!' I made some gag that I might end up having plenty of time to get my hammy right, and he laughed. I suppose the bottom line is I wanted Paddy to have a strong debut – but not too strong – and for us to be still in contention in two weeks' time, when France come to town.

It didn't turn out as anyone wanted. Scotland beat us 12–8, our first Six Nations loss in Edinburgh since 2001. To be fair, I thought Paddy had a decent debut in most parts of his game. He spilled a ball early on and missed touch off a penalty at a critical point in the second half, but his general out-half play was sound and he put Luke Marshall through a couple of holes. The problem was his place-kicking – we needed better than one on target from four shots in a low-scoring game. I don't think anyone will point the finger at him. He hasn't been kicking regularly in games, and his recent injury stopped him practising for at least a few weeks. I know from experience that not having enough practice can really affect a kicker. It can take a few weeks and a few games to get back in the groove. I remember tearing my quad before my first Six Nations and it really affected everything with my kicking. I couldn't practise for three weeks and then only had a couple of days before my first game. Imagine a golfer going into a major having not played a competitive round or even hit a ball in three weeks. Bad habits creep back in and everything feels alien. I really felt for Paddy because I was there only a few years ago and it is tough.

Not that we should have needed to win by place-kicks. We carved Scotland apart on numerous occasions but could only finish once, when Gilly scored in the second half. We should have been twenty points up by half-time. It was head-wrecking to watch and I was going bananas on the sofa, screaming at the telly. Scotland hadn't much to offer but the longer it went on, the more they sensed an upset, the more the crowd got into it. We handed them a gift and they grabbed it gratefully. God, it was painful to watch.

It's incredible to think that it's only three weeks since we were running Wales ragged in the first half at the Millennium. We haven't been helped by injuries. The list is almost freakish: since the Six Nations started, we've lost Zeebs, Darce, Mike McCarthy, Chris Henry and myself, while Cian has been suspended. That's on top of Paulie, Stevie, Tommy and Straussy, all of whom were already rehabbing. And we're supposed to have the best player-management system! Jason Cowman, our head of strength and conditioning, is top class and has been doing everything to look after us. I doubt there is anyone better in the business than him. It is just bad luck. Freak injuries. Nothing could have been done to prevent them.

I'd like to think I'd have made a difference against England – if I'd stayed on for more than half an hour – and against Scotland. But is it gratifying to hear pundits say, 'We would have won if Johnny was playing'? Not really, to be honest. All I can think about is the fact that we're in the process of blowing what was a great chance to win a Slam. I genuinely thought this could have been a dream season – the Heineken final scheduled for the Aviva, and a favourable draw in the Six Nations, with both England and France at home. We'd win everything and I'd stroll into the Lions tour. Now, it looks like everything is going down the toilet.

Sunday 3 March

Carton House

Six days out from the France game and after a lot of hard work to get myself right, things are looking positive. Deccie announced an extended squad of thirty-two players to assemble in Carton this evening and I am one of three out-halves included. The big news is that Rog is not. Mads went well again for Leinster when they won away to Dragons on Friday night, and his form has been acknowledged.

If this is the end of the road for Rog – and that's how it looks – it seems a sad way to bow out. In fact, he doesn't even get to make a final bow. He comes off the bench against Scotland and tries this bizarre cross-kick which lands us in all sorts of bother. We lose and a week later, on a Sunday evening, he is quietly omitted from a squad of thirty-two. So, having played 128 times for his country and scored over a thousand points, he just disappears? That's how it must feel to him.

I ring him to commiserate. Strange though it may sound after what we've been through, I'm going to miss him. I always admired him growing up and although we went through a rocky start in our relationship we have become good pals. He's such a competitive animal that we have clashed a bit at times. That's only natural because neither of us would back down if we had an argument. He's good crack, too. Every Test week, we'd probably have spent six or seven hours together in kicking practice, travelling to and from the Aviva or wherever. You grow close to someone in that situation, even if you're competing with him. He's got a wickedly dry sense of humour. He might come across as serious in interviews, and when he's been in a bad mood, everyone in camp has known about it. But he's been very popular, a good laugh. So it's going to be strange this week, my first week in Ireland camp with him not around. I've thirty-six caps for Ireland and he's been there for every one of them. Already Rala, our bagman, doesn't know what to do with himself. He's had Rog there for every camp, every tour and every Test for the last thirteen years, without exception.

We had a good chat on the phone. Rog was very down, naturally. He felt that it was a big risk to have two rookie out-halves. Mads is going well for Leinster but he hasn't even started a Heineken Cup match at 10. Meanwhile, Paddy isn't even place-kicking for his province. Even though Rog himself isn't happy with the way he's playing, he did well against the Ospreys last night, and feels there's an argument for keeping him involved. He did admit that there's another side of the coin. We're out of the running for the Six Nations now, so it's as good a time as any to bring younger guys in and give them some experience. I don't know if he'll be this diplomatic in print, however. Despite everything he's been through with Deccie, they have a prickly relationship.

Right now, I feel sorry for him, though. A legend deserves an appropriate exit. In Wales, it seems like they organized a farewell series of matches especially for Shane Williams, so that he went out on a high. A career like Rog's ought to be acknowledged properly. He deserved a standing ovation in a packed Aviva for his last game, but sport can be cruel and unsentimental. Deccie has to make tough decisions and this was one of them.

Tuesday 5 March

Carton House

Five days to go and my first proper fitness test. I only started running last Thursday in Carton – some long-distance stuff at around 60 or 70 per cent – and I've been happy with progress. Every strength test on the hamstring has shown an improvement, even if its endurance is still right down. On Sunday morning I did some kicking drills with Dave at the RDS, just a reintroduction to kicking, really, but still encouraging.

So I'm confident enough doing what they call a closed session with Jason Cowman. By 'closed', they mean a carefully controlled environment, where you know every exercise and every run before you do it. (An 'open' session is joining in with everyone, and subjecting the injury to spontaneous situations.) My straight-line sprints are going well, but just as I'm beginning to think I could be in business, Jason tugs me off-line without warning and I feel a bite in the hammy. Shit. It's still there. So they're not going to risk me. Jason says I could be OK by Saturday, but there's every risk that I could do it some real harm if I play. They want me to do another closed session on Thursday and aim to play in Rome next week.

It's very frustrating because France are there for the taking. The pre-tournament favourites have lost their first three games, something that they haven't done since 1982. We feel we owe them one after last season, when we drew a game we dominated for long periods. The word is that they're going to pick Freddy Michalak at 10 and I'd love a crack at him. But there's no point in me taking risks

at this stage. It's reassuring to get a text from Brian, who's had his
own hamstring problems over the years.

> We all want you back but you don't want to do your
> hammy again. Your season will be over.

I come across a few other compliments this week. On the Planet
Rugby website François Trinh-Duc says it's good for French rugby
that I am coming to Racing. Maxime Machenaud says something
similar – but then he has to be complimentary, seeing as he'll be my
scrum-half next season! And people close to me tell me not to be
rushing back, because I'll only blow my Lions chances. They say I
don't need to play any more Six Nations rugby to get on the plane.
I just need to be fit at the end of the season.

I tell them I'm afraid of Gatland. Rob and Jamie and Paulie know
him from the last Lions tour, which seems like an advantage. I've
never even met the man. I still don't know what he thinks of me. My
plan for this season was always to get on the tour, and then get two
or three chances in warm-up matches to make the Test team. Because
I've been out injured, he's undoubtedly been looking at the alternatives. He could go with Farrell, Wilkinson and a utility back. Dan
Biggar's been going OK for Wales. Who knows? Maybe that's me
being paranoid. Turns out he's going to be in camp with us next
week – he's been doing a tour of the four countries during the Six
Nations. At least I'll be there for that.

Saturday 9 March

Aviva Stadium (Ireland 13, France 13)

I may have missed this game but it's nice to know I provided some
entertainment, thanks to Paul O'Connell and Mick Galwey. O2 asked
me to do a Q&A with some clients in the Shelbourne at around
lunchtime, and by the time I got there Mick and Paulie had the guests
all lined up to ask me the most awkward questions about my move to
Racing! Then the two lads hammered me for a good twenty min-

utes, at every opportunity. I was a sitting duck. There was more Q&A out at the stadium before the game, but they went easier on me this time. It was good to catch up with Paulie, who is making good progress with his back and hoping to be back playing soon. I hadn't seen him for a while so we'd plenty to catch up on.

The lads played much better than in Edinburgh but this was another opportunity missed, another case of running out of puff in the second half, and another crap day weather-wise. We adapted well at first, mauling them off the park to set up a try for Jamie barely ten minutes in. Even better, Paddy landed the conversion and then kicked two long-range penalties, superb kicks in the conditions. Meanwhile, Michalak was missing kicks for France – he was a strange choice of place-kicker, given Morgan Parra was playing. We led 13–3 at the break, and France looked broken. Had we scored first after the break, I'm convinced we'd have won.

The danger was that it would turn into a slug-fest, for they had some seriously beefy ball-carriers to bring off the bench – Mathieu Bastareaud, Sebastien Vahaamahina and Antonie Claassen. Their muscle told in the final quarter, as Louis Picamoles bashed over for a try, while our guys began to drop. Luke Marshall had to go off with concussion, then Reddser fell awkwardly and broke his leg. It was typical of him that he got up and tried to run before collapsing in awful pain.

My initial thought was that this was the end of his season and that I'll never get to play with him again – he is behind Conor Murray in the Ireland pecking order, and if I return to Leinster he'll be at least thirty-four or thirty-five – but he assures me he's planning on playing for a few more years yet. I reckon it's Brad Thorn's fault. Because he won a World Cup at thirty-seven, now everyone in Leinster thinks they can go on for ever. It's brilliant how one guy can change the perception of what is meant to happen. Brad proved if you look after yourself you can play into your late thirties. Amy and their new-born daughter Sadie were at the game, and everyone is reading it as Drico's final game at Lansdowne Road. I wouldn't be so sure. The bloke is still as hungry as ever, even if he was battered and bloody and taped up by the end of the game.

Before his injury, Reddser had almost set up a winning score for Earlsy with a lovely chip into the right corner. We felt Earlsy had been taken out illegally but, having looked at the replay, it was no penalty try. In fact, we were lucky that Michalak grubbered the ball dead on the final play, for France looked like scoring had they kept the ball in hand.

I didn't hang around afterwards. As far as I'm concerned, I'm playing in Rome next week. It's a wooden spoon game for Ireland but I can't wait to show that I can make a difference. So I've been training in the morning – some more work on the hammy, some kicking. How keen am I? Mustard.

Monday 11 March

Carton House

I knew Warren Gatland was going to be in camp this week, so why do I freeze when I walk into the restaurant this morning and there he is, with the Lions operations manager, Guy Richardson? I merely say, 'Good morning,' and head over towards the breakfast cereals. Maybe I don't want to seem too keen? But what's wrong with just going over and shaking hands? When I see other guys coming in and doing just that, I curse into my porridge.

Training goes well, but Warren's presence seems to bring out the child in all of us. When we're doing a drill near where he's standing, I say silly stuff like, 'Great pass, Rob KEARNEY!' just so he'll hear. Everyone is chirpy. We notice that, with Warren sitting in on a team meeting, Peter O'Mahony seems more animated and enthusiastic than usual when he delivers an analysis on Wayne Barnes, who's refereeing the game in Rome on Saturday. We let him know about it too, just as we slag anyone who is seen to be trying extra hard in training. To be honest, it's difficult to figure out whether Warren notices any of this. Most of the time he seems deeply engaged in conversation with Alan Quinlan, who is there reporting for RTE's *Against the Head*.

That afternoon, as a few of us are walking through reception, I see

Warren sitting with Gerry Thornley. I keep walking but he calls me over so I turn and point to my chest. Me? I don't want to look like an eejit if it's someone else he's looking for. But no, it's me. He wants to know if I'd do a session with his kicking coach, Neil Jenkins, if he were to come over. I tell him sure, I'd love it. 'OK,' he says. 'All right, thanks,' I say, and off I go.

Did I leave too soon? Should I have shot the breeze for a minute? Christ, I must be making a bad first impression on this guy. A little later, I called Gerry and asked him to pass my number on to Warren and to reinforce that I'd be delighted to do a session with Neil. Gerry tells me not to worry. If Warren is openly offering his kicking coach to me, I should take it as confirmation that I'll be touring. I'm still a little uneasy, though. Have I created a bad impression? And why is he sending Jenkins over? Because he thinks my kicking needs to be worked on? Well?

Thursday 14 March

Sports Surgery Clinic, Santry

This is nuts. Training has gone really well all week and my hammy felt good. Then, in the final session before departure for Rome, I reefed a tendon in my left foot. I'm being told that I'll be out for around six weeks and in a protective boot for maybe half that time. Six weeks? Gatland is naming the squad in seven weeks' time! I feel like I'm going to be sick.

Before this season I'd barely had one serious injury in my professional career, and suddenly it feels like my body is beginning to fall apart. The way it happened was so innocuous, too. We were just running a move and as I ran 'around the corner', I felt this strange pop in the side of my foot. I could still run on it but when I took off my boot and sock to show the doc and the physio, the foot felt loose and slightly strange. I'll admit the foot has been a tiny bit stiff every morning for the past week or so but it seemed a minor irritation compared to the hammy, and it always loosened out when I warmed up. I'd had some physio on it, but what happened this afternoon doesn't feel like a muscular problem, more like something has snapped. I get it strapped and try to finish the session but it's now officially sore, especially under my big toe. So while the lads are getting ready to head for the airport, I'm whisked to Santry to have a scan done – purely precautionary, I'm told. Like, I'm able to walk into the scanning machine so it can't be that serious, right? Sure enough, the scan shows that I haven't fractured a metatarsal or anything like that. Grand. Anti-inflammatories and a bit of strapping and I should be fine.

But then the radiologist says there's some fluid at the side of the foot that needs looking at. On closer inspection, there's a slight tear in a tendon. They get Johnny McKenna, the leading foot specialist in Ireland, to have a look at it, and that's when I'm slapped in the face with what seems the worst possible news: I have to wear this big black boot for ten days and then they'll have another look. Johnny says the earliest possible return for me would be the Munster match, but that's very optimistic. Gatland announces his squad on Tuesday 30 April. Christ! Johnny also wants me to see a foot-and-ankle specialist in London next Monday.

The lads heard the news on the way to Dublin Airport – Paddy to start, despite me having run almost everything in training for the past four days, with Mads on the bench. I get reassuring texts from everyone. The Leinster physios get in touch to tell me it's a blessing in disguise, that this was too early to be risking the hamstring anyway, because that was more like an eight-week injury. My dad and my brothers were the same – a blessing in disguise, they insist. Bloody well disguised, so it is.

Saturday 16 March

Goatstown

A good one to miss. That's the line I'm getting, in numerous text messages, as I sit watching our Six Nations campaign unravel in Rome. Friends and family get in touch to assure me that it would have been very hard to make a positive impression when everything was falling apart so dramatically and players were dropping like flies. And it's true, if we thought we'd had bad luck with injuries earlier in the championship, today was ridiculous. To lose three backs – Luke Marshall, Luke Fitzgerald and Earlsy – in one quarter was unbelievably bad luck, and meant that Peter O'Mahony ended up playing most of the game on the wing. In keeping with the bizarre nature of the game, we had three players binned – Brian, Conor and Donnacha Ryan – which has never happened to an Ireland team before. Mad stuff. Brian went for stamping on their flanker, who was lying all over the ball. It was very unlike Brian, but I could understand his frustration. At least he showed some fight. I would rather someone who loses it the odd time than someone who you need to rile up when things aren't going well.

If I'd been out there, I'd like to think I would have stayed positive. As I was sitting watching, I was thinking of situations where I might have used Peter to come off the blind-side wing and truck it up. I got excited when we had our purple patch coming into the final quarter, when Mads at 12 and Cian and Seanie were thundering onto the ball and Paddy was kicking his penalties, gradually reducing Italy's lead from 16–6 to 16–15. But we ran out of gas, and soon started running out of players, as Barnes showed Conor and Donnacha yellow. Our first-ever championship loss to Italy. Our worst finish in the Six Nations, above bottom-placed France but only on points difference. Kind of depressing, when you think of all the positive energy that was bouncing about our meeting in the Aviva last August.

It felt very much like the end of an era. During the week, there had been talk that Deccie might hold on to his job if we'd won today, given there had been positive aspects from the French match and because there have been mitigating circumstances in general. After today I am not so sure. I have mixed feelings on the issue. I get on well with Deccie and I feel really sorry for him. You think back to our performances against Argentina and in the first half against Wales, and you wonder what we might have achieved if we hadn't had such a ridiculous run of bad luck with injuries. Then another part of me thinks that even if we'd won a Grand Slam, it might still have been time for a change, time for new ideas.

The guy I feel sorriest for is Lukey Fitz. To have worked so hard to get back from serious injury and then to pick up another almost immediately is horrendously unlucky. He is an incredibly professional guy and he doesn't deserve the luck he has been dealt in recent times. Already it looks like he'll need surgery on his knee, which means he'll have to write off the rest of this season. Knowing him, he will make a phenomenal recovery again due to his dedication. He is still so young. I honestly feel once he gets a run injury-free he will show everyone what a world-class player he is. He will look back at this tough time and it will be the making of him. It's a timely reminder not to be feeling sorry for myself.

There are a couple of positives to come out of this weekend. My brother Jerry played for the Irish Under-20s in Italy and scored a try as they salvaged a draw. London Irish have offered him an academy deal and will set him up with a college course. He's mad keen, naturally. I also draw hope from the fact that Wales have stuffed England 30–3 in Cardiff, as I predicted. It means Wales win the championship for the second year in a row, and it means they'll definitely have more Lions than anyone else. But we were the only team to beat them, so I'm hoping that will count in our favour when it comes to selection. I just need some positive news when I see this specialist in London on Monday.

SIX

Strange Days

Monday 18 March

Fortius Clinic, London

I didn't recognize any of the other sportsmen waiting to see James Calder, but I'm guessing they're footballers. Like Johnny McKenna, James is an orthopaedic surgeon specializing in foot and ankle injuries. Specialists can be surprisingly blunt when it comes to giving you their prognosis. James is a reassuring sort, but that doesn't make the news from the latest scans any easier for me to digest. He says I'm going to be wearing this bloody boot for another four weeks and it's doubtful whether I'll be back playing before the Lions squad is announced on 30 April. Maybe I could be fit to play the Ospreys on 4 May. That's just under seven weeks from now. As he spelled it out to me, I got that sick feeling in the pit of my stomach again.

James says that I've got to think of the bigger picture. The main thing is being fit for the Lions tour, rather than for the squad announcement. It's nice to meet another person who's convinced that I'll travel if fit, but from where I'm sitting, doubts about my physical fitness and durability create doubts about my selection. I need to know what I can do to hasten the healing process. James says I can take the cast off to get some electro-stimulus work done on my calf, so the muscle doesn't waste, but the main thing to do is be patient, do some upper-body work in the gym, and find ways to keep myself distracted. There's another scan he wants me to have done before I leave the clinic, and when he looks at that he's going to pass on his opinions to Johnny McKenna, whom I'm seeing ten days from now.

Stay positive. Find distractions. At least there was one of those this evening at the Grosvenor House Hotel: Drico's testimonial, organized for him by the great and the good of the Irish business world – and Bono, of course. Brian had Bono on one side of him, Prince William on the other. There were around 800 people there, which shows the amount of love that's out there for our greatest-ever player, and a brilliant ambassador for rugby and for Ireland. Patrick Kielty, the MC for the evening, opened with, 'It's the day after St Patrick's Day, we have a room full of Paddies, a free bar, and the future King of England. It's going to get messy!'

The entertainment was very slick, with a performance by the cast of *Riverdance* and some singing by Emeli Sandé, one of the faces and voices from last year's Olympics. Even the charity auction was good crack, with the auctioneer tearing a few of the celebs in the audience to shreds. Ferg was at my table, keeping everyone amused, as he does. I was glad to be there, even if it was by default – originally, the plan had been to be in Dublin, preparing for Glasgow this weekend. A fair few of the internationals were there, with some of the lads letting their hair down after the stresses of the Six Nations. I was minding myself, naturally. That's the theme for the next few weeks. Mind yourself.

Saturday 23 March

RDS (Leinster 22, Glasgow 17)

Not the first Leinster game I've watched from the stand but the first one I've gone to as 'the guy who's leaving at the end of the season'. I wondered what it would be like coming back into the Leinster set-up, seven weeks since the news broke. With Ireland, it was the week before the Six Nations so everything was out in the open straight away – all the questions, the answers, and the slagging. Besides, I'm not leaving the Ireland set-up, or at least I hope I'm not. I *am* leaving Leinster, which feels like leaving a family. While I've contacted everyone who deserved an explanation, and while I've been in and out of UCD to see the physios, it's only in the last while that I've been around the place more to test the temperature. Has it cooled?

It's different, definitely. Mostly, it's slagging. 'Who are you going to hang around with in Paris when we're not there to be your pals?' 'You know we're going to smash your head in when Leinster draw Racing in the Heineken, don't you?' And so on. All very light-hearted, though I'm sure a few people feel betrayed.

The news is out that Isa is leaving, too. The Leinster players have known about it for a while, but somehow the public announcement creates a stronger sense of a break-up. I can't say his departure had nothing to do with mine, because while I was weighing things up I realized that Leinster wouldn't be the same without him. He has been by far Leinster's most influential foreign player, and when you consider some of the characters who have passed through, that's saying something – Contepomi, Elsom, Whitaker. He's incredibly consistent and a wonderful example to us all in his hardness and his professionalism. I'm not surprised that his body is beginning to show signs of wear and tear, for he has put it on the line for us for five years now, and played more rugby for Leinster than any of us. I know Simone is missing New Zealand – like Laura, who gets on well with her, she has an identical twin. All things considered, it makes sense for Isa to quit while he's ahead, even though he's only thirty and had another year on his contract. I have sympathy for Zane Kirchner, who looks like coming in as Isa's replacement. He has a ridiculously hard act to follow.

Also arriving will be Jimmy Gopperth, an experienced Kiwi out-half from Newcastle Falcons, and, of course, Mike McCarthy – to think that I was on at him around the time of the November internationals, convincing him to join us because of what we could achieve together in the next few years! As things stand, there are more people going than coming. Andy Conway is heading to Munster, which will be annoying to Leinster fans, seeing as he is a Blackrock boy, a classic Leinster Academy product, with huge potential. Fionn Carr is returning to Connacht, so that's four backs leaving in total, so far. Heinke van der Merwe will also be a big loss to the squad. He has been phenomenal since he arrived and played a massive part in our back-to-back Heineken Cup wins. Then you've got the uncertainty over Brian and Leo, neither of whom have decided whether they're going to carry on, plus the fact that everyone in the country wants to know whether Joe is going to take over from Deccie as Ireland coach.

All things considered, victory over Glasgow this evening was the perfect tonic, even if it was only secured after a few palpitations. Glasgow arrived as the Rabo leaders, on the back of seven straight league wins. They have become a quality side under the influence of Gregor Townsend, hard to break down and threatening around the fringes where their scrum-half, Niko Matawalu, is a serious handful. They were leading 17–12 with ten minutes to go before they made the fatal mistake of taking their eye off Mads for a split second, and he nipped in for a typical try. He is lethal in those situations. He scored all our points tonight and was man of the match. Victory means we replace Glasgow as league leaders. Naturally, I get plenty of stick as I'm sitting there in the players' area in my big black boot. Who needs Johnny anyway? In the back of my mind, I'm half-thinking how I would have done things differently out there, but I keep smiling and soaking up the slags. As if I have a choice!

Wednesday 27 March

Sports Surgery Clinic, Santry

Good news. I went back to see Johnny McKenna today and he says I can remove the boot. That's two and a half weeks earlier than expected. Maybe when James Calder described it as a seven-week injury, he was 'managing my expectations'. Johnny scanned the foot again today and said that there has been good healing and that there is encouraging flexibility in the injured area, so I can walk on it but not run. He says I'm not to test it too soon, which is what I do at the first opportunity, of course. I don't run, just gently apply some weight. It feels better than I'd expected.

According to Johnny, the Munster match on 13 April might come around a bit quickly for me (we'll see about that) but I should be ready for Zebre away the week after that, which is nine days before Gatland announces the winners of the golden tickets. I'm a happy bunny, and even happier because Laura and I are heading off to Dubai for a week tomorrow. Laura's on her Easter holidays from school and Brian has generously offered us the use of his apartment so we're going to get some sun on our bones. Things are looking up.

Saturday 30 March

Dubai

Où est l'hypermarché, s'il vous plaît? (Where is the supermarket, please?)
C'est un plaisir de vous rencontrer, monsieur. (It's a pleasure to meet you.)
Combien cela coûte? (How much does that cost?)

I studied French for six years at St Mary's and got a B3 in my Leaving Cert. Or maybe it was a C1? Either way, it was eight years ago, so I've been brushing up while I'm out here. I'm using interactive language-learning software called Rosetta Stone. I start lessons with a personal tutor in UCD next week, but there's no harm in doing some work here beforehand, especially as we have so much time on our hands. I'm trying to encourage Laura to get into it, but she's dodging it for the time being – Spanish was her European language in school, so learning a new one entirely from scratch is a bit daunting for her.

The weather is just perfect – mid-twenties – but there's only so much sitting by the pool that I can do. So I've been dusting off my French conjugations, doing upper-body weights in the gym and flying through a box-set of *Game of Thrones*. Fantasy has never been my thing but this is fairly raunchy, violent fantasy and I can see why it's so popular. I still need my rugby fix, however, and I got it this evening – Leinster's Pro12 game against Ulster at the RDS, which I caught on the RTE website tonight. It wasn't easy to watch.

Losing up in Belfast in December was a low point of our season, so to allow them to complete a league double on us – and win in Dublin for the first time since 1999 – is very annoying. I know that we were missing Drico, who received a three-week suspension for that stamp in Rome, and that Leo didn't start, while Darce pulled out sick on the day of the game. That's our three most experienced players. Still, it doesn't excuse us being so out-muscled on our own patch as we were this evening. We still nearly nicked it at the death but it would have been a steal. Ulster scored two tries to none and controlled the flow of the game for long periods.

The result pushes us down to third in the table with three games left before the play-offs, so we've a job to get ourselves a home semi-final, seeing as one of those games is in Thomond Park two weeks from now. I'm an outside bet to play that game but at least the end is in sight for me. It's now six weeks since I did my hammy against England. I'm gagging to play a game or at least train in a competitive environment.

Wednesday 3 April

UCD

As expected, the IRFU announced yesterday that they wouldn't be renewing Deccie's contract and that they intend to name his successor in the near future. Kissy will act as interim coach for Ireland's games in Houston and Toronto in June. I texted Deccie to wish him all the best and thank him for all he's done for me. I won't forget that he gave me the opportunity to play for Ireland A in February 2009 when I wasn't getting a sniff at Leinster and was considering the possibility of leaving. That was a real turning point for me. It's a pity that his reign ended so disappointingly, but a lot of that was down to bad luck with injuries. Over time, I think he'll be remembered as the coach who delivered Ireland a rare Grand Slam.

Like everyone else, I'm fascinated to know who will take over. No prizes for guessing who I'd appoint. I met him this afternoon, as a matter of fact. He must have spotted me doing a weights session because he popped in for a quick hello. It gave me the opportunity to hop a ball, 'Well, Joe, how are you going to turn things around?'

He misunderstood me, or at least pretended to.

'What, how can I lift the spirits of Leinster's international players after the disappointment of the Six Nations?'

'No, Joe, how are you going to turn *Ireland* around?'

He laughed. 'Don't you start! Nah, to be honest, Johnny, I'd find it very hard to leave Leinster right now. We're in a bit of a transition period.'

'Is that a dig at me?'

'You bet it is!'

It's just light-hearted banter so I'm really none the wiser as to whether he'd consider taking the Ireland job if it was offered to him. He's always very diplomatic when talking about the performances of the Irish team, but I do know he's excited by some of the young talent that's coming through across the provinces. The national job would be less demanding on his time and therefore kinder to his family, which is a huge consideration for him.

He'd do a brilliant job. I'm biased, I know. Were Joe to move up, it would be an outstanding result for me, as it would allow me the chance to continue working directly with the best coach I've known, for large chunks of the season. I've talked about it to some of the lads, naturally, and the international players at Leinster are caught in two minds – yes, they'd love to see what effect Joe could have with Ireland but they'd miss him in the day-job.

It should be a no-brainer for the IRFU. Joe has a successful track record, he knows the players and he knows the system. Giving him the job would be such a positive news story after such a depressing Six Nations, and would surely boost the sale of ten-year tickets at the Aviva, which is a huge source of revenue for the Union. The press are reporting Ewen McKenzie as the favourite. I have been really impressed with the job he has done with Queensland. They play a great brand of rugby and winning the Super 14 a couple of years back with such a young squad was an incredible achievement. He could be a good candidate if Joe decides he is not going to put his name forward.

Sunday 7 April

Paris

It's a beautifully warm spring afternoon on the outskirts of Paris and I'm house-hunting with Laura. I reckon that a bit of snooping around some tasteful accommodation will get her more excited about the prospect of moving here. She has been very supportive, but it's only when the whole thing becomes a reality that you're faced with what a big deal this is for her, too. She won't be working because she doesn't have the language and besides, if I'm selected for Test matches in November, February and March, she'd hardly fancy being alone and tied to a job in Paris while her husband is away for six weeks. I've reassured her that there will be plenty of English-speaking wives and girlfriends of my new team-mates, but the prospect of building a whole new social circle is a daunting one for her.

Our search wasn't going particularly well this afternoon, either. Racing have been very helpful in finding four or five houses or apartments that we might rent, all fairly close to the training centre in Plessis-Robinson, and Julien Albinet, the club's director of administration, kindly drove us around to see all of them. They are all impressive, but each had its own drawback, whether in terms of layout or location. We were on the verge of travelling into the centre of Paris to check out an apartment mentioned to us by a friend when Julien suggested we have a look at one more option online. It's a big old country house which has been divided into two flats, only five minutes from the club's training centre and the same distance from the railway station – the train journey into town is about twenty minutes. The online pictures weren't that appetizing, but the house was on our way into the city, so Julien convinced us to swing by and have a look. It was love at first sight.

What the images on the website couldn't capture was the sense of space inside and out. We'll be on the ground floor. It's long and narrow and has real charm, with guest rooms for people to come and stay, which is a particularly attractive feature for Laura.

So this is one benefit of being injured: that I'm able to come over and choose where we're going to live. We actually arrived yesterday, because I had to undergo a medical at the club, so we got to spend some time in the city, too. For the first time, I got a sense of what an adventure it is we're about to experience – the language, the culture, the food. And the wine, of course. Monsieur Lorenzetti's main business interest is property but he also owns several vineyards in Bordeaux, so I've asked if it would be possible for him to do me a good deal for the wines for our wedding. I suppose you could say this is a case of me investing in my new club!

The longer I go without playing for Leinster, the more I wonder how I will be welcomed back. How will people take to being ordered around the place by someone who's leaving at the end of the season and hasn't played for the team since the middle of January? In fairness to Mads, he's making the most of his opportunity. On Friday we beat Wasps over there, 48–28, in the quarters of the Amlin, and he had a great game. He passed well, kicked well on and off the tee, and looked as dangerous as ever as a runner, stepping dangerously and scoring a good try. It was the best I've seen him play for Leinster, because he varied his game so well. You'd have thought he was a fair bet for man of the match but Shaggy was on commentary for Sky and he gave it to his old buddy Darce. Good man, Shaggy!

We have Biarritz in the semi, at the RDS in three weeks' time. I'm hoping to play some part against Munster next week but it might be a game too soon for me. Mads's form is another reason to get back as soon as possible. I'm sure there are some Leinster supporters who feel that he should be handed the number 10 jersey for the rest of the season, given that I won't be around next year. But I feel I've a lot to give. We're still in two competitions and I'm determined to go out on a high.

I'll do whatever's necessary. I'm actually due in Paris again tomorrow with Padraig Power, the IRFU's commercial and marketing director, to meet with Eden Park, who supply formal wear to the Ireland team, and choose a suit for the players. But I'm not staying over, because I have a physio session on my foot in Dublin tomorrow morning.

Tuesday 9 April

UCD

Whispers in the changing room.

Kearns, did you get a Lions letter? Yeah? OK, say nothing.

Seanie? You get a letter?

It sets the heart racing when you open an envelope and see the Lions crest peeping out at you, even though you know the squad announcement isn't for another three weeks. Sure enough, the first sentence of the letter gets things straight: 'This is not a selection letter.' It was just to say that I'd been included in an extended squad, though it didn't say how large that squad is. There were contracts to be signed, sets of conditions, bank forms to be completed, the whole rigmarole. We were asked to keep everything confidential but it's unrealistic to expect that bits and pieces won't start leaking out. Based on nods, winks and whispers in the dressing room today, I'm pretty sure as many as nine Leinster players are walking around with unusually big grins on their faces – Cian, Straussy, Rossy, Seanie, Jamie, Mads, Drico, Kearns and myself. Naturally, there is some interprovincial communication via texts to see who else is in the mix. So how large is the extended squad? Fifty? Sixty? Seventy? Depends who you ask.

This is my first week back as part of the larger Leinster group and it strikes me how much I've missed being part of the dressing-room culture – even if I'm the butt of all jokes today. Apparently it was reported in yesterday's *Midiolympique* that I'll be the best-paid player in France next season, earning more than even Jonny Wilkinson, supposedly pulling in €55,000 a month. I protest that this is an inflated figure, but when I try to explain the various reasons why it's inaccurate, I get shouted down. I'm Johnny Big-bucks, and that's the beginning and the end of it.

It's reassuring to have people taking the piss out of you. If there was no slagging I would be worried. As far as training is concerned, I'm still on the outside looking in, though. My foot is still tender so there's only so much I can do. Drico says he's had a phone call from Rob Howley, the Lions attack coach, to see whether I'll be playing in Limerick on Saturday because some of Gatland's team are thinking of making the trip. I'd love to play, especially as it could be a while before I play in another Leinster v. Munster derby. It occurs to me that I may never play in this fixture again. Still, I don't want to rush things. I'm meeting Johnny McKenna on Thursday. If he passes me to play against Zebre next week, that will do me. I'll be able to work on my kicking this weekend.

Saturday 13 April

Goatstown

So, Munster v. Leinster at Thomond Park – another match viewed from the sofa in my apartment, but at least I get a mention on the RTE panel discussion beforehand. It's the latest Great Out-half Debate. Not me and Rog, or Rog and Paddy, but me and Mads. George Hook is in the Madigan corner, saying that I shouldn't get a look-in for the rest of the season, seeing as I'm moving on and Mads needs as much experience as possible in big games. Shaggy stood up for me, so there was some balance to the debate!

If Joe were to stay on as Leinster coach next season then I could have no argument if he decided to go with Mads for the rest of this one. That's the sort of thing that often happens in professional sport. I'm just hoping that my contribution to Leinster over the past six years hasn't gone unnoticed, and that Joe realizes that moving on doesn't diminish my desire to go out on a high, or my ability to help Leinster win more silverware.

Today was another chapter in Mads's education and he will be better for it – a dirty old day down in Thomond with a wall of red in front of you, without the hint of a chink of attacking space. We had the elements in the first half but didn't make great use of them. We were only 12–10 ahead at the break and Munster took the lead early in the second half when Ian Keatley knocked over a gale-assisted penalty from well inside his own half. They must have been feeling good about themselves at that point, especially on the back of a brilliant win away to Harlequins last week, in the quarters of the Heineken Cup. But our guys stuck in there and played possession really well, with Isaac Boss controlling things brilliantly. Once they got close to the Munster try-line in the final quarter, Drico stepped forward and did the needful from a metre out – one of his specialities. I've never had to try to stop him from that distance, but I might get the chance next season!

We won 22–16 in the end. It was fiery stuff – maybe it was just as well I wasn't playing as I might have lost the cool. I was raging just sitting in my apartment, watching the TMO disallow a try for Rob early on, which was an outrageously bad call. But the real controversy was sparked in the second half when Paulie swung a boot at the ball and caught Dave Kearney on the side of his head – Dave had fallen awkwardly a second earlier having tried to regather a high ball. He lost consciousness temporarily and had to be stretchered off. I don't think for one minute that Paulie meant any harm, but it was reckless by him and, as often happens, it looked even worse on slow-motion replay. Nigel Owens, the ref, didn't even penalize Paulie for it but I'm sure the citing commissioner will be on the case. It won't just be people in Ireland who'll be watching the outcome on this one. Paulie's only three games back from a long lay-off but he looks in superb nick. In fact, he's my bet to be Lions captain – as long as he doesn't land a hefty ban over this.

Sunday 14 April

London

Drico, Seanie and I are in London on a top-secret mission. We're here to shoot an ad for Adidas, along with a selection of other likely Lions and a few members of the England cricket team – I recognized Alastair Cook and Stuart Broad. There are some Gaelic footballers there as well, Eoin Cadogan and Kieran Donaghy, who will be competing in the compromise-rules series against the Aussies. The idea is that Australia is the common enemy this summer, so the theme is that we 'Stand Together' and take out our desire to win on anything and everything coloured yellow. So Drico melts a yellow ice pop just by staring at it, Seanie squashes a yellow melon by slamming on it with his fist, and I – wait for it – place-kick a yellow toy train off a railway track.

So who was there from the other countries? Tom Croft, Manu Tuilagi and Ben Youngs from England; Sam Warburton, Leigh Half-penny, George North and Alex Cuthbert from Wales; and Stuart Hogg and Richie Gray from Scotland – someone said Sean Maitland was supposed to be there too but couldn't make it. The Adidas guys said they had been given a list of fifty players and given the go-ahead to do some 'commercial activity'. I was unhappy with the whole idea. It's OK for Brian to sit there in a Lions jersey. He's already toured with the Lions and played Tests for them. I don't want to tempt fate.

Big day tomorrow. My first open session in a month, two weeks before the Lions squad is announced. Nervous? You could say that.

Monday 15 April

UCD

This morning I chaired an IRUPA meeting, which went on for a few hours. I may be heading to Paris next season but I'm keen to carry on as chairman, seeing as I only started in the role this season. The meeting was about the thorny issue of sick pay. As things stand, once a player is out of action for six months, the IRFU can cut his salary by 75 per cent. There is anecdotal evidence of players returning from injury early in order to beat this deadline, just so that they can pay their mortgage, or mortgages in some cases. It's something we need to sort out with the Union.

I haven't started a game for just over two months and I was taking a bit of a risk having a first 'open' session this afternoon, where we simulate match situations. Last week Johnny McKenna described it as a four-to-six-week injury and we are now in week five, so I could have left it another seven days and still played the Amlin semi against Biarritz before the squad is announced. I didn't want that to be my first game back, though, so we taped up the foot and gave it a lash. A proper lash it was, too. The lads reckoned it was the toughest field session they've done this season, as there are a few lads playing against Zebre who weren't playing in Limerick and Joe wanted to put them through their paces. He ran us into the ground. I came through OK, which was a big relief. I was a little sore afterwards, but happy.

I've been so obsessed with my foot that I forgot to mention Dave Kearney is recovering well, having spent the night in hospital in Limerick on Saturday. The citing commissioner has decided that Paulie doesn't have a case to answer, which is good news for him and for Munster ahead of their Clermont game.

Tuesday 16 April

Goatstown

Joe has let rip at the citing commissioner, Eddie Walsh, and the entire disciplinary process in the papers this morning, saying that Paulie's kick last Saturday was the 'ugliest incident' he'd seen 'in 12 years of professional rugby'.

Paulie has been quoted as saying that he had absolutely no intention to harm Dave, which is how I read the incident. He has contacted Dave to say as much and to wish him a speedy recovery.

The more you see the kick – and apparently the clip has had 90,000 hits on YouTube – the more you realize that Joe did the right thing in criticizing the decision not to cite. It's a brave thing to do also. A more selfish person might have considered the political implications of criticizing a Munster legend like Paul O'Connell at a time when the Ireland coaching job is up for grabs.

Joe has put his name forward for the job. Word has it that Leinster's professional game board gave him their blessing last week, with the proviso that he didn't bring any of the current support staff with him. With limited time to find a replacement, Leinster obviously want as little disruption as possible. So Joe will be interviewed for the Ireland gig on Thursday. A couple of other candidates will be interviewed – Kissy's name has been mentioned, so too the Queensland Reds' coach, Ewen McKenzie – but Joe would be a very popular appointment. It would be brilliant for Ireland and brilliant from my point of view.

Sunday 21 April

Reggio Emilia (Zebre 22, Leinster 41)

I've never been to the Stadio del Tricolore before, and I never imagined it would provide the backdrop for one of the happier days of my season, but there you go. We won with a bonus point on top, which puts us back at second in the league table and in line for a home semi-final. I got through sixty-five minutes of good work on a sunny afternoon in this less-than-half-full soccer stadium, and my foot feels fine. Sore, but fine.

I enjoyed everything about the trip, actually. I'm determined to make the most of the last couple of months with Leinster and this two-dayer to Reggio Emilia, about half an hour from Parma, reminded me of the crack that I'm going to miss. I was rooming with Ferg, who's always entertaining. It was stinking hot and probably the worst hotel we've stayed in – tiny beds, faulty air conditioning – but we somehow managed to turn its general crapness into a source of amusement.

Zebre haven't won a league game all season, so the fact that they held us to 17–17 at half-time suggests we made a meal of it. It's true that we defended poorly to let them score two tries in the second quarter, but to be fair to Zebre, they were up for it, maybe too up for it at times – Drico was furious to have been tip-tackled off the ball by Mauro Bergamasco in the first half. From a personal point of view, I was delighted that they put it up to us. I was pleased with my kicking also. It was strange lining up my first shot, as I was conscious of the two-and-a-half-month gap since Cardiff, the last time I place-kicked in a match. I landed six out of six that day and felt like I couldn't miss. Today, I hit seven out of seven and it felt exactly the same.

I was called ashore after landing a touchline conversion following Isa's score, which put us out of Zebre's range. I was never going to play the full eighty on my first game back and I felt knackered at half-time. But I recovered well and was happy with my performance in general. No doubt the big story next week will be who Joe is going to pick at 10 for the Biarritz game – me or Mads. It's good to have competition. It brings out the best in you. But I feel I made my point today.

Thursday 25 April

UCD Commerce Department

'*Sortir les poubelles.*'

Sortir: verb, irregular, means 'to go out'. *Je suis sorti* = I went out.

Les poubelles: Pubs? Could '*Sortir les poubelles*' mean to go out on a pub crawl?

No. Actually, it means 'Take out the bins.' Not to worry. I feel that I'm making good progress with Baptiste, my tutor, who lectures to second-year commerce students here in Belfield. That's a bit above my standard, but I have to push myself. I'm doing an hour with Baptiste three evenings a week – Monday, Tuesday and Thursday. There will be plenty of English-speakers at Racing, but as out-half I have to be able to communicate with everyone. Jonny Wilkinson is Toulon captain and I've seen him delivering team-talks in French, so I've got to think along similar lines. That's why I'm going hard at it with Baptiste, who will only speak French with me, and listening to the Rosetta Stone CDs in the car. I'm actually really enjoying it, and excited by the prospect of being able to speak a second language.

Turns out Joe had an easy solution to his out-half conundrum. Darce hasn't recovered from a calf strain so I'm at 10 and Mads is at 12, which could suit him. He played there against Italy in the Six

Nations and he really stood out. He's small compared to Damien Traille, his opposite number on Saturday, but his running and passing could give us something a little different in attack.

So I'm officially back running the show against Biarritz, even if I'm no longer in the Leinster inner sanctum. This is confirmed by the fact that I only hear it second-hand that Leo and maybe a couple of other players have met with Matt O'Connor, Leicester's head coach, over the past few days. Apparently, they were showing him around our training facilities yesterday and it looks as though he's the front-runner to take over on the assumption that Joe steps up to Ireland – though every day that goes by without an announcement on this is another reason to worry, as far as I'm concerned. Leinster are obviously convinced he's gone, but the O'Connor deal is all hush-hush as he's still contracted to Leicester and nothing is finalized yet. It feels strange not to be part of that decision-making process, but then everything feels a bit strange these days.

Friday 26 April

Goatstown

Joe *is* the new Ireland coach, but I only heard confirmation from the unlikeliest source, and I'm sworn to secrecy. Laura is the super-sleuth. She called me this afternoon to say that she'd just seen a man she recognized walking out of Joe's house, wearing casual clothes but carrying a briefcase. She'd been stuck at the traffic lights there in Churchtown and got a decent look at him. IRFU, she thought, definitely knew him from after-match dinners. When I heard a brief description, I thought, *I bet that's Philip Browne and they've just done the deal.* So I took a chance and sent Joe a one-word text:

Congrats.

He texted back immediately, flabbergasted that I knew already. He'd only signed the contract five minutes previously! I explained what had happened but he was still amazed. What were the chances? Still, we had a good laugh about it. It's great news. I have to keep it secret until Monday, when there's a press conference to announce Joe's appointment. That won't be a problem. I have tomorrow's semi-final to distract me.

Biarritz are struggling in the bottom half of the Top 14, but they are the holders of the Amlin Cup and if they win it again, it's a route into next season's Heineken. They have quality players like Traille, Dimitri Yachvili and Imanol Harinordoquy, and pace to burn out wide with Takudzwa Ngwenya. This also just happens to be the final round of games before Gatland announces next Tuesday. Think I'll take a sleeping tablet tonight.

Saturday 27 April

RDS (Leinster 44, Biarritz 16)

I had another one of those surreal place-kicking moments during the first half yesterday, thanks in part to Baptiste but also thanks to the RDS wind. I had a penalty shot lined up when the breeze suddenly picked up from the left, so I waited as long as I could get away with for it to die down. Then I could hear one of the Biarritz players – I think it was Yachvili – complaining to the ref, Wayne Barnes, that I had gone over the allotted time. *Soixante secondes, monsieur! Soixante secondes!* And so I find myself in French translation mode, instead of concentrating on my job. I lost my routine and ended up rushing the kick and tugged it badly to the left. A complete mis-hit. *Merde!*

Apart from that, today went pretty well for me. Very well, in fact. I was a bit annoyed to kick one ball out on the full – again, I'm blaming the wind for catching it. As soon as I saw that it had flown too far, Neil Jenkins's face flashed up on the giant screen in the corner – he was sitting beside Rob Howley and Graham Rowntree in the stand. Great.

But it went well for me today, apart from those two hiccups. The plan was to play with pace, to move the big Biarritz pack around the park, and although it took us a while to wear them down, we were excellent once we clicked. Two minutes before half-time we were only 10–9 up with that breeze mainly at our backs, but we sneaked in for two tries before the break. Rob put me in for one of those, and I celebrated with a bit of the emotion that I had bottled up for the past two months.

I certainly wanted to show the Leinster supporters that I'd be giving my all until the end of the season, which is why I was unhappy to be called ashore after fifty minutes, just after Isa had scored a lovely try after a nice 1-2-3 move between the two of us. I was tackled making the scoring pass and took a bit of a bang on the calf, so Garreth Farrell, our physio, was sent on to give me the shepherd's hook. I was stretching the muscle as he arrived.

'Are you OK, Johnny?'

'Yeah, just got a knock on the calf.'

'OK, you're off.'

'What? I'm 100 per cent, it's fine, just a knock.'

'No, Joe wants you off.'

'Tell Joe I'm fine. [Mads offers to take the conversion.] Yeah, Mads, you take the kick and I'll just stretch this out.'

'Johnny, you're off.'

'No, I'll take the kick. Just to prove I'm OK, all right?'

'Johnny, you're off!'

I tried to jog back to halfway to show that I could play on, but that was when Andrew Goodman appeared and the game was up. At least I finished on a good note, and we'd the result wrapped up at that stage. In fairness to Biarritz, they were up against it, when you consider that ten of us had the added incentive of trying to impress Gatland. If there was any doubt about Jamie going, he removed it by completely outplaying Harinordoquy, who lost his rag well before the end. Brian looked incredibly sharp, mugging Biarritz players for possession and scoring a try for good measure. As Mads was lining up the conversion, our supporters started a chant of 'One more year!' aimed at Drico, who's yet to finalize his plans for next year. One more year? I reckon he could be around for a bit longer than that.

We've got Stade Français in the Amlin final, three weeks from now, and it's at the RDS, the day before the Heineken final at the Aviva. Not quite how we'd planned to spend that weekend but hey, at least we won't just be sitting around, doing nothing. Always good to be busy.

Sunday 28 April

Goatstown

I don't envy Owen Farrell. OK, so Saracens were beaten 12–24 by Toulon in today's Heineken Cup semi-final in Twickenham and Jonny Wilkinson had the better of their so-called 'duel', but Sky aren't very subtle in the way they describe these things. It's all or nothing, win or lose, nothing in between. Owen didn't have a bad game at all, but once it became apparent that Jonny was going to come out on top I thought they were unfairly critical of Owen. The guy is only twenty-two and he's had to put up with Wilkinson comparisons for the past couple of years.

I suppose it's to be expected that he and Jonny would be the story today, given that Gatland has apparently stated he's only taking two 10s to Australia – I'm assuming he'll also bring a utility back with experience of playing out-half. This was in an interview on Sky Sports which I studiously avoided. I'm keeping my promise to myself not to read or watch anything Lions-related, though it's not easy at the moment. Today I received a text from someone 'close to Gatland' who said I was 'quids in'. Lovely to hear, but no real comfort, to be honest. I won't relax until the squad is announced and it's 100 per cent. This isn't false modesty. I'm not the only Leinster player who's up to 90 on this one. We've been trying to decide what we should do Tuesday at 11 a.m. when Lions manager Andy Irvine is due to announce the squad on Sky News. We're off that day, so we have to find a way to fill the time. Should we meet in a cafe where there's no TV? But what happens when the text messages start coming through and some of us get good news and others get bad? I'm considering just taking a sleeping pill when I wake up on Tuesday morning so that when I come around again, it will be all done and dusted.

Tuesday 30 April

RDS

I love the fact that the thirty-seven lucky rugby players who have their names read out by Andy Irvine this morning will be getting the news at the same time as everyone else in the world. No heads-up, no text the night before, just switch on Sky Sports same as everyone else and keep your fingers crossed – very old school, and different from Ireland selections. I couldn't sit beside the telly, though. Today is our day off, and on days off I do kicking practice. I'm not going to change my routine. It's a very welcome distraction.

So I set the machine to record from eleven onwards and headed down to the RDS, where I'd arranged to meet Richie Murphy. There's no escaping Sky, though. Richie has brought out his iPhone so he can tell me the squad as I'm warming up – kind of what I was trying to avoid, but I appreciate his thoughtfulness.

He asks, 'Do you want me to tell you the names as he reads them out?'

'No, just tell me at the end.'

After a few more warm-up drills, I stop beside him.

'Well? Am I in?'

'Yes, well done.'

Later on, I'd process all the other info: how Sam Warburton is our captain, as expected; how Leinster have six Lions – Drico, Jamie, Seanie, Kearns and Church; how Conor Murray has got the nod, as have Tommy Bowe and Paulie, of course. No luck for Rory Best, who must be gutted, or Rossy, who I expected to get picked, seeing as the Wallabies' scrum is a perceived weakness. Gatland was true to his word in picking only two specialist 10s – myself and Owen Farrell – with only Stuart Hogg as back-up, and he hasn't played there since school, apparently. It wouldn't surprise me if Jonny Wilkinson joins us after Toulon's season is over. I kind of hope so in a way, because it would be cool to get to work with someone I admired so much growing up.

For the rest of our kicking session I was on autopilot, filled with an enormous sense of well-being. When I finished, my phone showed six missed calls and fifty-five texts, including one from Rog, and also messages from other former Irish Lions like Ollie Campbell and Tony Ward, which was really cool. My uncles from Kerry were on, saying how well I looked in a red jersey, and that I was welcome to come and play for Munster at the end of my career!

I saw what they were talking about when I watched the announcement later on tape. When my name was read out, up popped the photo that was taken out in Carton back in January, when everyone in the squad dared to dream that they might make it. Believe me, there is no sense of anti-climax when this happens, no matter how many people have told me that I was definite to travel. As Ian McGeechan says on those Lions DVDs, this feels special. I'm reminded of watching the 1997 Lions Tests with my dad in Ciss Madden's in Donnybrook, when I was only twelve, seeing Scott Gibbs barrelling through massive Springbok props and Keith Wood on one of his rampages. I remember wondering in 2009 if I'd be good enough four years from then to challenge for selection. I'm reminded also that Lions selection has been one of the main driving forces of my season. So, happy? Very.

Friday 3 May

RDS (Leinster 37, Ospreys 19)

All going to plan, I'll have four more games before departure for Australia. The good thing is that they'll all be important games, with something at stake. There may be a sense of the group breaking up, with Joe, Isa, myself, Heinke van der Merwe and other players leaving at the end of the season, but there's a real drive for us to finish in style, and that means securing the double – maybe not quite the double we had in mind at the beginning of the season, but a double all the same.

We needed a win tonight to secure a home semi in the Rabo. The Ospreys were long shots to make the semis but they like nothing better than to win at the RDS, having won two grand finals here already. Whereas Joe mixed his selection up a little bit, giving starts to promising youngsters like the McGraths, Luke and Jack (no relation), the Ospreys had three Lions in their starting pack – Adam Jones, Alun-Wyn Jones and Justin Tipuric. There were no high fives with these guys during the warm-ups. All that bonding stuff can wait. Dan Biggar did come over and congratulate me, though, which I thought was a really nice touch, especially seeing as he was a contender for selection, having finished the Six Nations so strongly. I wished him all the best and also commiserated with him a little.

Sure enough, the Ospreys didn't make things easy for us. We set off like a train, setting up two tries for Andy Conway, but then allowed them back into it with some poor defence. We led 17–12 at the break but then pulled away, with Andy completing his hat-trick – how has this guy been allowed to go to Munster? Cian secured the bonus point in style, running in from thirty metres – he is not your average prop. We will face Glasgow in the semis here next week, while Ulster host Scarlets.

Personally, I was happy. I kicked five from five, including one corker of a penalty from the left touchline thirty metres out, and had a hand in a couple of our tries. This was my first full eighty minutes since returning and it was a proper workout. I made eleven tackles – a decent number for an out-half – and kept myself busy. Try and hold yourself back, or mind yourself, and you've probably a better chance of getting injured. That said, I could have done without having to try to stop the Ospreys' centre, Ben John, who ducked his head and charged straight through me to score in the first half. He managed to simultaneously wind me and crush the family jewels, leaving me in a heap and puking my guts up in the in-goal area. A few of the lads surrounded me, as if to protect me from sight, but I could hear a kid in the front row of the stand making a sound like he was revolted. I'm not surprised. I wasn't a pretty sight.

SEVEN

Awards Season

Saturday 4 May

Mansion House

Leaving Leinster was always going to be hard, but only tonight did I realize just how hard. Not because they made a fuss of me at the annual team awards bash, which has 500 people all glammed up in a massive function room, loads of video clips and presentations. More because they didn't make a fuss of me. The stars of the show were Mads, whom the guys voted as Player of the Year, and Isa and Joe, whose contributions to Leinster were celebrated with tributes and interviews and more video clips. I was up on stage briefly, to receive a commemorative Leinster cap along with the seven other lads who are leaving at the end of the season – Andy, Fionn, Damian Browne, Mark Flanagan, Tom Sexton, Jamie Hagan and Heinke van der Merwe. And that was it. As soon as the formal aspect of the evening was over, I legged it.

Sore? On the way home in the taxi, yes, a little. Here's how I was thinking: I've contributed a lot to Leinster in the past five years, a period when we've won three Heineken Cups and a Magners League, and it feels like they've barely acknowledged that. Mads as Player of the Year? Fair enough, he's having a great season, but it's an award I've never won. Are the players trying to tell me something? Is it because I annoy everyone by constantly barking at them? Maybe they don't rate me. Fine. I'm glad that I'm going. This only makes me hungrier to be successful with Racing.

I've cooled down a little now, though, and I'm thinking with a clearer head. It was me who made the decision to leave Leinster, so they owe me nothing. Yes, we've had some great success but professional sport is a business, with little room for sentimentality. I should

know that. I would like to have said a few words tonight, to have
expressed to the many Leinster supporters in the room how much
the club means to me, to say that I never expected to leave and that I
wouldn't have left if I'd been made a fair offer initially by the IRFU.
I realize that I haven't got my side of the contract story out in the
public domain yet, and tonight would have been a good opportunity,
if I'd asked for it. I didn't.

I get the impression people think I'm going to Paris on sabbatical.
During his speech, Leinster president Ben Gormley wished me the
best during my two years in Paris, which I really appreciated, but I'm
not thinking of Racing as some sort of career break from Leinster. I'd
be mad to think that way. I may love Paris. I'm determined that
Racing will be successful during the next two years and that the
squad develops a winning culture, and if things go on from there,
well and good. Besides, two years from now, the Union may not
want to push the boat out for an out-half who is approaching his
thirtieth birthday. Leinster might have moved on and won another
Heineken Cup with Mads or Gopperth at 10. They might not want
or need me back. But that's another matter. The more I think about
it, what happened tonight – or what didn't happen – should actually
make leaving Leinster a little easier.

Wednesday 8 May

Burlington Hotel

It's awards season, so here we are in our monkey suits again – for the
IRUPA awards. The difference is that I get to say my piece here,
albeit reluctantly and in a totally different context. After all the
awards have been made – Ulster's Nick Williams as Players' Player,
Connacht's Robbie Henshaw as Young Player of the Year, and so
on – part of the 'entertainment' is me sitting up on stage being interviewed with Andrew Mehrtens, the former All Blacks out-half, who
also played with Racing a few years back. As IRUPA chairman, I'm
in no position to object. They wanted me to make a speech but I

negotiated them down to a Q&A – a bit more light-hearted and doesn't need any preparation. It's late enough in the evening by the time we do our thing. Andrew is more of a character than you might have thought by watching him on the rugby pitch. Who will he be rooting for when the Lions play the Wallabies? Neither of us. He hates Australians and he hates Poms. 'I hope you beat the shit out of each other,' he said.

Earlier today, I was interviewed up in St Mary's Rugby Club by Vincent Hogan, a colleague of my godfather, Billy Keane, in the *Irish Independent*. I've kept a low media profile recently, but my Adidas contract involves some media work and I was happy to chat with Vincent, who lent a sympathetic ear on the contractual issue. I was as diplomatic as possible about the Union's position but made it clear that all I'd been looking for was what others had got in Leinster and Ireland. I never asked them to compete with the French market. I also stressed how I'd always seen myself as someone who would be with Leinster until my mid-thirties but that business had got in the way. The interview will appear over the weekend so it will be interesting to see what kind of a reaction it gets.

Working with Adidas means getting to spend time with Dave Alred, and I'll do three ninety-minute sessions with him this week, which is great. That one rush-job against Biarritz has been my only miss since returning from injury and my confidence is soaring. Since the start of the year, my stats are 42 out of 46 – over 91 per cent. I'm striking the ball so well, it makes me nervous. Does that make sense?

Saturday 11 May

RDS (Leinster 17, Glasgow 15)

Bloody wind at the RDS. It kind of made a mess of my kicking stats for 2013 this evening, as I landed only four from seven. But, this being a Rabo semi-final, it also saved us from extra time, and Glasgow would have fancied themselves if it had gone that far. They would have had the momentum, plus the advantage of having scored two tries to our one in normal time, which could have won it for them if we were still level after the extra period.

How did the wind save us? When they scored their second try, five minutes from the end, it left Stuart Hogg with a fairly straightforward-looking conversion, about fifteen metres to the right of the posts. But no kick was straightforward out there tonight. The wind was gusting like mad, more unpredictably than I'd ever experienced it, and his angle was the toughest, towards the Dublin Mountains. It was a difficult kick for a regular goal-kicker – and Gregor Townsend had taken a gamble in not bringing a recognized kicker. I was relieved, but not surprised, when Stuart's kick stayed right.

So we're relieved to be through to our fourth consecutive grand final, and this one will be against Ulster, who beat the Scarlets in Belfast last night. The final will be here at the RDS in two weeks' time, even though Ulster finished top of the league. Ravenhill is being redeveloped and doesn't have the 18,000 capacity you need for a grand final, so they've chosen to play the match here, which seems a bit cheeky to me. Maybe they think that because they've won here before this season, they can do it again. We'll see.

They could very easily have been playing Glasgow here in the final, which would not have been good. There was a disappointing crowd this evening, which suggests that some Leinster fans are saving themselves up for the two finals. They should know better than to underestimate Glasgow. The last three games between us have been decided by seven points or less and when they played here in March, they felt they'd been robbed by the referee calling forward pass on the final play of the game.

We didn't play particularly well, but, to be fair to Glasgow, they didn't let us. They ran hard and offloaded cleverly, which allowed them to control the game into the wind in the second half, even though we'd turned around with an 11–10 lead. Scoring opportunities were scarce, which made it annoying to miss those kicks at goal. I'm not too upset, though, because I struck the ball well. And I also delivered with the toughest kick of all, ten minutes from the end, from just inside our half, which turned out to be the match winner.

The dressing room was fairly subdued, as we have a few injury worries. Drico had to be subbed in the first half because of back spasms, while Darce has had a recurrence of his calf problem and Straussy's knee is at him. I think Joe is a bit tetchy because we have a European final next week, but his Lions will be missing all day Monday, too, because we're over in London for an organizational day. Me? I don't think I've ever been so excited about a day of admin!

Monday 13 May

Syon Park, London

The Lions' logistics people call it Messy Monday. You have thirty-six players – Drico couldn't travel – assembled in one enormous room with six or seven stations that we all have to visit. Fill out this questionnaire. Try on these compression tights for long-haul flights. Collect your nutrition supplements from the S&C staff. Try on your Thomas Pink gear – three suits, eight shirts and two pairs of shoes. Try on your Adidas gear, including special Lions red, blue and white boots. Sign a million replica shirts. Have your mugshot taken for Fox Sports Australia. Fill in this visa application form. And do it all quickly, because you've a return flight to Dublin at four o'clock.

It's all a crazy rush, but thankfully there is time to take stock and confirm that yes, this is all now real. Leinster still have two games to play but already we're getting a flavour of what it's like to be a Lion. I was even excited last night, when it was just us five from Leinster, sitting in a hotel bar in Heathrow – Rob, Seanie, Jamie, Cian and myself. We flew in the night before to make sure there were no delays today. There we were, full of excited chatter, like Under-15s on their first representative trip.

Then this morning we had our first address from Andy Irvine, from Warren and from Sam. You feel you've been air-dropped into one of those Lions DVDs except that it's not a DVD. It's for real. You're actually sitting in a very grand room with all these blokes that you've been trying to outwit for the past couple of seasons, all in Lions tracksuits, looking like a unit for the first time.

Sam made a very strong first impression. He spoke to us without notes and kept it simple. He had two points. First, to embrace the challenge of playing for the Lions, rather than being nervous about it. Second, to realize just how fortunate we were. He talked about a recent hospital visit where he met a guy of his own age who is dying of cancer, and how thankful it made him for the opportunities he has been given. I thought he struck the perfect tone. He's incredibly composed for a guy who's only twenty-four.

After lunch, Owen Farrell and I had a few strategic meetings together with the coaching staff, just so that I'm clued in as to what the squad will be working on over the next two weeks, while the fourteen lads from Leinster, Ulster, Leicester and Northampton are still busy with their clubs. They're doing a week in the Vale of Glamorgan before moving over to Carton, so there's obviously a fair bit of prep they can get done in that time.

Straight away you can see what an influential character Andy Farrell will be in the whole set-up. Like I said before, he was a bit of a hero of mine when I was growing up. I can remember him smashing his nose in a big game against Leeds, going to the blood-bin and then returning with his face covered in a bandage, looking like the Lone Ranger. He's our defence coach, but even though we were focusing mainly on attack today you could see how much he loves talking rugby.

We agreed calls for switches, wraparounds and so on, and went through the general attacking plan. It's very structured, which makes sense when you're trying to build a side in a very short space of time. Rob, who's in charge of attack, explained the basic pattern, whereby if we're moving the ball from right to left, we keep moving in the same direction, using the full width of the pitch to stretch their defence, then realign quickly so we have strike runners running at some of their tight forwards. 'So it's Wales, basically?' I said, smiling, which got a laugh. I explained I wasn't being smart and that I knew from experience how difficult the pattern is to defend, especially when you've got carriers like Jamie Roberts and George North charging at you.

After one meeting, I already feel like I have a relationship with these guys. There was a complete sense of openness about sharing ideas and talking about what works in our respective set-ups – I was reminded of Earlsy's comments at our meeting in the Aviva last August. Given the power runners we have in the squad, the general idea is to try and dominate opponents physically. We'll play plenty of rugby in the warm-up games and then see how we're fixed for the Tests.

I was wondering whether I'd get a clue as to whether we'd be joined by a third 10 at some stage on tour – perhaps a certain chap from Toulon – but based on what Warren said today, myself and Owen can expect to be involved in every game. 'You've barely played for the past three months and Owen is young, so you'll manage,' was the gist of what he said. Fair enough.

So we packed a fair bit in today, and still made it to Heathrow in time for our four o'clock flight. When I turned my phone back on, I picked up a few texts from people saying that the *Indo* interview read well, and that it was good to see me getting my side of the contract story out there. It's been a tiring day, but a productive one.

Tuesday 14 May

Goatstown

Rog calls today, out of the blue, and tells me there's a possibility he might be going to Racing as a skills coach next season! How bizarre is that?

He didn't say it immediately. Probably felt he needed to build up to it. There was some small talk about the Lions and about Munster's Heineken semi a couple of weeks ago, when they gave Clermont a serious run for their money. Then he tells me he needs some advice on the French tax system! I asked him was he thinking of playing for a year or two over there. No, he says, coaching. I told him that was a great idea, and that's when he broke it to me.

Here, you're going to laugh, Johnny, but I might be talking to Racing Metro!

I laughed, but straight away I knew he wasn't joking. He wasn't asking my permission, either – not that I'd have expected that. He just said he wanted to get into coaching and this would be a great way to get some experience. He said if it happened, it would be good for both of us and I agreed. I also thought that the media would have great fun with the story, given our history, but that wasn't a problem for me. We'd be working together, rather than against each other, which would be a nice change.

At the same time, it's too crazy to be true. Me and Rog, together in Paris? He said nothing was definite yet and he'd be sure to let me know either way. We'll see. There have been other rumours about him floating around, including one which had him joining Stade Français for a season – though from what I'm hearing, Morne Steyn is joining them. Pick any day of the season and there's a rumour about somebody or other joining a French club. We'll see.

It will be interesting to see Stade close up on Friday, as they'll be Parisian rivals next season. The word is that Stade are back in the money again, having had financial difficulties for a while – Digby Ioane is their other big signing for next season. There are two theories about how they will approach Friday. The one that Joe has been impressing on us is that winning the Amlin is Stade's only route into the Heineken for next season, and that they'll desperately want to be involved, given the final is scheduled for Paris and given that they can't be seen to fall behind Racing. Joe also makes the point that they won both their quarter-final and semi-final on the road.

The other theory is that they are free-wheeling at this time of the year, seeing as they have avoided relegation in the Top 14 but are out of contention for the play-offs. They might give it a lash for half an hour but chances are they're already almost in holiday mode.

I'm not sure which theory to believe. After Rog's phone call today, anything seems possible.

Friday 17 May

RDS (Leinster 34, Stade Français 13)

It's confirmed. Rog will be Racing's kicking coach next season. I found out around three hours before kick-off when I walked into the physio room up in UCD and people started giggling. The *Independent* had confirmed it on Twitter – a two-year deal, same as me. Apparently the *Examiner* have the full story tomorrow, a column by Rog, the lot. Then I heard from the horse's mouth. He sent me a picture of himself and Monsieur Lorenzetti, shaking hands, big smiles! He's a gas man. Three hours before an Amlin final and he's sending me this – although he probably doesn't even know Leinster are playing tonight!

People assume I'll be pissed off, because they're assuming that our relationship hasn't changed since May of 2009 when I roared at him in Croke Park. We're friends now, and I can see us becoming better friends in Paris. I knew Laura would be delighted, as she gets on well with Jess, so she'll have a friend in Paris and will enjoy helping to mind the O'Gara kids! In fact, I could only see good things in it. But the Amlin final was only a couple of hours away, so I needed to screw my game head back on.

Stade didn't roll over, as some people had expected, but we still won in some comfort, despite spending most of the game in defence. It was the perfect counter-punching performance – soak up their pressure and then stun them with a few perfect combinations. We were really clinical when we had the ball. The first try came in the third minute from an inside pass from Bossy and a perfectly timed run by Isa, who fed me to set up Mads. Sean Cronin scored the second try after Andy did really well to gather Bossy's box-kick. Two pre-planned moves that we worked hard on all week, and we pull them off – the coaches must be happy – and Rob got our third after Isa had run onto my cross-kick. Rob celebrated with an extravagant dive, and was captured mid-air by photographer Dan Sheridan, with the sunset behind him creating almost a halo effect! A great picture on a beautiful evening in Ballsbridge.

About an hour later, the sky was lit with fireworks and the RDS was rocking. Leo and Jenno and Jamie, who was captain for the night, insisted that myself and Isa received the Amlin trophy afterwards, which was a nice touch, and very much appreciated. With the presentation ceremony and the champagne and the group pictures and the lap of honour and more crack in the changing room, it was after eleven before I did some media outside the changing rooms. The journos politely asked me a few questions about the game before eventually asking about Rog. I made only positive noises, which probably wasn't what they wanted to hear! So I said I was looking forward to Rog carrying out the kicking tee for me – which will give him a giggle.

It's important to celebrate wins like this as a team, so we did. We just didn't go mad, like we've done after winning Heineken finals. We've learned from our mistakes there. We partied hard on the night of those finals, then met in the pub the following afternoon. We had the Monday off and Joe ran the booze out of us on the Tuesday, so you'd only be starting to actually prepare for the Pro12 final on the Wednesday. Basically we wasted a lot of valuable time. We're fortunate that we have an eight-day turnaround this year but we're still taking it handy. We had a bite to eat in the family room at the RDS, and then went for a couple of beers in Kiely's, nothing more. There's still business to take care of.

Monday 20 May

UCD

There's some hilarious stuff going around on the internet about me and Rog. Dad sent the picture of me roaring at him in Croke Park, except now there's a speech bubble and I'm shouting at him, 'QUIT FOLLOWING ME, WILL YA?'

A bit of light relief is no harm because this will be an emotional week, and not just here, with so many of us leaving the club, but also in Ulster, where I'm sure they're dedicating their efforts to Nevin's memory. I had a quick chat with Joe this morning and he talked about the importance of not letting ourselves get emotional in the build-up to Saturday, but even while he was saying this I could sense a bit of emotion in his voice. He asked me did I want to speak before the game and I said I didn't. Isa's the same. We're all agreed that it's best to keep things businesslike.

I know this from experience. The night before the 2010 Magners League final in Dublin, quite a bit was made of the fact that it would be the last Leinster appearance for Mal O'Kelly and Girvan Dempsey, two guys who gave so much to the province. When a coach tells you that you have to win the next day for these guys, it puts a bit of added pressure on you that you probably don't need. A couple of years later, we played Munster in a Pro12 final and it was a farewell match for Hinesy and Stan Wright. The two lads spoke to us the day before the game in Thomond and there was barely a dry eye in the room. It was draining, really. We were ready to play the game there and then, which means we were wasting energy. I don't want to put the guys through that this week. It's much more important to concentrate on the process of how we win a game, rather than the reasons we want to win it.

Even so, I'm acutely aware that I'm doing a lot of things for the last time, things that have been part of our weekly rhythm. Mondays are generally when we prepare our attacking plays, so as we were walking out today I mentioned to Isa that this will be our last Leinster attack session together. He said he was thinking the same thing. Tomorrow will be the final defence session, Wednesday the last time the kickers meet up, the last time we'll have our weekly place-kicking competition.

I joked last Friday about getting Rog to bring out my kicking tee for me next season. It's going to be weird not having Johnny O'Hagan there, because he's been doing that job for me since I started with Leinster. He's our bagman, and so much more – dispenser of kit, wit and kindness, salt-of-the-earth. I've actually known Hago all my life. He's a friend of Dad's from Bective, and became Bective bagman as soon as he stopped playing – so not only have I known him since I was a nipper, I've only known him as a bagman! Richie might bring out the tee if Mads or Ferg were kicking, and used to do so for Isa too. But Hago always does it for me and it's a great comfort to have him there. He'll give me little bits of advice as I'm lining up the kick, like 'Keep her nice and low now into the wind, now Jonno.' Sometimes it's exactly the opposite of what I'm actually telling myself – he'll be saying, 'Head down, now, son!' and I'll be thinking of standing tall! But there are times when the wind is blowing when I'll ask his advice on the wind, so Hago's a bit like a caddy for me. He knows his sport – he was a decent soccer player in his day, or so he says – and he's been part of the Leinster set-up since the game went professional. He got on great with Cheiks, giving him plenty of advice, whether it was wanted or not. When Cheiks arrived, Hago introduced himself by saying, 'Just remember, pal, I'll still be here long after you're gone!' And he was right. Now Hago's going to out-last me, which feels a bit weird.

He'll be tickled by the idea of Saturday's final being a home match for Ulster – on our patch. There's a YouTube clip going around, with some Ulster supporter going on about turning the RDS into 'OUR DS'. It's not something that was mentioned in today's meeting. There's a perfectly good reason for them choosing our place as their nominated stadium. They had to choose a venue a couple of weeks ago and Celtic Rugby had already ruled out the Aviva as an option just in case Glasgow made it to the final, in which case the stadium might not even be half full. So it was either the RDS or Thomond Park, and Dublin is much more accessible for Ulster supporters.

We'll be motivated by the fact that Ulster have done a league dou-ble over us this season, and bullied us in both games. Next Saturday is more important to us than last weekend's final. That's no disrespect to the Amlin. The Pro12 is not only our bread and butter, but it's caused us a fair bit of heartache: we've lost the final three years in a row. So regardless of the fact that some of us are making our fare-wells, there's a big itch there and it needs a proper scratching. It's no coincidence that Joe had picked his strongest and most experienced available side, with Brian, Leo and Cian all due to start. Seanie won't play, having twisted his knee last Friday. It's a big loss to the squad, but not an injury that's going to put his tour in danger. Speaking of which, we've an appointment with the Lions in town tomorrow night.

Tuesday 21 May

Bear, South William Street

Twenty-two of the Lions squad have been training for over a week now, and seeing as fifteen of them are Welsh there's probably not much bonding that needs to be done. But that's the idea behind heading into town this evening to Jamie Heaslip's restaurant, Bear: for players, management and support staff to get to know each other a little bit better. It's also a chance for the Leinster lads to do a bit of mingling, after another day of preparing for the Rabo final.

I got there a bit early, so ended up walking the streets, killing time like someone on a nervous first date. I didn't fancy sitting there on my own in the restaurant when the Lions coach pulled up outside. I had arranged with the Leinster lads to meet at an appointed spot so that we could all arrive at the same time. I don't know about the other Leinster guys but I felt a little bit uncomfortable walking in to see how relaxed everyone looked in each other's company, having spent a week in the Vale of Glamorgan and a couple of days in Carton. They're having a few beers and laughing about stuff that happened in training. I didn't know whether I should go in and shake hands with everyone. Would that be over the top? I've met a few of the lads at post-match functions, but I couldn't say I was on close terms with any of them. To begin with, I stuck pretty close to the Leinster boys.

I needn't have worried. Everyone was keen to make us feel welcome. Guys who have already toured with the Lions were leading the charge when it came to making introductions and breaking any ice, which melted pretty quickly anyway. I had a chat with Owen Farrell, who impressed me as a really decent bloke. It was nice to shake hands with Jamie Roberts and Dan Lydiate, who will be team-mates not only for the next two months but for the next two seasons in Paris. I'd met Jamie before and exchanged texts with him when the news broke about the two of us being signed by Racing. We chatted about accommodation, learning the language, and the excitement of stepping into the largely unknown.

You could see there are a few characters involved, and not just in the playing squad. I knew about Paul 'Bobby' Stridgeon from watching the DVD of the 2009 tour. He's an S&C coach who worked with Gatland as far back as his days with Wasps, and a former Olympic wrestler. He doesn't look anything out of the ordinary in terms of his own physique but he's phenomenally strong, judging by the 'horizontal hold' he performed for me on the street outside the restaurant. Grabbing a lamp post, he extended his body parallel to the ground and suspended it there for a few seconds, which requires phenomenal strength and technique. That he'd do this in a public place suggests that he'll be a strong personality in the group – he'll hold himself up, but he won't hold himself back, sort of thing.

This was as we were leaving the restaurant. I felt a bit jealous that most of them were heading off to Kehoe's for pints. I had chores to attend to: I had to drive Rala – Paddy O'Reilly, bagman for Ireland and now the Lions – out to Carton to pick up Lions kit-bags for myself and Rob. Then I drove home and squeezed in some casual gear for the tour, before dropping my bags all the way back out to Rala in Carton again. It's funny to think that I won't see them again until Hong Kong, where we're playing the Barbarians on Saturday week, but also reassuring that I've got that job out of the way. I don't want anything to distract me from what we've got to do on Saturday.

Saturday 25 May

RDS (Ulster 18, Leinster 24)

Back in the autumn, when I committed to the idea of recording my thoughts over the course of a season, I had certain goals I thought were achievable. One of them was to end up on stage in the middle of the RDS pitch on the last day of the season, going mental with my team-mates while fireworks exploded all around us. This came to fruition today, but I'd no idea of the intensity of emotions it would arouse in me.

I don't think any of us could have handled watching opponents celebrating a grand final victory for a fourth year in a row – and a third time on our own patch. Losing to the Ospreys last year was particularly annoying and took a lot of the good out of winning the Heineken the previous week. From a personal point of view, beating Ulster in front of our supporters at the RDS gave me some sense of closure. Delivering a second trophy in two weeks made it feel like I'd given them all I possibly could give before heading off.

So that's why there was a certain manic intensity to the way I celebrated on the pitch after the presentation ceremony, doing the lap of honour in a blue Afro Isa wig. There had been all sorts of emotions jostling to get out – regret, frustration, anger and love – but now they had all been trumped by relief and happiness. As farewells go, this one was a bit memorable.

Earlier, even Joe had been struggling to stay composed. We'd agreed to focus on process and not let emotion intervene, but in the dressing room, ten minutes before we went out for our warm-up, I kept my head down as much as possible for fear of losing it. I could hear the emotion in his voice and see the tremble in his lip as he addressed us. Beside me, I could sense Isa was struggling too. At times like this, you want to fast-forward to kick-off so that adrenaline can take over, so that the game can absorb all conscious thoughts. My last game in blue in the RDS. I'd be lying if I said there weren't a few tears. A pat on the head and a few words from Jenno got me back where I needed to be.

Before that, there were distractions. Rob tweaked a hammy in the warm-up to force a rejigging of the backline, with Isa moving to full-back and Andy coming in on the wing. You couldn't help but notice the white flags dominating the stand at the city end, or the fact that our normal PA announcer had been replaced by some bloke with a northern twang. But once the game started, I don't think we could have made a more emphatic statement of ownership than Jenno's try, right in the faces of those Ulster fans.

It came from a lineout, which in turn came from a penalty. For me, the most enjoyable bit was managing to punt a penalty as deep as possible into the right corner without putting it into touch in goal, a bit like a golfer taking on the pin rather than aiming for the middle of the green and two-putt territory. Leaving it twelve to fifteen metres from the try-line makes it that much easier for the defending team. In that situation they're more comfortable contesting the throw. Five metres out and they'll usually all stay on the ground to repel the maul. That's what they did here, but our organization was spot-on. I converted from the right touchline and we had the perfect start.

Soon we were 10–0 up and flying, knowing that we needed to take the game away from Ulster because they'd had a week's rest and would probably finish stronger. We took unnecessary risks, though, and did well to stop Robbie Diack from scoring a try during a period of heavy pressure before the break. Ulster wouldn't back down, however. They had so much emotion invested in this game themselves. The game was slipping from them early in the third quarter when Diack was binned for killing the ball at the ruck, and we went 19–6 ahead. But Paddy Jackson swung the game back their way with a brilliant break. While he didn't finish it off, he was caught illegally by Isa, who joined Diack in the bin. Ulster cashed in when they had momentum with Ruan Pienaar banging penalties over from everywhere, and heading into the final quarter, they'd brought it back to 15–19.

Then came the attack which won the game for us. For the second time in the match, I looked to send a line kick as close to the corner as possible. For a split second, as I saw assistant ref Peter Fitzgibbon jump into the field of play at the corner-flag to judge the flight of the ball, I wondered if I'd bitten off too much. Thankfully, referee John Lacey reckoned I'd got my angles right and we had another five-metre lineout. We had to work Ulster a little harder this time, but eventually Jamie was driven over to the left of the posts.

I missed the conversion – I'll blame Hago for giving me a bad line.

I hit it exactly where I wanted to and hoped the strong breeze would bring it in slightly. Good strike, executed as planned . . . just unlucky, move on. Ulster could still have nicked it. Poor Jamie Hagan gave them an opening when he dived over the top at the ruck in the final couple of minutes, but while Pienaar tried to set his side up with an attacking lineout, he did bail out a little with his line kick and Ulster barely got into our twenty-two. We held on pretty comfortably from there.

And then we celebrated. It seemed like we were out on the pitch for an hour afterwards before returning to the dressing room, where we drank beers and sprayed each other with champagne but still took time to say a few words. It was great to get the chance to tell the lads how much I'd loved my time with Leinster, how I would have liked to stay but that we had so many positive things to look back on – like six trophies in six years! The great thing about having an afternoon kick-off was that we had time together afterwards, at the official function and in the family room, which was jammers. I think this was the part Laura found toughest, because this was when we made our farewells to so many people who mean so much to us. We could have stayed there all night – except for the fact that I had an 8.45 flight to London the next morning.

EIGHT

Lions

Sunday 26 May

Royal Park Hotel, Kensington Gardens, London

I should really be getting some sleep. I'd only a couple of hours of shut-eye last night before Laura dropped me and Rob at Dublin Airport for the early flight to London, and while anyone who played yesterday was excused training, I was almost nodding off on the bus from our hotel to the Lions' farewell dinner at the Royal Courts of Justice. Yesterday was physically and emotionally draining, so I've been looking forward to getting my head on the pillow. But when you're rooming with a new team-mate, it would be rude to just hop into bed, flick the switch on the bedside lamp and clock out. Besides, I'm in a chatty mood. Maybe it's because Owen Farrell is my roomie and we're getting on really well.

Not that I thought there would be any problems between us. Yes, we are both chasing the same jersey. I've read how England's hooker Brian Moore wouldn't talk to the other hookers in the 1989 Lions squad because he saw them as the enemy, but we simply don't have the time for that sort of stuff. We need to get our heads around the game-plan as soon as possible – which is why I spent this morning's flight swotting up on calls and plays.

There is still plenty of speculation that at some stage we may be joined in Australia by Jonny Wilkinson, who helped Toulon beat Toulouse comfortably in the Top 14 semi-final yesterday, and who captained his club to their first Heineken Cup title last week. But all Owen and I have been told is to expect ourselves to be involved in all ten games on tour. It's not going to be to anyone's advantage if we're at odds with each other.

As it turns out, Owen is pretty easy to get on with. He's a bit spiky, like myself, as you can tell from watching him play. But I think that just shows he's passionate about what he does. He is competitive, and it's what makes him the player he is. He's a character, full of chat, and while his accent is pure Lancashire, he reminds me that he must have a fair bit of Irish in him – his dad's a Farrell and his mum's an O'Loughlin. That's Colleen O'Loughlin, older sister to Sean O'Loughlin, who played rugby league for Wigan and Great Britain, like Andy, so there's some footballing pedigree in the family.

We have loads to chat about. We're not flying to Hong Kong until tomorrow evening and already we've lost one player – Dylan Hartley, the Northampton and England hooker, who was sent off in yesterday's Premiership final for verbally abusing the referee, Wayne Barnes. I haven't seen the incident – there's barely been time to draw breath – so I have no idea whether Hartley deserves the punishment of missing out on the tour. However, I'm delighted for Rory Best, who got some good news after the disappointment of losing the Rabo final. Twelve months ago, a lot of people were tipping Besty to make the Test team, but he wasn't helped by Ireland's poor Six Nations. Seeing as he narrowly missed out on selection four years ago, he deserved a break.

Wednesday 29 May

Grand Hyatt, Hong Kong

The heat here never fails to shock you. Walk through the sliding doors at hotel reception and it's as though an oven has suddenly opened before your face. The temperature is in the low thirties, but it's the 90 per cent-plus humidity that really gets you. Just walking a few blocks from our hotel you can feel it sapping your energy. In training, at the Aberdeen Sports Grounds, there have been times when we've gone high intensity and it feels like you're burning up, but when we look at the read-out from the GPS monitors stitched into the back of our shirts, the numbers tell a different story. I think that to go through this sort of discomfort is good for morale and that we'll benefit from it sometime later in the tour. I know it's not a very scientific way of thinking, but some pain can be good for the soul.

Not that this is the reason we're in Hong Kong. We're here to play the Barbarians on Saturday, the first game of our tour and a stop-off which I understand has strong commercial possibilities for the Lions' brand. The team won't be announced publicly until tomorrow, but we've already been informed. Predictably, none of the starting XV was playing last weekend. It reads as follows: Hogg; Cuthbert, Davies, Roberts, Maitland; Farrell, Phillips; Vunipola, Hibbard, A. Jones; Gray, O'Connell (capt.); Lydiate, Tipuric, Faletau. Replacements: Youngs, Healy, Stephens, A.-W. Jones, Heaslip, Murray, Sexton, North.

It's hard to see anyone playing eighty minutes in this heat, so I assume I'll get some time on the pitch. It's a 7.30 p.m. kick-off but apparently that won't make much of a difference – the stadium will be like a giant sauna and already the match officials have agreed to allow water breaks. Our S&C staff have been working flat out to help us avoid dehydration and overheating in training. At the side of the pitch they've set up huge electric fans blowing cold air, and just to stand in front of them is heaven. Then you are handed ice jackets – basically, Adidas body-warmers that have been kept in ice buckets. Again, the immediate effect is to reduce core temperature, but the effect only lasts for a couple of minutes. The heat dominates everything here.

It's been hard work, but already it's clear that we'll be looked after very well by the support staff. Everything is done for us. There's no checking in bags at the airport, no queuing at the reception desk in hotels. Everywhere you turn, Bobby Stridgeon is there, handing you a protein shake or an electrolyte drink or vitamin supplements or whatever is appropriate to the time of day. Every morning you are weighed on high-tech scales and asked a series of questions to check on your sleep patterns, your hydration levels, any niggles, your mood – basically every detail relating to your general well-being is logged on computer, so the management are always fully briefed.

The best way to avoid heat exhaustion is just to stay in the hotel, of course. I'm rooming with Richie Gray, who's as unobtrusive as it's possible to be when you're 6'9". He seems to spend most of his free time watching the box-set of *Homeland*, but we've had some good chats about playing in France. Richie's off to Castres next season, so I've been slagging him about his sense of timing. Castres are in the Top 14 final next week against Toulon, but the guys who have been given most credit for this are the two Laurents, Labit and Travers, who are leaving for Racing, of course!

Saturday 1 June

Hong Kong Stadium (British and Irish Lions 59, Barbarians 8)

A pretty emphatic win against a decent enough Baa-Baas side but the sort of occasion that left me feeling a little hot and bothered. Partly it's to do with the conditions here and partly it's the fact that I missed a few shots at goal towards the end, having been in good place-kicking form over the past few weeks. Nothing to worry about, but still not the ideal start to the tour for me.

I don't think it was really the ideal start for anyone. Mike Phillips must have been pretty happy with his game, and already I can see that he actually plays on the image of himself as being a big-head – 'Stick with me, kid,' he says with a wink. 'I'll make you look world-class.' He looked world-class here, scoring a couple of tries, but despite everyone in red working their tails off to impress, the occasion lacked something. It lacked atmosphere, for starters – the stadium was only half full – and it lacked any real edge, except for one moment in the first half when Schalk Brits, the Baa-Baas' hooker, launched an incredible assault on Owen. Yes, Owen was holding him back illegally at the side of a ruck, but this was a Baa-Baas game, and the two are club-mates at Saracens, so to throw a haymaker at your team-mate's jaw at the beginning of a Lions' tour was astonishing. I thought Owen did well just to push Brits in the face, because his blood must have been boiling.

I received a couple of texts afterwards from pals saying that Owen had a poor game, probably intended to reassure me. I thought he'd done pretty well in ridiculously humid conditions, with a ball that was like the proverbial bar of soap. It was a little like watching Paddy Jackson in Edinburgh during the Six Nations, hoping he'd go well but not too well. The important thing is that we win the warm-up games, build some momentum and put ourselves in the best possible shape for the Tests.

You could see how keen I was to please by the way I was flinging my body into contact as soon as I came off the bench in the second half. The one part of my game I was unhappy with was place-kicking. Two out of five is a pretty poor stat to start with, even if four of those kicks were from difficult angles, wide on the right and outside Dave's 'red zone'. I got the first, the easiest of the five, and struck the second well, but it faded just to the right. The third was in almost exactly the same spot, right on the touchline, and I pulled it left, probably over-compensating. I was on target with the fourth, from roughly the same area, giving me a 50 per cent success rate, which doesn't look so bad, but then Alun-Wyn Jones scored with the last play of the game – in the right corner, naturally – giving me the opportunity to finish positively. I was too quick into the kick, though, and it stayed right. Shit. I'd agonize on one missed kick after any game. But three? That will eat away at me, especially as I'd been kicking so well – 85 per cent accuracy since the start of the year and only two kicks missed in two finals with Leinster. At least we're out of Hong Kong tomorrow, and the tour can start properly.

Monday 3 June

Pan Pacific Hotel, Perth

This is probably the part of the story where the Aussie customs official is supposed to warn me about what the Wallabies are going to do to us but, as it turns out, the 2013 British and Irish Lions have got a very quiet, polite welcome to Australia. Partly it's because we touched down in Perth International Airport at around 6.30 on a Monday morning, and partly it's because this is Western Australia, and not exactly prime rugby union territory. I believe they're expecting a crowd of around 30,000 for our game against the Western Force on Wednesday, but this is still mainly Aussie Rules territory. It feels like we have slipped into the country almost unannounced.

It's good to be here. I love Australia. Rob and I first came here with an Ireland Schools team nine years ago, but this is my first time on the west coast. Perth is beautiful. It has a couple of skyscrapers, as if to prove that it's a proper city, but the thing that strikes you is the sense of space and the relaxed pace of life. After the claustrophobia and humidity of Hong Kong, this place is heaven. It's officially the middle of winter but the temperature is in the high teens, and after training the kickers convinced one of our security guys to bring us down to the beach in one of the Lions' Land Rovers, so we could do our warm-down in the Pacific Ocean. What a spot.

I'm rooming with Toby Faletau, who's very relaxed and into his music – he even brings his travel speakers into the bathroom with him. I'm beginning to get a handle on the Welsh guys. You've got the slightly older blokes like Adam Jones, Mike Phillips and Gethin Jenkins, who are a bit old-school, would maybe go out for a beer after matches – they're very professional in their own way but fond of the crack. Then you have the ultra-professional younger crew like Sam, Justin Tipuric, Leigh Halfpenny and Dan Lydiate – very nice blokes but really serious in how they go about their business. I know I have to stop thinking of them as being Welsh. We're all Lions, right? Right. Still, I can't help but notice that there is a particularly Irish feel to the side that has been picked for Wednesday: Halfpenny; Bowe, O'Driscoll (capt.), Tuilagi, North; Sexton, Murray; Healy, Best, Cole; A.-W. Jones, Evans; Croft, O'Brien, Heaslip. Replacements: T. Youngs, Vunipola, Stevens, Parling, Faletau, B. Youngs, Farrell, Maitland.

The only Irish players not involved are Paulie, who started in Hong Kong, and Rob, who won't get a run until next week because of his hamstring. He can take some comfort from the fact that Gats is giving him an extra week to recover, which is a sign of how highly Gats rates him. He'll still have a lot of ground to make up if he's going to make it into the team for the Waratahs game on

Saturday week – seven days before the first Test and traditionally dress-rehearsal night. If anyone can do it, Rob can. He was sick for a couple of months before the last Lions tour and only played a couple of games before the Test series, and then produced some remarkable performances against the Springboks.

There is no question of easing yourself into a tour like this. Every opportunity is golden. I know people are unhappy that the Force will have a weakened team out on Wednesday – their coach, Michael Foley, has annoyed everyone, including Gats, by resting players so that they can play against the Waratahs next Sunday, even though that match has no bearing on where they will finish in the Super 15. Seven of the team we're playing haven't even played Super 15 rugby. People are predicting a landslide, which isn't good for the whole concept of Lions tours. Does that mean we'll take it handy against them? Quite the opposite.

Tuesday 4 June

Pan Pacific Hotel, Perth

Not happy.

Leigh is going to take the place-kicks tomorrow and it's bugging me. It's only one part of my game, but it's a massive part and to have it taken away from me is unsettling. Leigh is a world-class kicker, as everyone knows. But I was still cranky when Neil Jenkins gave me the news towards the end of our kicking session at the stadium.

I didn't really hear him at first. 'What?' I said, which may have sounded more like disbelief. When he said it again, I just said OK, though he must have known that I was unhappy, because he asked me about it. I explained that I would have liked to kick, that I've been striking the ball well and that I wanted to erase the misses in Hong Kong. Jenks reassured me that there would be plenty of opportunities, which I accepted. But I can't deny that I'm annoyed and, I'll admit, conscious of the fact that Leigh works with Jenks on a regular basis. Does this give him an advantage over Owen and me? Maybe, but what am I going to do? I had an opportunity in Hong Kong and I made a mess of it. Get over it. Given the way Leigh is kicking, I can have no complaints.

Maybe Jenks is right – there will be opportunities. I can't let it upset the rest of my game. At the same time, I couldn't just accept it meekly. I see place-kicking as a strength of mine and I want the coaches to know how much I want the responsibility. I think they probably got the message. It doesn't affect my relationship with Jenks at all. We are getting on really well. He is a top guy and he had to make a decision.

Wednesday 5 June

Patersons Stadium, Perth (Western Force 17, British and Irish Lions 69)

It looks like Cian's tour is over. I was about five metres away from him when he twisted horribly on his ankle and his yell will stay with me for the rest of my life. X-rays have shown that his ankle isn't broken, and if there's anyone who can recover quickly from such a terrible injury it's him, so no decision has been made yet. But the fact that Alex Corbisiero has been summoned from England's tour of Argentina doesn't look good. It's cruel, because Cian had been flying in training and to my mind was a banker to start the first Test, especially seeing as Gethin Jenkins is already struggling with a calf injury.

To add insult to injury, Cian has been cited for biting the arm of one of the Force players, Brett Sheehan. As I've been told it, Sheehan had his arm squeezed against Cian's mouth at the bottom of a ruck, in a sort of a headlock – no surprise there, seeing as Sheehan had been stirring up a bit of aggro in the local papers before the game, talking about 'getting under the Lions' skin'. Cian doesn't wear a gumshield, so there were teeth marks – from his top teeth only – on Sheehan's arm. That doesn't constitute a bite, but because Sheehan brought this to the referee's attention during the game, the citing commissioner reckons that Cian has a case to answer. I think it's a disgrace. He's going to be made to sit through a hearing and have his name dragged through the mud, all the while knowing that his tour is probably over. It's awful for him. I know how hard he has worked to get here.

It was really the only blemish on what was a good night for us. We scored nine tries, all of them converted by Leigh, who also kicked a couple of penalties in a faultless display. Fair play to him. It was a world-class performance by a world-class goal-kicker who is also playing very well in general. He might not be the biggest lad in the squad – we've decided he looks like Bilbo Baggins – but he plays with real assurance. With Rob unfortunately out of action for the time being, Leigh has laid down a real marker for the 15 jersey.

We have plenty of big blokes to do the power running, as we showed tonight. Jamie Heaslip, Sean O'Brien, George North and Manu Tuilagi all did plenty of damage – it's taking a while to get used to having all these monster backs around me. The Wallabies had a couple of cameras there anyway, which is only to be expected. Everyone does their research on the opposition these days and we know we'll be scrutinized for clues over the next few weeks – there was even a lone cameraman at the captain's run yesterday and our security staff got him to delete the footage, just in case he felt like passing it on to the Wallabies' coach, Robbie Deans.

Our general plan is to play fairly expansively in the provincial games and then to be more direct in the Tests. I found it easier to run and handle tonight, because kicking from the hand is difficult at an Aussie Rules 'oval' like this, with only a few advertising hoardings to give you your bearings. From a personal point of view, I was happy to score early on with a dummy pass inside. I might have had a second soon after, only Brian failed to spot me running a support line inside as he raced for the left corner. He scored two in the end, and linked well with Manu. Already it's clear that Gats is going to have some incredibly tough calls to make, especially in midfield and in the back row.

So it was a good start, before a crowd of over 35,000, with plenty of Lions jerseys on view. Rod Kafer, the former Wallaby, interviewed me afterwards for Fox Sports and greeted me like a long-lost pal. I smiled to myself as only a couple of days ago I'd seen a rugby maga-zine article quoting him as saying he's 'never been convinced by

Sexton'! I thought I was convincing enough in my sixty-odd minutes, and I'm confident that I've laid down a marker. I'm just interested to see how much of a part I play against the Queensland Reds on Saturday. At least I know I'll be playing some part. Poor Cian will probably be on his way home by then.

It turns out I've escaped playing Leinster in the Heineken group stage next season. The draw was released today and Racing have been pooled alongside Clermont, Harlequins and Scarlets. An incredibly tough pool. Avoiding Leinster was my main concern. They have drawn Ospreys, Northampton and Castres, who shocked everyone by beating Toulon in the Top 14 final last weekend – quite a send-off for the two Laurents, and quite a disappointment for Jonny Wilkinson, who has a groin injury. It has been reported that he definitely won't be joining us out here, which ends all that speculation. On with the job.

Friday 7 June

Hilton Hotel, Brisbane

Just heard that Cian has been cleared of any wrongdoing, which is a relief, but no surprise either. The surprise is that he had to sit through a four-hour hearing. And the shocking bit is that despite having his name cleared, some mud will inevitably stick. If you type 'Cian Healy' and 'bite' into a search engine, something will still come up, just because some bloke made an allegation that proved to be unfounded. Is that fair?

We flew into Brisbane yesterday. The Hilton is smack in the middle of the city. This is how it's going to be for most of the tour, with the team accessible to the supporters. We're still in our first week in Australia, but already there are plenty of red jerseys in and around the hotel. I like being in the centre of town because it's easy to pop out for a coffee and a mosey around. It's mid-winter here, which means it's dark by six in the evening, but it's up around twenty degrees in the middle of the day. No wonder the Aussies are such a healthy-looking people – they get to spend so much time in the open air. Stroll down to the Botanic Gardens and it seems like every second person is either jogging or cycling.

Andy Irvine describes Brisbane as the capital of Australian rugby union. Not that this makes it the most popular winter sport. League is king here. Brisbane is in mourning today because Queensland lost the opening State of Origin game in Sydney last night, and this dominates the sporting headlines. Come Saturday, however, we should get top billing. Andy says we should expect plenty of verbals on the streets and from the stands – which is the best way to gauge whether you have registered in Australia's sporting consciousness.

Judging by where we trained today, rugby union is very much a posh sport around these parts. The kids who go to Anglican Church Grammar School – or Churchie, as it's known – wear blazers, long shorts and wide-brimmed hats, and enjoy amazing sports facilities, with fifty- and twenty-five-metre swimming pools, multiple cricket squares and top-quality rugby pitches. We did our captain's run there this afternoon and the good news was that our captain took part. I'm delighted for Sam, who's been struggling with a knee problem but has got on with his rehab without complaining and is ready to start against the Reds tomorrow. The team is as follows: Hogg; Cuthbert, Tuilagi, Davies, Bowe; Farrell, B. Youngs; Jenkins, T. Youngs, Stevens; Gray, Parling; Lydiate, Warburton (capt.), Faletau. Replacements: Hibbard, Vunipola, A. Jones, O'Connell, Tipuric, Murray, Sexton, North.

Gats reckons this will be our toughest game outside the Tests, even allowing for the fact that seven of the Reds' best players are controversially unavailable for selection, as they have been bubble-wrapped in Wallaby camp up in Caloundra on the Sunshine Coast. That number includes Will Genia and James Horwill, but even more controversially doesn't include Quade Cooper, whose presence tomorrow night is one of the reasons the Reds will be up for it: to help Cooper prove to Robbie Deans that he was wrong to omit him from the national squad in the first place. The Reds have been going well in the Super 15, and they think of Suncorp Stadium as something of a fortress. They're also proud of the fact that they beat the 1971 Lions and they want to repeat the dose tomorrow night.

Suncorp is a great stadium, a little bit like the Aviva except that it looms above you to equal height on all four sides, making for a cracking atmosphere when it's full. I played there with Ireland three summers ago, when we ran the Wallabies close, despite fielding what was virtually a second-choice forward pack.

Kickers end up having a tour of their own. After the captain's run, Leigh, Owen, Jenks and myself hop into a Range Rover with one of our security guys and head off to the stadium. We might get back to the hotel two or three hours after everyone else, and on a tour like this that might happen two or three times a week. We have less free time and so we miss out on a lot of the touristy stuff that's on offer, but I'm not that worried about sight-seeing while I'm on this trip. I can do all that some other time. We have work to do.

Saturday 8 June

Suncorp Stadium, Brisbane (Queensland Reds 12, British and Irish Lions 22)

'Oi! Sexton! You've got shoulders like a snake!'

This is more like it. Andy Irvine said we'd get some abuse in Brisbane, so when it comes it's almost a relief. I'm sitting on the bench, and during a break in play during the first half this Aussie three rows back is giving me a serious earful about my not-so-impressive shoulders. The other subs are loving it. My avatar on our specially commissioned Lions smartphones is a bottle of Heinz tomato ketchup, because of my sloping shoulders, so this is giving the lads fresh ammo. But I'm not the only one who's getting it. 'Oi! Jones! You're the best fat prop in Europe!' Suncorp feels like the Australian version of Thomond Park.

The Queenslanders gave it to us on the pitch, too. Not with the traditional biff, but by giving us the runaround. Remember, the Lions have already been characterized as the physically biggest side to tour Australia – 'great slabs of raw, red meat', according to one newspaper – and the Reds obviously decided that the best way to beat us was to outrun us. They owned the ball for the first twenty minutes and I don't think I've seen a quarter with such a rapid tempo. Cooper was in his element, all quick taps and long cut-out passes deep inside his twenty-two. But the Reds' real star was their winger, Luke Morahan, who prevented two tries with heroic defence and then counter-attacked for one of the individual scores of the season.

The only way for us to quell them was to out-muscle them, play for territory and for penalties, and squeeze them in the scrum, where Mako Vunipola chose a good time to have a big game, seeing as both Church and now Gethin Jenkins are heading home. The scrum was directly responsible for Ben Youngs's try, and Owen place-kicked beautifully for seventeen points, six out of six. Even when the Reds scored their second try at the start of the final quarter, we had the composure to ride out the storm, thanks in no small part to the settling effect Paulie had when he came off the bench.

It was quite a battle, which was what we needed, but there were casualties. Tommy Bowe cracked a bone in his hand early in the second half and his tour is now in the balance, while Manu received a 'stinger' in his arm and had to be replaced in the first half. I have my own issues, too. With half an hour to go, I was trying to keep up with George North when I felt my hammy bite just a fraction – in and around the scar tissue from the injury that kept me out of action for five weeks in the spring. I probably would have gone off, but for the fact that we were already down two outside backs and Owen, who had moved to inside centre, was beginning to cramp up too. Besides, the game was still in the balance. I got some heat rubbed into it on the touchline and made it through to the end, keeping the ball in behind the Reds and defending hard. But staying on wasn't ideal. I know I won't make Tuesday's game in Newcastle and I'll do well to make the Waratahs game next Saturday.

Back in the changing room I did a strength test on the hammy, which went OK, but we went for a scan in the medical centre beside the stadium, just to be sure. The scan was clear, 'but you need to rest for a good ten weeks!' says the radiologist, with a big smile. These Aussies and their sense of humour, eh?

Sunday 9 June

Hilton Hotel, Brisbane

A slow day. I had been booked in to play golf up on the Gold Coast this afternoon, but now everything I do is determined by the state of my right hamstring. So I spent a fair chunk of today icing it and spending time with our physios, with a view to getting myself ready to play the Waratahs next Saturday – if selected, of course. During the morning, I tried to watch Ireland v. USA on a live feed from Houston, Texas, where it was still Saturday evening, but the feed was stop-start, a bit like the game, from what I could see, which we won 15–12, all penalty kicks, with Mads kicking five from six. I got in touch with Ferg by text later on, who says that Joe has arrived but is only observing at this stage. They're off to Toronto next, though not with Simon Zebo, who's being flown out here as cover for Tommy. Back to our full complement of Irishmen!

Next, it's Newcastle, which is north of Sydney, for an 'old school' tour match, against a Combined New South Wales/Queensland Country XV, made up mostly of amateurs. It will be different, but maybe just a bit too different from what we'll be facing in Sydney next Saturday, and especially from what we'll encounter seven days after that in the first Test. Deans revealed six additions to his squad this afternoon and it was no surprise that Cooper wasn't one of them – if Deans wanted him in the side, he would have included him in the original squad. While he has left out one magician, he has recalled another in Kurtley Beale. Beale can cut you apart, but I'll be glad if he's involved in the series, because you want to try and beat the best that Australia has to offer.

It's almost impossible to figure out the shape of their backline, though. I'm guessing they're going to pick Berrick Barnes at 10, seeing as Deans used him there quite a lot last season, but there's talk he'll go with James O'Connor, who's played most of his Test rugby in the back three. Adam Ashley-Cooper looks nailed on at 13 and I'm assuming they'll pick a stopper like Pat McCabe to deal with the threat of Jamie Roberts, who is our most obvious pick at 12. The Aussies can be hard to read, though. I think I need to talk to Alan Gaffney, who coached me at Leinster and with Ireland, and who's helping Cheiks to coach the Waratahs. The Waratahs beat the Force in Perth this afternoon so Riff should be in good form. I noticed an old Leinster wraparound move worked quite nicely for them, too. So I sent him a text:

> Liked the Ireland Shuffle, Riff. We'll be ready for it
> next week.

To which he responded:

> We could have done it better with you there. See you at the
> weekend.

The old charmer.

Tuesday 11 June

Hunter Stadium, Newcastle (Combined Country XV 0, British and Irish Lions 64)

It's good to be reminded occasionally of how highly regarded Drico is across the rugby world. I'm used to having him beside me at training with Leinster or Ireland, so perhaps I take him for granted a little. It's different out here. Turn on Fox Sports in your hotel room and there's a decent chance you'll see him scoring that famous try in the first Test in Brisbane in 2001. George North describes it as his first sporting memory. You can sense a respect verging on awe from some of the Lions whenever he speaks to the group. Guys' eyes light up. You get the sense they want to write down what he's saying. So if the Lions get excited about sharing the same air as him, imagine what it must have been like for the part-timers of the Combined New South Wales/Queensland Country XV? No wonder their outside centre, Lewie Catt, made sure he swapped shirts after the game and was still wearing the red 13 jersey at the press conference an hour after the final whistle. In fact, it looked like he had no intention of taking it off for quite some time.

Playing 'up-country' is part of what Lions tours are traditionally all about. It's nice to get outside the main Australian cities for a change, though Newcastle was a little sleepy yesterday on account of it being the Queen's official birthday and a public holiday over here. There wasn't really much to do for those who weren't playing in the game but go to the beach. A couple of reputations were enhanced tonight – Sean Maitland and Stuart Hogg both looked sharp. These games are tough. Play well and people will tell you it was a ten-try turkey shoot, which it was. Play poorly and you'll be damned for failing against amateurs.

The most frustrating thing was to see George icing his hamstring afterwards. He's been one of the players of the tour so far here and the Combined Country boys must have been relieved that he didn't reappear after the break, having scored two tries in the first half. We're still hopeful that he will have recovered in time for the first Test but Gats has already summoned more backline cover, with Billy Twelvetrees the latest to have been called here from Argentina. Once we get a new addition, there is no standing on ceremony. Alex Corbisiero must be suffering from jet lag but it didn't stop him from playing this evening. We're told he is also a brilliant rapper, so Zeebs will have some competition.

I need all the distraction I can get from the worry of my hamstring. Needless to say, I've been looking after myself. I'm confident that if I stay fit, I'll start the first Test, but I'm not sure if I need to start this Saturday to make sure. Clearly, I'm not in a position to ask if this is the case and Gats has said nothing to let me know either way – though Dad tells me the vibe coming through the media is that he wants me to play another game before he'd risk me in a Test. I desperately want to play. I'd love to get the chance to play against a side coached by Cheiks and Riff, but mainly it's my opportunity to nail a Test spot. The key for me will be this Thursday morning, when I'm due to test it properly. Fingers crossed.

Thursday 13 June

North Sydney Oval

Gats can be hard to read at times. My understanding was that I was having a fitness test this morning, before the team to face the Waratahs was announced. But then in our morning meeting, Gats reads out the team and I'm already included! I glance over at Bob, one of our physios, and he gives me a surprised look. I say nothing. I decide it's best to go to training, do the fitness test, and go from there. I'm happy enough, anyway, as I wanted to play this game to put in a good performance ahead of the first Test. As it turns out, I come through fine, and train fully, so no worries. But then Warren tells me that if I have any doubts at all, to pull out. I'm not to push myself if I feel I'm not 100 per cent. I'll still be 'in contention' for the Test team, whether or not I play Saturday or next Tuesday in Canberra. I'm confused, not sure where I stand.

I like Gats but I don't really feel as though I have what you could call a close working relationship with him yet. The guys I'm dealing with most are Rob and Andy, both of whom I have a lot of respect for. Rob reminds me of Joe, in the way that he attends to the finer details of attack. I feel really comfortable talking to him and discussing various moves and options. I love working with Andy, too. I now realize why England are so hard to break down.

Anyway, the good news is that I'm fit and available to start. I even did a full kicking session after training – not that I'll be given the place-kicking duties, with Leigh also starting. The team reads as follows: Halfpenny; Maitland, Davies, Roberts, Zebo; Sexton, Phillips; Vunipola, T. Youngs, A. Jones; A.-W. Jones, O'Connell; Croft, Warburton (capt.), Heaslip. Replacements: Hibbard, Corbisiero, Cole, Parling, Lydiate, B. Youngs, Farrell, Kearney.

You couldn't call that the definite Test team. On previous Lions tours, the aim was always to use the Saturday before the first Test as a dress rehearsal, but there is uncertainty in quite a few areas. Sam surely feels he needs a big game on Saturday to justify his selection.

Like him, Dan Lydiate only played his first game on tour last Saturday and is still short of a gallop. I realize that I have yet to start a game between Mike Phillips and Jamie Roberts, two players so critical to the Gatland attack-plan. This can be boiled down to the basic idea of recycling continuously and at high pace in the same direction to eat up the full width of the pitch, before reloading and getting big, quick backs to run at whichever slow forwards are isolated in the middle of the pitch. If I'm going to implement it in the Tests, then myself, Jamie and Mike need to spend some time on the pitch together.

But I also need something to take my mind off selection matters. I get it on the way back to the team hotel. It's the glorious view from our Land Rover as we're crossing the Sydney Harbour Bridge on the way back from training, with the Opera House down to our left. We're staying right on the Harbour, a couple of blocks away from Circular Quay. The sun is shining and we're in one of the greatest cities in the world.

Friday 14 June

Brookvale Oval, north of Sydney

As a rugby league fan, I thought it would be good to go see a game, so together with Owen, Seanie and a good few others I went along to Brookvale this evening. Owen is quickly becoming an honorary Irishman on this tour. The joke is that it's because most of the English blokes are from Leicester and he'd rather hang around with us than with them. He's also Lancastrian, with league in his blood, so it was good to get some insight into what was going on out on the pitch. Unfortunately the match was a bit one-sided, with Canterbury getting the upper hand, so most of the entertainment was listening to the abuse being flung at the Manly players by some of their own supporters. The Bulldogs were out of sight by the time we left with twenty minutes to go.

I've sympathy for Seanie that he's not playing tomorrow because everyone knows it's the most important game so far. He's played really well on tour and the locals are surprised he's not a nailed-on starter after the carnage he caused in our World Cup game against the Wallabies two years ago. Even though he's not playing, he's still looking out for his out-half.

'You know they're going to go after you tomorrow night, Sexto, don't you?'

'Why do you say that?'

'Because Cheika will tell them to go after you.'

'He wouldn't do that. Sure he knows I'm hoping to play in a Test match next week.'

'Wise up, will you?'

I suppose Seanie's right, but it's not as though Cheiks is going to send someone out to do a Duncan McRae on me. McRae has been in the papers during the past few days, talking about the time he gave Rog a thumping here in Sydney twelve years ago. I think Cheiks is more interested in showing the advances the Waratahs have made since he took over at the start of the year. They've been playing some exciting rugby, and while they're not going to make the Super 15 play-offs, he's definitely turned them around from last year, when they finished down near the bottom of the table. His big problem for this game is that he has a dozen players either in Wallaby camp or out injured – though he has succeeded in getting Dave Dennis and Rob Horne released for tomorrow's game. They'll be up for it, no matter who's playing, but I think I know how to look after myself at this stage.

We arrived back at the hotel to hear that we missed the best finish in the entire NRL season. Manly scored three tries in the last fifteen minutes but missed a kick to win it, with the Bulldogs kicking the 'golden point' to win it in extra time!

Saturday 15 June

Allianz Stadium, Sydney (Waratahs 17, British and Irish Lions 47)

It turns out Seanie was spot-on with his prediction. I was hit hard four times tonight, all of them verging on late, had my ankle stamped and had a prop lean on my windpipe to the point that I thought I was going to pass out. When I saw Cheiks being interviewed on the side of the pitch afterwards, I called him a name that I can't repeat here.

I said it with half a smile on my face, though, because there was a lot to be happy about tonight. This was a fairly complete performance and we produced some cracking rugby, helped in part by the refereeing of Jaco Peyper, who showed again that he rewards sides who play positive rugby. We scored five tries in total and, seven days before the first Test, before a full house at the old Sydney Football Stadium, we sent out the message that we are not just boshers. We can play. No wonder Gats was beaming in the dressing room afterwards.

His selection job has been made interesting by several fine individual performances. Paulie and Alun-Wyn Jones are set in stone as the second-row combination. Sam easily did enough to ensure that he leads us out next week, and after playing a full eighty Jamie looks nailed on at number 8. Tom Croft and Tom Youngs both had massive games and made it very difficult for Gats to leave them out, while Mako must now be favourite to start at loosehead, with Adam Jones at tighthead.

Leigh is heading towards a point-scoring record with a total of thirty tonight, including a couple of tries. He now has twenty-two successful place kicks from twenty-three attempts on tour. Despite Leigh's heroics, Jonny Davies was probably man of the match, as Drico pointed out afterwards. Zeebs even put himself into contention if George's hamstring doesn't heal in time and would have scored the quickest try in Lions history had he not brushed the touchline while touching down with less than a minute on the clock. The one big negative was another hamstring injury – to Jamie Roberts, late in the game. He'd been flying too, showing his power and skill in setting up Leigh's second try. He must be very doubtful for next week, so my guess is that Jonny and Drico will now start. It's not ideal to have two 13s in a side, but both are adaptable and playing really well.

I was just happy to survive forty-eight minutes in one piece before being called ashore. Actually, that's not altogether true. I felt I slotted in well between Mike Phillips and Jamie Roberts and that we looked sharp. It was pleasing to get on the scoreboard, too. It was six minutes in, a counter-attack moving right to left – after Zeebs sent Jonny down the touchline, he found me with a lovely inside pass off his left. My try-scoring celebrations were pretty ropy – very 1970s, sliding over feet-first. At least it was an 'honest' celebration. I don't practise my routines like some people I could mention!

I was delighted and relieved that my hamstring had passed an early test, but not quite so rapturous about some of the stuff that went on after that. While I rate Peyper, I thought his assistant refs might have been a bit more vigilant about some of the stuff that Mike and I had to put up with. The heaviest hit came from the biggest bloke on the field – Will Skelton, an absolute monster of a lock, who apparently has slimmed down from 160 kilos to a trim 135! This was early in the game, when I took the ball to the line and passed inside to Jonny. Skelton was committed to tackling me, but he hit me with a shoulder to the jaw and then drove me into the ground, just to make sure I knew he'd got me.

I complained to the match officials but it carried on after the break. When I went down on a loose ball, they gave me a good old-fashioned shoeing – this was where I was stamped on the ankle. Then came my near-asphyxiation, after their second try. There wasn't a red jersey in sight – my team-mates were off in a huddle discussing what they were going to do from the restart. This big lump had his forearm right on my windpipe, and he had a number of his mates with him, so I let my hands down by my side, in submission. Hello, lads? Calling all Lions? Ref? Assistant ref? I promise I won't be so lippy in future? Eventually, the cavalry arrived and I was set free.

I was gone soon after, not so much to protect me from the Waratahs as to protect myself from doing further damage to the hamstring, which had tightened up again. It's been getting a lot of work since I started playing again. That was eight weeks ago and I've played some part in ten games since then. I just need it to behave itself for another few weeks. So there was no Saturday-night party for me in Sydney. Just chats and a quiet beer back at the Intercontinental with Drico, Owen and Jamie. And another large bucket of ice ordered up to the room.

Sunday 16 June

Ribs & Rumps Restaurant, Manly

Newsflash – Shane Williams is to join the tour, so too Brad Barritt and Christian Wade. Together with Zeebs, Alex Corbisiero, Ryan Grant and Billy Twelvetrees, that's seven replacements in total, and with five games left on tour, there may well be more. Shane is by far the most newsworthy, not only because he's a rugby legend but because he's currently playing in Japan and was on his way to join the tour as a radio analyst with TalkSport. Now he'll be playing against the Brumbies in Canberra on Tuesday.

Around fourteen of us took the ferry to Manly for lunch. It's a half-hour trip and the poor man's Sydney Harbour cruise. Very pleasant. The plan was to go for a swim but the water was pretty rough and I have my leg heavily strapped, so in the end I watched a game of beach volleyball between the Lions and four local girls, two of whom had represented Australia at the London Olympics. With Paulie involved, it became ridiculously competitive. He was up front with Geoff Parling and nearly killed one of the poor girls with a spike. He queried nearly every line-call. The rest of us were sitting on this high wall, cheering them on. Just watching Paulie was great entertainment.

Earlier on there was terrific news from Toronto, where Ireland beat Canada 40–14 – an excellent result, given how many players they were missing. I texted Peter O'Mahony to congratulate him on leading a successful tour as captain, and I was delighted for a couple of my close pals, too: Ferg scored a hat-trick and Kev had his first Test start in a couple of years. A nice end to the season for both of them.

Tuesday 18 June

Canberra Stadium (Brumbies 14, British and Irish Lions 12)

I felt for Rob tonight. He was one of the stars of the 2009 tour, but because of bad luck with injury, his first start on this tour came behind four three-quarters who are barely a day in Australia, and a non-specialist out-half, Stuart Hogg. It's no surprise that there was a defensive mix-up in the back three early in the game which allowed the Brumbies to score a try, and in a tense, low-scoring game, that turned out to be critical.

The Brumbies have been the most successful Australian side in this year's Super 15 and under the guidance of Jake White, a World Cup-winning coach with South Africa, they are certainly well organized, so that when the Lions looked to haul them in with some help from a strong bench in the final quarter, the Brumbies held on for a win which, judging by their celebrations, meant a lot to them.

It's disappointing to lose our unbeaten run on tour, but to be honest, you can feel a bit detached from a game like this if your focus is on the Test match in four days' time. You're in a different world. During the afternoon, when some of the guys playing are so nervous they're struggling to keep their pre-match meal down, you're playing ping-pong in the team room, whiling the hours away. It was nice to meet Shane Williams – I've always been a fan – but our two-day hop to Canberra hardly goes down as a tour highlight. As Kearns said afterwards, this week is all about the Test. If we win on Saturday, the Brumbies game will be forgotten fairly quickly – except by the Brumbies, of course.

Wednesday 19 June

Hilton Hotel, Brisbane

Thought for the day from the top of the team bus was from my roomie, Mike Phillips, on the subject of Aussie pop diva Kylie Minogue.

'Funnily enough, a few years ago, there was a bit of a rumour that me and Kylie were seeing each other. It was big news at the time. She was quizzed about it.

' "Kylie, is it true you're going out with Mike Phillips, the international rugby legend?"

'She turned to the guy and said, "I should be so lucky." '

This is just another variation on Mike Phillips's one gag – how he is just numero uno, the best. He's actually a very nice bloke and rooming with him is quite relaxing. He has been giving me a few French lessons, too. He doesn't seem to get perturbed about anything, certainly not Test selection. I suppose it was kind of obvious that we'd be the half-back combination when we were roomed together for the second half of the week. Sure enough, I heard Gats read my name in the team room at around nine this evening, sixth on the list:

Halfpenny; Cuthbert, O'Driscoll, Davies, North; Sexton . . .

Once you hear your own name, you kind of switch off. It's an amazing feeling, and a relief. After I click back into real time, I discover that the rest of the team is as follows: . . . Phillips; Corbisiero, T. Youngs, A. Jones; A.-W. Jones, O'Connell; Croft, Warburton (capt.), Heaslip. Replacements: Hibbard, Vunipola, Cole, Parling, Lydiate, B. Youngs, Farrell, Maitland.

I'm delighted to be one of four Irishmen and one of three Leinstermen, sorry for Rob because I thought the coaches might fancy his experience and versatility on the bench, and especially sorry for Seanie, whose form has been so strong. I have to wait a while before texting home as it's still a bit early in the morning over there, but soon I get on to everyone – Laura, Mum, Dad, Mark, Jerry and Gillian. They are all delighted for me. Dad would have made the trip but for slipping a disc playing golf. As for Mum, she travelled all the way to New Zealand for the World Cup two years ago and I think she's still recovering from the experience. Not to worry. Laura has enough on her plate preparing for a wedding and a move to Paris. I know they're all rooting for me.

Thursday 20 June

Anglican Church Grammar School

Inside the makeshift conference room to the side of Churchie's main pitch, Andy Irvine is announcing the Test team to a massive media gathering. I'm out on the pitch, kicking with Leigh and Owen, to the soundtrack of Christy Moore's 'Ride On', which is booming from Rala's pitch-side sound system. He has converted all sorts of people into Christy fans.

After kicking, I have some radio interviews to do, and one of the questions is about how I'm coping without the place-kicking duties. I reckon I'm coping pretty well, actually. One part of me misses the pressure, the enjoyment of kicking well in a game. However, it's interesting to get a taste of what it's like to go into a game with probably half the nerves I'd normally feel. Only without the responsibility do I realize just how stressful it can be. I would never sleep easily after a game if I had place-kicked badly but done everything else well. I've often kicked seven from seven but played a poor game, though only our coach and a few team-mates might have spotted the flaws. That would eat me up, but not to the same extent as a poor place-kicking display. Why? Because that can be the difference between winning and losing, and everyone's response tends to be conditioned by the result.

So would I like to be place-kicking on Saturday? Of course. But is it any harm that Leigh will do the job, and do it very well? No. With the worry that my hamstring might go again at some stage in the game, I'm probably better off without that extra pressure.

The feeling is that we have an advantage in this area, as no one is absolutely sure who will be taking the place-kicks for Australia – they have picked Berrick Barnes, Christian Leali'ifano and James O'Connor, any of whom could do the job, with Kurtley Beale another place-kicking option on the bench. I'm a little surprised that they have picked O'Connor at 10, but unpredictability and fluidity are two Wallaby strengths. Robbie Deans has picked three debutants in flanker and lineout expert Ben Mowen, Leali'ifano at 12 and Israel Folau on the wing, who's a big unit and a serious athlete, according to Riff.

The bookies have us as favourites, I'm told, which is a little surprising, given that the Wallabies won the Tri Nations only three years ago and they're on their own patch at Suncorp, where they have a great record, against a team that has been together for a very short span of time. But we'll take it as a positive sign. We did two field sessions today, so we're feeling tired, but ready.

Friday 21 June

Hilton Hotel, Brisbane

It's the shortest day of the year in the southern hemisphere, but it was still warm when the rain stopped this afternoon, so after the kickers completed our final pre-Test session at Suncorp, we warmed down in the lagoon on Brisbane's South Bank. We'd only been in the water a couple of minutes when the beach was thronged with Lions fans, all snapping away merrily. The hotel lobby was full of red jerseys when we got back and I imagined Queen Street, the main pedestrian hub just a couple of blocks away, would be absolutely humming.

It turned out I didn't even have to imagine it. We could hear the singing and chanting this evening from the team room when Ian McGeechan came in to do the jersey presentation. 'O Flower of Scotland', 'The Fields of Athenry', and so on. McGeechan is quite soft-spoken, and someone had to shut the window so we could hear him. Once again, I felt like I'd been parachuted into a Lions DVD. I'd heard a version of his speech before, but now McGeechan is actually speaking to me. It was surreal, but special. That's a word he uses a lot. He said to play in a Test match for the Lions would change us but that we would have the memory for ever. He also urged us to make sure that when we took the jerseys off, it was after winning the Test match. As I listened to McGeechan speak, the enormity of what we're about to do really dawned on me. Twenty-four hours to go and for the first time I could feel the flutters in my stomach.

When he was finished, you could still hear the punters out on the street, eight floors below. Thankfully, our corridor is on the other side of the hotel and we are another three floors up. Still, I'm taking a sleeping tablet. Why change the habit of a career?

Saturday 22 June

A lot was said before, during and after this Test match, but the words I thought were most accurate, or relevant, came from Rob Howley. He told us beforehand that if we scored two tries, we'd win the game, and he was right. But Christ, we did our best to hand the game back to the Wallabies.

As everyone now knows, we won only after Kurtley Beale lost his footing with the final kick of the game, just inside our half but within his range. The Suncorp pitch took a lot of rain before the game and much was made of the fact that Kurtley was using moulded studs, rather than metal ones. I use metal studs 99 per cent of the time, but I'm reluctant to criticize him. I'm told that he has worn them all his career. I know Rog has worn mouldies a lot, and he has obviously played on a lot of wet pitches. I felt for Kurtley. He has a good record of landing last-minute kicks to win big games and I thought it was written for him tonight, after all his well-publicized personal problems with alcohol. He has had a tough time of it and as I watched him line up the kick, I was thinking, *This will be his redemption*.

To slip was cruel. If you miss a kick, you can blame your technique. If you slip, you'll never know. Ultimately, it came down to the fact that the penalty had been awarded for a scrum offence and the ground in that part of the pitch was badly churned up. The ref was watching him closely to make sure he didn't steal a yard, so the nearest clean piece of turf was back a metre or two and he'd have been reluctant to move further from the target with a kick at the edge of his range. So it goes.

As ever with big games, I end up lying in bed, processing the various words, images and actions of the day. It was a late kick-off Australian time – eight o'clock, to facilitate the TV audience at home – so you spend the greater part of the day trying to make the hours go by quicker – up for as late a breakfast as possible, back to bed, up for lunch, then back to bed for some *Game of Thrones*. I toyed with Rosetta Stone for a while during the afternoon but couldn't concentrate on conversational French.

There are nerves, of course. Leave your room to go down for breakfast and you can see the bar in the lobby is already heaving. Look through the window of the team room and you can see that a tape of one of the Tests from the 1997 tour of South Africa is being projected onto a giant screen at the side of the hotel. This can only get you going. But the more Test rugby you play, the better you get at stopping yourself from thinking about the game until you need to.

I don't need an emotional build-up because I'm trying to keep a clear head, but there will always be passionate words spoken before Test matches, perhaps even more so when you have players from four nations thrust together on the far side of the world. I thought Gats handled this aspect of our preparation cleverly by bringing our families into it. We had a room set aside for any mums, dads, brothers and sisters and other relatives who had travelled out here, and as Gats wrapped up his speech just before we left the hotel, he suggested we should walk through that room on our way to the lifts. These are the people who put us here, he said. He turned to Paulie and pointed out how cool it is that in years to come, his young son Paddy will be able to say that he was here to watch his dad play for the Lions against the Wallabies. I had a quick glance at Paulie and saw that he was struggling to contain himself. He wasn't alone. I'd say it got to the guys who don't have kids, or who don't have their folks here, for various reasons, but the effect would have been all positive. It was done at exactly the right time.

We walked through that family room, into the lift and out into the foyer and the place just erupted. Judging by the flags, the crowd was mainly Welsh and Irish but there was only one word on their lips, roared repeatedly, 'Lions! Lions! Lions!' It was bedlam but good bedlam, if you know what I mean. Travelling from team room to bus to training to kicking practice, you're in a bit of a bubble; but when you're hit by this explosion of red noise, you realize how much the whole thing means to so many people.

At the stadium, out on the pitch as we kickers went through our routines, I was struck by how the blocks of red in the stand were offset by roughly equal amounts of yellow. A lot has been written about how the Wallabies felt ambushed by the Lions supporters in Brisbane twelve years ago, so this time they have issued thousands of distinctive yellow 'Lion hunter' pith helmets. In this atmosphere, we didn't need any more stirring words. The dressing-room talk was functional, with Warby talking about the intensity we need to bring. During the captain's run, I talked about how we couldn't afford to sit on a lead as we did here against the Reds. If only we could have followed through on that.

Leali'ifano's concussion, less than a minute into the game, was terrible for him, and difficult for the players on both sides, who had been just let off the leash only to be restricted again by a five-minute stoppage. When the match started again, the action was at times frantic, crazy; words were yelled but inaudible. In an atmosphere like that it can be hard to organize people, but I was helped by some good messages from the coaches relayed onto the pitch via Jenks, when he came on with the kicking tee for Leigh. We spotted how the Wallabies were using Genia in the backfield on our ball and managed to drop some balls onto their key player, or alternatively attack the empty chip-space area behind their defensive line. Both tactics earned us good field position.

I thought we were harshly treated by referee Chris Pollock in the first half. He gave us penalty advantage when we were attacking during the first quarter, but when that advantage didn't accrue, he didn't go back and give us the penalty. Instead it went the other way, and Genia's quick tap shredded us down the right, with Folau being allowed to run behind the posts and make O'Connor's conversion easy. Then when Wycliff Palu wilfully killed the ball metres from his own line at the end of the half, Pollock gave the penalty but not the yellow card that was clearly deserved.

Earlier, the game had been transformed by George North's brilliance on the counter; he missed out on a second due only to Folau's superb defence – they were having a great battle. The next time Folau got the ball in attack, he hurt us again. I showed him the outside, assuming I had cover on the inside, but his brilliant step, plus our lack of shape, let him in for his second. I tried to force a more difficult conversion for O'Connor, which turned out to be an important detail. It meant we held the lead going into the second half.

It was now the Wallabies' turn to be unlucky as they had two more backs stretchered off – Berrick Barnes and Leali'ifano's replacement, Pat McCabe. Freakish misfortune, which meant they had to move Michael Hooper, their flanker, to inside centre – a great defender off the side of the scrum but an obvious target out of position in midfield. Our problem was that attacking platforms remained hard to come by. I wanted ball off the top of the lineout, so that I could release our big wingers quickly, but the Wallabies were crowding the middle and the tail, forcing us to keep it simple but limited at the front. Even so, we managed to manoeuvre ourselves to call a 'Hendo Tune' in midfield – named after Rob Henderson, the Lions and Ireland centre, and Ben Tune, the Wallaby winger. It's a 'split centre' move, where I put the blind-side wing into a hole created by Drico's decoy run and, in this case, by Hooper's over-enthusiasm. We didn't get our timing quite right, but Alex Cuthbert's pace did the trick.

Eight points up with half an hour left against a makeshift backline and with a dominant scrum? It should have been a formality. But we gave them three points back immediately by being sloppy at the restart and then blew an attacking scrum under their posts – mind you, it didn't help that Corbs strained his calf or that Adam Jones ran out of gas. We needed some breathing space coming into the final quarter but instead the game was opening up, which suited the Wallabies, especially now that Kurtley was on the pitch. He improved their penalty kicking, too, landing two shots, then missing an easy one, before his famous late slip.

Did we deserve to win? I'm torn on this one. Yes, they left fourteen points out there in missed kicks, whereas Leigh was off target just once. At the same time, I'm not sure that either of the two penalties Kurtley missed should have been awarded in the first place – if anything, Australia should have been penalized for illegally wheeling and shunting that scrum in the final minute. It made sense just to enjoy the win, which we did. Some went out for a few beers, some fell into bed almost immediately, absolutely shattered. A few of us watched highlights of the game again on a laptop in the team room –

Drico, Jamie Heaslip, Jonny Davies, Leigh and myself. We had a couple of quiet beers and someone did a McDonald's run. Personally, I'm happy with the way it went. I could have done better for the Folau try but I thought I kicked well from the hand and a couple of my chip-and-chases worked – and might have worked out even better had the bounce been kinder. Of course, I wish we could have played a bit more rugby, but this was a proper Test match. We'd agreed on a fairly cautious game-plan based on territory and pressure, though we probably could have managed that aspect a bit better. Most of all, I'm delighted that my hammy held and I lasted the full eighty minutes.

There will be some fall-out from the game over the next twenty-four hours or so, I'm sure. Alun-Wyn Jones had to have stitches inserted in his eyelid after an incident early in the game and was lucky not to lose his eye – there's a feeling that James Horwill, the Aussie skipper, has a case to answer. Meanwhile I'm concerned about the way Paulie needed so much treatment near the end after taking a bang on his forearm. I've seen him play for forty minutes against France with what turned out to be a torn medial collateral ligament in his knee. It has to be something serious for him to stay down. But for now, it's about sitting back and relishing victory. Happy bunnies, so we are.

Sunday 23 June

Grand Hyatt, Melbourne

The advantage gained by last night's win seems massively reduced twenty-four hours on. Paulie fractured his forearm towards the end of the game. Just as he will be a huge loss to us, spiritually and physically, the Wallabies will be lifted by Horwill having been cleared this evening of stamping – according to the commissioner, the reason Horwill stood on Alun-Wyn Jones's eye was because he lost his balance. In other words it was an accident. It's not a decision that has been met favourably within the camp, but we've decided there's no point in complaining publicly as it won't change anything. The only comment has come from Drico, who described Horwill as 'a lucky boy'.

So the Wallabies retain the services of an enormously influential second-row, while the Lions lose one – a classic fourteen-point swing. It's a measure of Paulie's importance to the squad that Gats has asked him to hang around to work with the forwards and especially with Geoff Parling, who's going to take over calling the lineouts on Saturday. But the Wallabies will be delighted to know that his only role for the remainder of the series will be an advisory one.

Late news: Tom Court is due to join the squad as cover for Alex Corbisiero and will be in the twenty-three to play the Melbourne Rebels on Tuesday evening. He received the call while on a family holiday in Brisbane.

Tuesday 25 June

AAMI Park (Melbourne Rebels 0, British and Irish Lions 35)

Another downtown hotel in another attractive Australian city. Melbourne is smaller than Sydney but seems just as cosmopolitan, quite arty, and has lots of side-streets with cool cafes where the only people who'll recognize you are wearing red jerseys. This place may now have a Super 15 franchise, but rugby union is well down the sporting list. Melbourne has nine professional Aussie Rules teams, one rugby league side and one union, two soccer clubs, one netball, three basketball and one baseball franchise. If you need any further proof that Melbourne takes its sports seriously, stroll about half an hour south of our hotel and you'll come across an extraordinary collection of facilities: the Melbourne Cricket Ground, the Rod Laver Arena, the Margaret Court Arena, the Hisense Arena, Collingwood's training facility in the Westpac Centre, Melbourne Park Tennis Complex, the Punt Road Oval and Gosch's Paddock, and our venue this evening, AAMI Park. And that's not mentioning the amazing Etihad Stadium, with its retractable roof, over in the Docklands, where we're playing on Saturday.

AAMI Park was close to its 30,000 capacity, which shows that the Lions can make a bit of a splash, even here. It was a big marketing opportunity for the newly formed Rebels, but they were up against a Lions team more than half of whom had genuine reason to believe they could force their way into the twenty-three for Saturday. Seanie, for example, put in a superhuman effort, and even if not everything he tried came off, he can at least claim that he emptied the tank. But this was also a massive collective endeavour. Quite a few of the team may have played their last rugby of the tour tonight, with just under two weeks still to go. By winning by five tries to zip, they ensured that they finished in style.

Wednesday 26 June

Grand Hyatt, Melbourne

Seanie didn't make the starting XV, but at least he's on the bench for Saturday and is virtually guaranteed to play some part. There are five changes in total – so much for sticking with a winning team – with two of them enforced by injury. Mako Vunipola comes in for Corbs and Geoff for Paulie, as expected. The other switches are all highly interesting from my point of view. Ben Youngs comes in for Mike, who has been struggling with his knee. This means I have to get used to another scrum-half with whom I have played for the grand total of forty-two minutes. That's no criticism of Ben, obviously, whose hard work means he is rewarded with the chance to start a Lions Test with his brother, Tom. Just means we will have to spend a bit more time chatting during the week about various things.

Tommy's return is a remarkable story when you think that he broke his hand against the Reds two and a half weeks ago. It's a compliment to his dedication and also shows how highly Gats regards him that he's brought him for Cuthy, a try-scorer in the first Test. The final change is Dan Lydiate for Tom Croft in a team that looks like this: Halfpenny; Bowe, O'Driscoll, Davies, North; Sexton, B. Youngs; Vunipola, T. Youngs, A. Jones; A.-W. Jones, Parling; Lydiate,

Warburton (capt.), Heaslip. Replacements: Hibbard, Grant, Cole, Croft, O'Brien, Murray, Farrell, Cuthbert.

It's been enlightening to watch Lyds at close quarters, seeing as we'll be spending some time together in France. After one training session earlier in the tour, Owen and I sat and watched him, Paulie and Seanie go through this scary chop-tackling drill that they'd devised themselves. The 'attacker' runs towards Lyds holding a tackle shield against his lower leg and then jumps up to safety at the last minute as Lyds comes in like a low-flying missile. He's practising his technique at full throttle, while they are protecting themselves from the damage that could be done by full impact. We wondered what would happen if Paulie or Seanie's studs got stuck in the turf – a broken ankle? A snapped shin? After a while, I couldn't watch.

Whatever the perils of the chop-tackle, one of the beauties of a Lions tour is that people freely swap technical information with guys against whom they're competing for places, and who will be enemies again in a matter of months. There's a generosity of spirit that's refreshing. I remember reading about Rog benefiting from Jonny Wilkinson's openness here twelve years ago, while others learned from Jason Robinson's rugby league experiences. Now Seanie is learning from the best chop-tackler in the world, while Lyds is getting a few tips from one of the best ball-carriers in the world. This pair are both farmers, too, so there is probably all sorts of information changing hands.

Word has it that a pair of pals in the Wallabies team have walked themselves into some bother after staying out a bit late in Melbourne last night. It was probably not a great judgement call by Kurtley Beale and James O'Connor to be in Hungry Jack's at 4 a.m., and definitely not wise to pose for a photo with a Lions fan. The photo appeared in one of the British tabloids, which heaps even more pressure on Wallabies coach, Robbie Deans. The word is they weren't drinking, but had just been out late with some of the Rebels after the Lions game. Will they be suspended? Probably not, especially when you consider that Australia have an injury crisis in their backline.

We must seem very well behaved by comparison. Tonight we gathered in the team room to watch the second game in the State of

Origin series, in Brisbane, with Queensland running out comfortable winners to square the series. Crisps, popcorn and chocolate all round! We are easily pleased.

Thursday 27 June

Grand Hyatt, Melbourne

Just two changes for the Wallabies, both enforced: Joe Tomane in for Digby Ioane, who has a shoulder problem, and Kurtley at full-back for Berrick Barnes. Christian Leali'ifano has been passed fit to play and will be the place-kicker.

So, relatively little disruption to the Wallabies despite having had three players stretchered off last week. The big story in Wallaby camp is how the International Rugby Board have appealed against the decision to clear James Horwill of deliberately stamping on Alun-Wyn last week. I have the feeling that Gats made a decision not to criticize the original decision for fear that he might turn Horwill into a martyr. Now it looks like he may have been martyred anyway. As you can imagine, the Aussie media are depicting the 'retrial' as a northern hemisphere conspiracy, driven by an organization that has its headquarters in Dublin. However, as the IRB lodged its appeal only today, it won't be heard until Monday, so Horwill will definitely play on Saturday.

We have our own cause to pursue. As I mentioned before, Gats encouraged Brian to talk to the entire group today, pushing the line that Lions Test series victories don't come around very often. He was part of a team that went one–nil up twelve years ago. Then, as captain in New Zealand in 2005, he was injured in the first minute of the first Test of what turned out to be an easy series for the All Blacks; and the Lions were pipped in South Africa four years later. He said we simply had to grab this opportunity. Then Gatty spoke about how Brian deserved to win a series with the Lions and how we had to do it for him. By the end of the meeting, there was a lot of emotion washing around the room.

I was a little worried that we were overdoing that side of things. Of course we wanted to win it for Brian, and for Paulie, but wanting something passionately will only get you so far. You can want it ten times more than the opposition, but if they are more accurate and take their opportunities, they will probably win the game. I've read in a couple of books about how Munster went overboard on emotion before their first Heineken Cup final, in 2000. Players ended up bawling at a team meeting the night before the game but then didn't play their best against Northampton the following day.

So my focus was on how we would win, preferably by producing some good attacking ball in their half, rather than on how much we wanted to win. I said as much to journalists who asked me about the chances of us making history on Saturday.

Saturday 29 June

Etihad Stadium (Australia 16, British and Irish Lions 15)

The stands are empty by the time I'm led from the changing room out onto the corner of the pitch to face the journos. Empty, except for one punter in the second tier, who's trying to get my attention. His voice is strangely insistent, so much so that I have to concentrate hard to hear the questions being fired at me. But he won't go away. 'Score tries,' he keeps repeating. 'Forget kicking penalties. Score tries.' Eventually, he gets to me and I look up in his direction. 'Yes,' I say. 'You're absolutely right.'

Of all the rugby matches I've been involved in, I find it hard to think of a more frustrating one than this. The Etihad is a brilliant stadium, as atmospheric as the Millennium but just a different-shaped space-ship. So many people paid so much money to come and see us play tonight but they were served up some awful rugby, an occasion that in truth was saved only by another dramatic endgame.

We came with ambitions to play positively, if only we could set up some attacking platforms in the Australian half of the field. But the Wallabies starved us of usable attacking ball at the lineout, giving us scraps at the front, which we could only drive in the hope of forcing a penalty. It's no way to play.

The scrums, meanwhile, were a shambles throughout, thanks mainly to the determination of both sides to spoil and unsettle and collapse and then start all over again. The first-half scoring consisted of seven penalty kicks, as many as four of them for scrum offences – two to each side. It didn't make much sense.

I have some sympathy for referees in these situations, and in general I think Craig Joubert is one of the best in the game, but for the second week in a row I felt we were harshly treated by the match officials. I was hopeful of us getting a fair shake when I saw that Joubert was allowing us to contest at the breakdown, where Sam caused havoc early on. But then he gave the Aussies six of the cheapest points imaginable at the scrum.

The scrum was such a lottery that we had the upper hand there for the second quarter, allowing us to go in 12–9 in front. Everyone was agreed in the dressing room – scoring next was critical. I look back on a kick through by Jon Davies six or seven minutes after the break, how we stormed onto Folau, how they hit the ruck from the side, yet somehow they came away with a cheap penalty for accidental offside against Mako. In the overall context of the game, this was a huge decision that went against us.

We did eventually get that first score of the second half, after another penalty awarded at the scrum, early in the final quarter. Unfortunately it coincided with Sam's departure with a hamstring injury. From that point on, I thought we were guilty of wishing the game to be over, trying to dog out a win, rather than going and grabbing it. In fairness to the Wallabies, that is precisely what they did. When they were needed, their key players imposed themselves – Folau popping up with a half-break here and there, Genia probing with menace. We made a couple of bad defensive reads and with four minutes to go Adam Ashley-Cooper ran a killer line onto James O'Connor's pass to score the only try of the game. Leali'ifano kicked the conversion and we were a point behind.

So began the five minutes of high drama, the only part of the game that made it memorable. O'Connor kicking the ball out on the pass-back gave us our first opening but again the officials let us down. Watch the replay and you'll see O'Connor kicked the ball seven metres from his try-line, yet for some reason assistant ref Chris Pollock marked touch around eight metres further upfield. Drico pointed this out to him but he was waved away. It made a significant difference to our chances of scoring. Defend a lineout seven metres from your line and you'll probably stay on the deck to repel the maul. Fifteen metres out, you'll contest the throw, as the Aussies did, and Liam Gill came away with the ball. That said, I'd still give Horwill credit for positioning himself at the very front of that lineout and thereby forcing us to chance a throw to the middle, where Ben Mowen spoiled effectively.

Our last bite came when we won a penalty in our own half, with the clock just about to head into the red. I was tackled on our ten-metre line but not held, so I scrambled the extra metres to half-way, where the Wallabies failed to release. Penalty to the Lions, bang on halfway, maybe fifty-four metres on the angle. I've seen Leigh kick them from that distance before. We were in the eighty-second minute so there was a fatigue factor, but we were indoors on a solid surface and the adrenaline must have been pumping. A Test series was there for the taking. But it was an incredibly tough kick. Even if he hits it 100 per cent he might not make it.

I stood directly behind him so I would know as soon as possible. We've spent enough time practising together at this stage, so I can tell from his posture at the point of contact if he's made a 100 per cent connection, which is what you need for a kick from that distance. I knew immediately that the kick was short. The poor bloke. He was inconsolable. You spend hours practising for moments like that so that you can deliver. He certainly put in the work – his work ethic is incredible. I can understand completely how empty he must have felt.

But you move on. We poured our heart and soul into this match and it didn't work. Do you accept that the momentum is now with the Aussies and whinge about our injury list? (Sam has no chance of playing next week.) Or do you see next week as an opportunity for the Lions to finally reach something like their potential as a rugby team? I look at it this way. Tonight was a cup final. We lost, but normally when you lose a final, you have a long wait before you get the chance to put things right. We only have to wait seven days. We have no option but to think positively.

I got some food back at the hotel with Jamie and Rob, went up to my room and chatted to my roomie Mike, watched some *Game of Thrones* and finally fell asleep at around four. Like I said, you move on. We have a job to do next week.

Monday 1 July

Sheraton Hotel, Noosa

Some of us are watching a movie in the team room but, even from here I can hear the racket from the hotel bar. Drinking games. Classic rugby-tour stuff. The Lions are still a bit old-school like that. It works for some blokes as a way to unwind. Even if I was that way inclined, it wouldn't be happening this week. I'm struggling with a chest infection so I'll be taking it handy.

I get the idea behind taking a couple of days off when we're all coming to the end of a long, hard season. We are here in Noosa until Thursday. It's small, remote and scenic, with a couple of nice cafes and restaurants. The hotel is right beside the beach and we have it entirely to ourselves. It's a prime spot for surfing and jet-skiing. Today a few of us visited the Steve Irwin Zoo, which was cool.

My only reservation about coming here is that I remember doing something similar in the final week of Ireland's tour to New Zealand this time last year, when we headed down to Queenstown for a few days to unwind. The idea was to recharge the batteries, but some of us probably turned the engine off altogether. I wouldn't use this as the reason we lost 60–0 in Hamilton the following Saturday, but I don't think it helped. So it will be interesting to see what energy levels are like when we start training again on Wednesday morning. Like everything else about the tour, if we win on Saturday, coming to Noosa will look like a great idea.

Word is that there will, again, be significant changes for Saturday. Wig has been having those 'difficult' conversations with a few forwards, including Jamie.

Tuesday 2 July

Sheraton Hotel, Noosa

I found out this morning from Kearns, before breakfast. There have been a few shocks, he says. I tell him I've heard that Jamie Heaslip has received the shepherd's crook. Yeah, he says, and Drico's not in the twenty-three.

It's a shock, a huge shock. Neither he nor Jonny Davies got to shine in Melbourne, but they were both restricted by our failure to produce quality ball. But Drico defended well and, like I've said, I assumed he was the natural choice as captain for Sydney. One reason it was so shocking was that we made last week all about Brian. In Melbourne, we were going out to win the series for ourselves but especially for him. Emotionally, spiritually, symbolically, he had been a reference point for players and management all week. Doing it for Drico had been our theme of the week, if you like. It must have been quite a load for him to carry about with him. Even at half-time at the Etihad Stadium, when we were leading 12–9, Gats urged us to go on and make history, and to do it for the bloke in the number 13 jersey, who'd put so much into that jersey over the space of a dozen years and gotten so little reward.

That's why I was so surprised that he has been discarded completely. But I have to be careful in how I react to this news. I'm playing in a Test match alongside Jonny Davies on Saturday, so it doesn't do our relationship, or the team, any good if I show that I am surprised by his selection. I remember the first time I was selected for Ireland ahead of Rog, for the 2009 Test against Australia, and how uncomfortable and self-conscious I felt when I saw some of the Munster players in the squad sympathizing so openly with him. So while it may sound strange, I have to show solidarity with Jonny. He has won a Grand Slam and a Six Nations championship with Wales. He is a world-class player. I have to keep that in mind. He must feel a bit strange that everyone in the squad is talking about the decision to drop Drico. Wait till they hear about it in Ireland.

But still, I wanted to commiserate with Brian. I went to his room on Tuesday evening and Seanie was there to do exactly the same thing. He was upset, naturally. It's the first time he's been dropped since school. He's strong, though, and I know he'll handle the situation with dignity. That's the bloke you're dealing with. He even agreed to take a coaching session this afternoon with Noosa Dolphins, the local club side, which was a classy touch. Somehow I don't think he'll be coming back to Noosa on his holidays, though.

Wednesday 3 July

Sheraton Hotel, Noosa

Ireland's three biggest sporting scandals:

1) Roy Keane leaving Saipan

2) Thierry Henry's handball

3) Gatland drops BOD

That's the text that I received tonight from Jerry. He tells me that the whole country is in uproar. It's supposedly the lead item on the RTE News. Keith Wood has had a major pop at Gats, so has Willie John McBride. Even non-Irish rugby legends joined the chorus of disapproval – Dan Carter, Matt Giteau, Sonny Bill Williams and David Campese have been giving it loads on Twitter.

It's been weird following the reaction to a story I first heard about over twenty-four hours ago. At training this morning, both Rob and I noticed how all the cameras were focused on Brian, because the snappers were all making the same assumption I had made – that he would later be revealed as captain for the third Test. I said to Rob,

'They're getting the pictures they want, but not for the reasons they think.'

Then it all kicked off at lunchtime, when Gats revealed the team: Halfpenny; Bowe, Davies, Roberts, North; Sexton, Phillips; Corbisiero, Hibbard, A. Jones; A.-W. Jones (capt.), Parling; Lydiate, O'Brien, Faletau. Replacements: T. Youngs, Vunipola, Cole, Gray, Tipuric, Murray, Farrell, Tuilagi.

That's another five changes between Tests but only one selection is of general interest, it seems. Brian had a good partnership with Jamie on the last Lions tour, but that is four years ago. Jamie has played a lot more rugby with Jonny and they complemented each other beautifully against the Waratahs, which surely influenced selection.

But I've put all such comparisons to one side. We have a Test match to prepare for and today's training session was a shambles. Andy must have spotted the anger in my body language because he took me aside at the end of the session. He said that today was always going to be a bit difficult. You've got fifteen lads who are happy, eight who probably think they should be starting but are happy to be involved, and then there are seventeen blokes who are pissed off. He said it should be tighter tomorrow.

In all the controversy over Brian's omission, it's almost been missed that Seanie will start – missed by everyone except the Aussies, who rate him so highly. Conor is one of the replacements and I'm also happy for Justin Tipuric that he has made the bench, for he has kept the highest standards in training throughout. That blue scrumcap seems to be everywhere. Of course, to a lot of sports fans back home, Tips is just another Welshman included by the Wales coach. We actually joke about the Welsh conspiracy theory. Because the simple fact of ten Welshmen in the starting team is so unmissable, the only way to deal with it is to get it out in the open and have a laugh about it. Those players not in the Test squad – dirt-trackers, as they used to be called – were out for dinner the other night and someone asked, 'Are there any Welsh here?' Ian Evans put up his hand, and the response was, 'You must be really crap if you can't make it into the Lions Test XV!' Everyone – including Ian – cracked up laughing.

Thursday 4 July

Noosa Dolphins RFC

The weather improved in Noosa today, but our training standards did not, and my patience cracked this morning. I know I'm regarded as cranky and pushy – a slave-driver, is how Jonny Davies described me to the media last week – but I've tried to stay positive. I lost it with the forwards today, and it didn't go down well. We were trying to nail these plays off lineout mauls that we hadn't shown in the Tests yet – I won't bore you with the details – but even allowing for the fact that there are four changes in the pack from last week, it was taking far too long for us to get it right. We'd already talked through the details of the play in a meeting pre-training, then stopped to go through it again during training, but still people kept ending up in the wrong spot at the critical moment. 'For fuck's sake, lads!' I roared. 'How many more times does it have to be explained to you?' Or something along those lines.

This sort of thing rarely happens on Lions tours, or certainly not on this one, because everyone is making a special effort to get on with guys they don't usually play with. So I was getting daggers from Geoff Parling and Richard Hibbard. I was annoyed at myself, too, because I probably should have handled it better. But sometimes it's hard to get the message across without being direct and I was determined to influence things for the better. I said there was no point in turning up for a Test match and expecting to win it on passion. We had to be positive, and we had to be accurate. Thankfully I was backed up by the skipper, Alun-Wyn, who said that it's only right of me to demand high standards. But I still apologized for losing my cool, just in case. The lads said it was OK, but I sense there is still a sour aftertaste.

Brian had a quiet word with me afterwards and suggested that I keep all my contributions positive for the rest of the week. It was a good call from a bloke who has kept his own standards high all week, who could have gone into his shell but who has continued doing whatever he can for the cause. I've been very impressed.

Friday 5 July

North Sydney Oval

Suddenly, clarity. After a couple of awful training sessions up in Noosa, everything seemed to fall into place today. I got to clear the air, too, to apologize again for going mad yesterday but also to explain why it happened, to put across my frustration at the fact that we haven't done ourselves justice as a rugby team in this Test series. Last week, in particular, it felt like we were just wishing the game to be won, rather than going and actively winning it.

I just wish we could set up an attacking platform so that we can take the Aussies on. Looking back over the two Tests so far, I don't think we've had one scrum that we've been able to attack off, and the lineouts haven't been giving us high-quality ball. Also, the Wallabies are playing cleverly and making it difficult for us. I'm just worried that we aren't going to get to show what we are about during this Test series. That would be an awful shame.

Reasons to be hopeful? With Hibbs and Corbs in tow, we have our biggest available front row tomorrow, and the ref is Romain Poite, who usually rewards the dominant scrum. I don't pretend to know much about what goes on in the front row, but a chat with Paulie has left me feeling that a good scrummaging performance is on the way. Jamie Roberts definitely offers us something different in midfield. He's not just an up-the-middle man. Yes, he does like to run over people, but there's more to him than that. He's probably the marshal of the Welsh backline. He'll definitely give the Wallabies plenty to think about.

I can't believe that the tour is almost over. I've loved the intensity of it, and how different it's been from anything else I've ever experienced. A part of me would like to sit back and savour it a bit more, but when you're in the middle of it, you're focusing on the next game, or on recovering from the latest injury. The best non-rugby thing I've done? I can come back here on holiday another time. As a kicker, you don't have the time to climb the Sydney Harbour Bridge.

You'd be off with Jenks at the stadium going through your routine. That's what we did this evening. It was a proper trip, an hour to get out to Homebush. Bobby had our packed rations for us – sandwiches, protein bars and drinks. Owen hooked up his sounds to the Land Rover, and he saved all the cheesy ones for the return trip – all the boy-band stuff that you pretend you don't like.

We were trying to figure out how many kicking sessions we'd done together over the course of the tour. We've done three or four in the Test weeks, so that's ten or twelve for starters. We've probably spent more time in that Land Rover than in the team bus. It's reassuring to know how much we've done, and how I have a 100 per cent record on tour – zero from zero! Rog texted me to see how I felt about the fact that I'm not kicking, and I told him that I'd felt a little frustrated, but also more relaxed before matches. He told me to keep working hard because it could come down to me having to kick a penalty to decide the series. I know I'm ready, if required. I just want the team to deliver. After this morning's session, I feel a bit better about things.

Saturday 6 July

ANZ Stadium, Sydney (Australia 16, British and Irish Lions 41)

LIONS! LIONS! LIONS!

Today was everything. Today was what decided whether this tour was a massive success or a massive failure. Any dirty old 6–3 win would have done it, but to have won so emphatically, and with such flair, was good for the soul, and good for the Lions. The big motivation as a player is to be remembered after you've hung up your boots, and that means winning as much as possible. Winning a Lions series puts you in an elite group, so to be there feels a privilege.

A confession. As I was running around behind the goal-posts to score the most important try of my career, who popped into my head? Only Rog. Will he ever stop haunting me? (Only kidding, Rog.) Specifically, I was reminded of the time he hopped over the advertising hoardings after scoring at Lansdowne Road and went to commune with the Munster supporters. Was I considering a reprise? Happily, it never became an issue, because Kurtley Beale bumped me just after I'd touched down so I was off balance and in no shape for any fancy celebrations. Then the sudden reduction in crowd noise made me realize that the TMO was involved. Ah, Jesus, no.

To be honest, I was almost expecting him to disallow it because I knew my short-cut support line had taken me ahead of Leigh and so I'd had to catch the ball behind me. Back in our half, all I could see on the screen was my face, though I knew the folks at home would be watching slow-motion replays to determine whether Leigh's hands had gone backwards in delivering the pass. The crowd conveyed the good news first – lots of them were using ref-links, so they heard the TMO deliver the news a split second before Poite signalled the try. Relief.

If the score that broke Aussie resistance was created by our backs, it was our forwards who had done virtually all the damage up to that point. They were, as James O'Connor described them afterwards, like men possessed – as riled up as last week but not distracted by emotion. After twenty-five minutes, by which stage we were cruising at 19–3, there was an almost eerie atmosphere in the stadium, as both sets of supporters were trying to believe what they were witnessing. Bewilderingly, sixteen of those points could be attributed directly or indirectly to the absolute dominance of our scrum – Corbs's first-minute try, which came four or five phases after a free-kick awarded for early engagement, and three penalties.

Ben Alexander had just departed to the bin, and the contest looked over. The Aussies came back at us, though. They always do. Five minutes after half-time, they were trailing us by a mere three points. This may not be the best Wallaby team ever, but they are scrappers.

Their comeback was mortifying from a personal point of view, too, as O'Connor left me flapping in first-half injury time before muscling his way over. The bottom line is that he's quick, elusive and strong and I didn't put him on the ground. I was convinced the winger, who was starting on the inside of O'Connor, was going to pop up on the outside – the opposite of a move they tried last week. I made another bad read and was left looking a bit silly.

Two cheap Leali'ifano penalties soon after the break, to go with his conversion of the try, meant we were looking a bit brittle. Two things saved us. First, the scrum delivered another three points and a little breathing room. Then we got an injection of energy off the bench, from Conor Murray and Tom Youngs in particular.

If there was a turning point, it was probably Toby's turnover under our posts, and a chip from me that bounced into George's arms. I'm not sure how the coaches felt about the idea of me attacking from deep when we were only six points ahead in the third quarter of the decisive Test match – certainly, risk-taking in our own half wasn't part of the general game-plan. I just sensed that George was open, and sometimes your rugby instinct takes over. It's amazing how much information you can process in a couple of high-intensity seconds. The obvious play was to get the ball to George with a lobbed pass, but one of their backs was looking for the intercept. When you've seen Joe Roff's try from 2001 played and replayed on every Qantas internal flight for the previous five weeks, it makes you particularly allergic to interceptions. The Wallabies' backs are all fairly tall, so if you consider that they are jumping with their arms above their heads, that's a nine-foot barrier to lob the ball over. The chip is almost the safer option. I had two chips in the first Test that worked well – I was able to collect the ball myself and make yards – but they could have been game-changers if I hadn't been forced to check my stride and reach to regain the ball. This time the ball sat up so that George didn't have to break stride. Jonny was supporting on the inside, bullocking into Australia's half to give us some precious territory. Result.

The try? It was just a variation on the 'Hendo Tune' that worked for us in Brisbane. Instead of Tommy being the strike runner, he released Jonny, and Leigh's injection of pace made the difference. We called the move 'TP'. We'd been falling over ourselves trying to get it right up in Noosa, but here it worked a treat.

I didn't expect to be called ashore six minutes later, and that much was probably obvious by my reaction. I'm actually a little ashamed about it. Owen has worked incredibly hard on tour and is a quality player. We have got on so well. I should have been happy for him. I apologized to Rob Howley later, though I think he was more amused than angry. Once I cooled down, sitting pitch-side was actually enjoyable. I could sit back and watch Leigh put George over for try number three and then Conor send Jamie over for number four. A hammering.

We went mad afterwards, of course – forty-odd players and over thirty support staff, all hugging and jigging and finally savouring the moment, including Brian, who hugged Jonny Davies and got his hands on the Tom Richards Trophy. It must have been a bitter-sweet moment for him but, as he pointed out, he'd played his part in a Lions series victory.

I was particularly giddy when I saw Daniel Craig, the actor, on the pitch. 'It's bloody James Bond!' I shouted, not thinking he'd hear me in the noise, but he looked up from his conversation and walked over to shake hands. I told him that I'm a big fan of his and he told me that I'd had a great series. A bizarre but beautiful moment.

The dressing-room celebrations were epic, but I found time to call home and share the moment with the people who matter most. I also swapped jerseys with James O'Connor, who was gracious in defeat. Then there was some partying to be done.

Later, on the bus to the post-match reception in the Sydney Opera House, Bobby got me up the front for a song. 'Don't Look Back in Anger' was drowned out by booing, so I gave them what they wanted: 'Bread of Heaven'. They joined in on that one! In the front seats, Rob and Gats were shaking their heads and smiling, but they knew it was all just good, clean fun.

The fun was only beginning.

Epilogue

My next sporting contest was a game of golf with Mark, Jerry and a few friends at Adare Manor the following Friday – the morning of our wedding. We were playing in pairs, better-ball Stableford, but I bottled it completely and had to head in after nine holes. I wasn't used to this sort of pressure.

I was far more nervous than I'd been before any of the Lions Test matches. Yes, I'm used to being on show, but not as part of this team – the most important team in my life. As I said earlier, Laura and I are a private couple, so it was daunting to be the focus of attention, to have family and so many close friends gathered together in one place, purely for us. I was nervous also because I wanted the day to be everything Laura wanted it to be.

We were so fortunate to have Father Paul Lavelle to guide us through the ceremony at the beautiful Holy Trinity Abbey Church. Father Paul is a friend of the family and a former referee so – sorry, there's no way of avoiding this – he kept everyone on-side. And we were lucky to be blessed with a beautiful Irish summer's afternoon.

The nerves returned when I realized I still had a speech to make. You can answer questions before a TV audience of millions but when it's just you and a microphone and 200 people, it's scary. Luckily, my job was fairly simple – to give thanks. There are so many people who deserve my gratitude.

Once the formal part of the day was over, Laura and I were able to relax and enjoy ourselves. It was great to have so many rugby friends there, but there were also friends I hadn't seen in over a year, people who'd travelled from New Zealand to be there. The younger crew ended up in a cellar-type bar downstairs, where there was a guy on guitar, and we sang until the sun came up.

I'm writing this from Las Vegas, where we are holidaying before heading to Paris – we'll do a proper honeymoon next year, when we have a bit more time on our hands. Everything has been so hectic, including the Lions' celebrations, which carried on well into the Sunday morning after the game and then started up again the following afternoon in Bondi. Great memories. The party barely let up before we boarded the plane two days later. Most of us slept the whole way home.

Laura was brilliant in getting things organized for the wedding, but there were still so many last-minute details to attend to. Now, on holiday, I'm constantly finding myself wondering what it is that I'm supposed to be getting ready for, and then remembering: *Nothing. You're on holiday. Relax.*

There is time now to reflect on a fairly crazy year in my life. There was a time back in March, when I was camped on the couch in Goatstown with my left foot in a ski-boot, when things weren't looking so good: Leinster out of the Heineken Cup, Ireland floundering in the Six Nations and my Lions chances on the line. Things worked out in the end.

The best bit? For Laura and me to find ourselves in that cellar bar in Adare, with all the people who mean the most to us, and with each other. Now there's a happy ending.

Index

He just wanted a decent book to read ...

Not too much to ask, is it? It was in 1935 when Allen Lane, Managing Director of Bodley Head Publishers, stood on a platform at Exeter railway station looking for something good to read on his journey back to London. His choice was limited to popular magazines and poor-quality paperbacks – the same choice faced every day by the vast majority of readers, few of whom could afford hardbacks. Lane's disappointment and subsequent anger at the range of books generally available led him to found a company – and change the world.

'We believed in the existence in this country of a vast reading public for intelligent books at a low price, and staked everything on it'
Sir Allen Lane, 1902–1970, founder of Penguin Books

The quality paperback had arrived – and not just in bookshops. Lane was adamant that his Penguins should appear in chain stores and tobacconists, and should cost no more than a packet of cigarettes.

Reading habits (and cigarette prices) have changed since 1935, but Penguin still believes in publishing the best books for everybody to enjoy. We still believe that good design costs no more than bad design, and we still believe that quality books published passionately and responsibly make the world a better place.

So wherever you see the little bird – whether it's on a piece of prize-winning literary fiction or a celebrity autobiography, political tour de force or historical masterpiece, a serial-killer thriller, reference book, world classic or a piece of pure escapism – you can bet that it represents the very best that the genre has to offer.

Whatever you like to read – trust Penguin.